D1101578

MARGUERITE
PATTEN'S

SUCCESSFUL
BAKING

MARGUERITE PATTEN'S SUCCESSFUL BAKING

COLLINS

CONTENTS

CHAPTER 1

THE ESSENTIALS

Page 8

Good cakes, bread and pastry depend upon the right ingredients, the right cooking utensils and correct oven temperature. Including all you need to know about ingredients, equipment, weights and measures.

CHAPTER 2

THE RUBBING-IN METHOD

Page 36

The simplest of all baking methods. Master Recipe – Rock Cakes, plus small and large cakes, shortcakes, puddings, crumbles.

CHAPTER 3

THE CREAMING METHOD

Page 64

This method is the basis for the largest group of cakes. Master Recipe – Victoria Sandwich, plus one-stage cakes, rich fruit cakes, cheesecakes, upside down puddings.

CHAPTER 4

THE MELTING METHOD

Page 108

Cakes made by this simple method are moist and keep well. Master Recipe – Gingerbread, plus various large and small cakes, cakes made using oil, biscuits.

CHAPTER 5

THE WHISKING METHOD

Page 124

These cakes are the lightest of all. Master Recipe – Sponge Cake, plus gâteaux, soufflés, Swiss rolls, Genoese pastry, batters.

CHAPTER 6

FILLINGS, FROSTINGS & DECORATIONS

Page 144

Recipes for filling and coating all types of cakes. Including glacé icing, butter icing, marzipan and royal icing, plus piping, Australian icing and tempting fillings.

CHAPTER 7

CELEBRATION CAKES

Page 156

Special occasions are not complete without one of these cakes. Including novelty cakes for birthdays, celebration cakes for christenings and weddings.

CHAPTER 8

MERINGUES, BISCUITS & COOKIES

Page 164

Mouthwatering selection of home-made treats. Master Recipe – Meringues, plus meringue gâteaux, truffles, biscuits made by rubbing-in, creaming, melting and whisking methods.

CHAPTER 9

SCONES, TEACAKES & YEAST BAKING

Page 180

Economical and elaborate fare to thrill family and friends. Master Recipe – White Bread, plus scones, teabreads and loaves, enriched yeast recipes.

CHAPTER 10

PASTRY AND PASTRIES

Page 196

All the pastries are included with delicious recipe ideas using them. Including large and individual pies, tarts and flans, quiches.

INDEX

Page 220

First published in 1984
by William Collins Sons & Co Ltd
London · Glasgow · Sydney
Auckland · Johannesburg · Toronto

© Marguerite Patten 1984

Copy editor: Barbara Croxford
Designer: Pedro Prá-Lopez
Layout: Kate Simunek
Line illustrations: Kate Simunek

Colour Photography by Charlie Stebbings (with home
economist: Joyce Harrison, and picture stylist: Elizabeth
Allen-Elsor) pages 4–5, 9, 109 and 181; and by courtesy
of Billingtons Sugar pages 37 and 165; Danish Dairy
Board (photographer: Sue Jorgensen; home economist:
Deidre Ryan) pages 65 and 197; Flour Advisory Bureau
page 85; Cadbury's Food Advisory Service page 125;
Kitchen Devils page 145; and Woodnutt's Ltd of Hove,
who made the wedding cake, page 157.

All rights reserved. No part of this publication may be
reproduced, stored in a retrieval system, or transmitted,
in any form or by any means, electronic, mechanical,
photocopying, recording or otherwise, without the prior
permission of the publishers.

ISBN 0 00 411270 9

Text set in Plantin by Rowland Phototypesetting Ltd
Bury St Edmunds, Suffolk
Colour reproduction by Intercrom S.A., Madrid
Printed and bound by
Graficromo, S.A., Cordoba, Spain

Introduction

For many years I have been a great advocate of home baking, for you can save money and at the same time give great pleasure to your family and friends. I hope I shall encourage all who read this book to become as enthusiastic as I am.

Baking is a satisfactory form of cookery and one that enables every cook to develop her, or his, culinary skills and artistic abilities.

Often I find that even accomplished and experienced cooks are nervous about making and baking cakes, bread and less usual pastries – they feel there is some hidden mystique about these recipes with which they are not familiar. I sincerely hope the information given throughout the various chapters will reassure less confident or less experienced cooks and give inspiration to fellow enthusiasts.

I think it is important to appreciate that baking recipes are somewhat akin to chemical formulae, for the ingredients should be chosen critically; weighed or measured accurately; handled and baked with loving care.

Let me explain how 'Successful Baking' is planned.

The Essentials, in Chapter 1, gives a great deal of information about the ingredients used in baking, how they should be handled and baked, together with details of the various equipment.

The other chapters cover baking recipes of all kinds. Sections start with a Master Recipe plus line illustrations that clearly show how to follow the specific technique upon which the recipes in that section are based; after that come recipes based on the simple Master Recipe. Did you know that when you have mastered the technique of making a perfect Victoria Sandwich, you immediately know how to prepare dozens of other cakes that will be equally delicious and successful?

After the relatively simple recipes, you will find exotic and exciting ideas (many of which come from other countries) for sweet and savoury baked dishes.

Obviously I hope all your results will be 100 per cent successful, but remember it takes time and practice to achieve perfection, so every chapter ends with an analysis of the kind of things that can go wrong with the particular group of recipes, for I hope to prevent mishaps happening to your cooking.

Modern freezers mean that batch-baking is practical and a way of saving time and effort; most baked foods can be frozen and I give full advice on the technique of freezing the particular dishes covered in each section of the book.

Over many generations we have achieved a high reputation for home baking in Great Britain and throughout the Commonwealth; I hope this book will help us to maintain this tradition.

Marguerite Patten

CHAPTER 1

The Essentials

Good bread, cakes and pastry depend upon well-balanced recipes, plus the right choice of ingredients for the particular dish; the right kind of cooking utensil and the correct temperature for baking in the oven.

These points can be termed 'the essentials' for success and they are covered fully in this chapter and summarised below.

It is worthwhile reading about these important points, for certain success depends not only on knowing *what* to do, but the reason(s) for doing this.

WHAT ARE THE ESSENTIALS?

Understanding what kind of fat, sugar and flour to choose for the various forms of baking. For example you should buy a different kind of flour if you are making bread from the type you would use to make a light sponge.

Appreciating the effect of using various kinds of raising agent, such as baking powder, bicarbonate of soda, etc.

Knowing how to look after the equipment used for baking, and selecting the right utensils for each kind of recipe.

Learning about oven temperatures and baking times, and how to check the baking progress when making various kinds of cakes.

Knowing about both metric and Imperial weights and measures.

Some of the foods used in baking (see pages 11–20) including flours, raising agents, fats, sugars, eggs, liquids, flavouring mixtures, fruits and nuts

Five steps to successful baking

Successful baking depends upon the following important points:

Step 1: Choosing a well-balanced recipe, then measuring and/or weighing the ingredients carefully. You can 'chop and change' the ingredients in a soup or stew without harming the dish, but the basic proportions of fat, sugar, eggs, flour and liquid in cakes and other recipes are calculated carefully and should be followed. Obviously, after trying the recipe, you can adjust the flavouring, such as spices or essence to suit your own personal taste; e.g. if you dislike the taste of cloves then use another spice, such as cinnamon.

Step 2: Successful mixing. The way in which the ingredients are incorporated makes a great deal of difference to the result. There are four basic techniques of mixing, these are: a) rubbing-in; b) creaming; c) melting; d) whisking. These are described on pages 23–24, in Chapters 2 to 5 and used in recipes throughout.

Baking recipes need other skills in mixing too, such as 'folding'. This can mean the way you incorporate flour in a sponge mixture or handle the dough for puff pastry. These important terms are described on pages 23–24.

Take time to learn about the correct methods of handling each kind of mixture together with the way to judge the correct consistency of the prepared cake, pastry or batter. The explanation of the various terms used to describe the consistency or texture of the mixture is given on page 24.

Step 3: Careful baking. The way in which you bake bread, biscuits or a cake is as important as the proportions in the recipe and the way in which these various foods are put together.

The temperature of the oven is the key to successful baking and the oven should be preheated, see page 33. In most ovens the position in which you place the food should also be considered, see page 33. Obviously the kind of recipe, as well as the quantity of the mixture determines the baking time and temperature. If you try and bake a rich fruit cake too quickly you burn the outside before the centre is cooked; if you cook a sponge too slowly it will be hard and dry.

There is another piece of advice given in the recipe which should be followed, this is the size of the cake tin or cooking container. If the recipe states 'bake in an 18 cm/7 inch cake tin' and you change this to a 20 cm/8 inch cake tin, you are spreading the mixture over a larger area and therefore you are producing a more shallow cake, which would cook in a slightly shorter time.

If, on the other hand, you reverse the procedure and put the mixture into an 18 cm/7 inch cake tin instead of the recommended 20 cm/8 inch cake tin, you are then making a deeper cake which will take a little longer to cook. In this case you may need to lower the heat slightly. You must also make quite certain the amount of mixture will *fit* into the smaller tin.

The way to adjust cooking times is given in the question and answer sections.

Step 4: Testing the cooked cake or loaf of bread. Never assume baked food is cooked without adequate testing. Many a good cake has been spoiled by either being taken out of the oven too soon, or left in a little too long. Inadequate cooking means a cake that could be heavy and fall in the centre; over-cooking produces an over-brown and over-dry cake. Methods of testing are given in each section.

Step 5: Careful finishing. The appearance of the food is very important so make well-shaped bread, biscuits, cakes and pastry and perfect your icing.

Following the recipes

The chapters in this book are clearly defined, so that both a beginner and an expert in baking, will find the kind of recipes they need quickly and easily.

Each chapter begins with the simplest recipes and where a basic technique is involved you will find a Master Recipe with line illustrations of the various steps to preparation. If there is no Master Recipe, there are full details, and often line illustrations too, that indicate exactly how a basic recipe is made or a particular stage is reached. In sections where a special process is involved, as in the case of flaky pastry, then line illustrations of each of the stages are included.

After the simple, or basic, recipes come variations on these, followed by more elaborate ideas. International and original recipes are included.

Sometimes a question may occur to you and you cannot find the answer in the recipe; in this case look at the question and answer page(s) at the end of each chapter. Included also in this part of each chapter are tips to 'put right' any results that do not reach the standard of perfection you would wish.

Most chapters end with advice on batch baking, freezing and defrosting, or reheating, the particular recipes in the section.

Portions in recipes

It is always difficult to say how many people any dish will serve, for it entirely depends upon personal appetite and the other courses, if the dish is part of a complete meal.

You will find I have described portions in three ways in this book.

Small Cakes: I give the approximate number the mixture produces; that does not mean you have to make that number, but if you make more smaller cakes then shorten the cooking time slightly. If, on the other hand, you make slightly bigger cakes, lengthen the cooking time by a few minutes, but do check in this case that the outsides of the cakes do not become over-brown with the longer cooking; it may be necessary to reduce the heat.

Large Cakes: I have given the size of the completed cake, but not the portions, for cakes can be sliced as thinly or thickly as required. As a general guide though, allow a slice of about 2.5 cm/1 inch when slicing a plain cake; but not much more than 1.5 cm/½ inch when slicing a very rich cake. Wedding cakes are, of course, cut into very small portions and you will find the amount given on page 97.

Desserts and Gâteaux: Many of the creamy cakes are suitable for desserts, as well as teatime, so I have given the approximate serving, so that you can plan a menu accordingly.

Savoury Dishes: The portions are indicated here, or the number made if they are of individual size.

Know about foods used in baking

There is such a range of fats, flours, sugars and other foods on the market that it can be very confusing as to which is the best to buy for each particular purpose.

Obviously the recipes state my recommendations and the foods are given in the order of preference, for example if I say 'butter or cooking fat' it means I prefer butter but cooking fat could be substituted, for it gives a very acceptable result in that particular recipe.

FLOUR

Flour is, of course, one of the essential ingredients for baking cakes, bread, biscuits and many other recipes. As there are various kinds of flour, it is important to select the right type for each group of recipes. Do not overlook the less-used flours, such as rye, maize, rice and oat flours: available in health food stores.

The majority of flours used come from wheat, and the chief division is as follows:

White Flours

These are produced by extracting the bran and most of the wheatgerm leaving between 72 and 74% of the whole wheat grain. White flour can be divided:

Plain flour: In baking this is used without raising agents for pastry, most biscuits, whisked sponges and rich fruit cakes. If you add a raising agent, such as baking powder, it can be used for all cakes.

Self-raising flour: In this flour the millers have incorporated baking powder. The proportion used is suitable for a wide range of cakes and other recipes. Soft Wheat Sponge ('S') flour is now made by a manufacturer. It is self-raising flour for light cakes and scones.

Strong flour: The wheats used have a higher gluten content than the weaker plain flour. Strong flour is particularly suitable for preparing yeast doughs, for a mixture made from this flour expands well, has a good texture and shape. It produces good puff, rough puff and flaky pastry.

Other Flours

Wheatmeal or wholemeal flour: Although wheatmeal or wholemeal flour can be used in many cake and bread recipes they are not the same. Wheatmeal flour contains most of the bran and wheatgerm and between 80 and 90% of the whole wheat grain whereas wholemeal flour contains 100% of the wheat grain with all the bran and wheatgerm.

These flours can be used in many recipes. You can buy 'strong' brown flours, suitable for breadmaking.

Wheatmeal and wholemeal flours give a less light result in cakes, but many people prefer the flavour they produce. You will find recipes based on these flours in most sections of the book.

Granary flour: The wholewheat flour has been treated to give a slightly sweet flavour which is excellent in bread. Some granary flours are a mixture of wheat plus a little rye flour.

Stoneground flour: This refers to a special milling process used to produce flours from wheat.

Maize flour: This is not used a great deal, although a little mixed with wheat flour makes interesting scones and cakes.

Cornflour: This is frequently used with wheat flour in biscuits, some kinds of pastry and a few cakes. It gives a particularly light texture to a cake, or crisp texture to biscuits or pastry.

Oat flour or the coarser oatmeal or modern rolled oats: These are excellent additives to wheat flour when making bread and some cakes.

Delicious biscuits can be produced from rolled oats, you will find recipes on pages 172 and 174.

Rice flour or ground rice: Less fine than the flour. An excellent additive to wheat flour in rich biscuits, like shortbread. It makes the shortbread deliciously crisp.

Rye flour: Used extensively on the Continent to make rye bread. There are several recipes based on this flour in the breadmaking section which begins on page 186.

Bran: This is an important part of the grain and is not only extremely good from a nutritional point of view but it can be used in a variety of different cakes, biscuits, breads and scones.

RAISING AGENTS

This term is used to describe the ways in which various mixtures are made light and therefore able to rise.

Raising agents can be divided into the following groups:

Eggs

Eggs plus the way in which they are whisked to aerate a mixture; excellent examples of the way in which eggs act as a raising agent are shown in the classic Sponge on page 126 or Choux Pastry on page 208. The more eggs, the lighter the mixture.

Yeast

This is a very efficient raising agent. There is full information about yeast and yeast recipes, beginning with home-made bread, on page 186.

Chemical Raising Agents

Baking Powder: This is the most usual agent. When you buy self-raising flour, the baking powder is efficiently blended with the flour. Self-raising flour is suitable for many, but not all, recipes. You can buy a container of baking powder and use it with plain flour. This enables you to adjust the quantity of raising agent according to the specific recipe. Always sift the baking powder with the flour.

Commercial baking powder consists of a good balance of acid and alkali ingredients. Often these are combined with a very small amount of starch, such as arrowroot, cornflour or rice flour. The purpose of the starch is to keep the mixture dry in storage, but it is important to close the container of baking powder firmly after use and to store it in a cool dry place.

The amount of baking powder required varies with the type of recipe. You will find that no baking powder is required with plain flour when making pastry or very rich fruit cakes; a smaller proportion than usual is needed for a moderately rich fruit cake. It is important to follow the advice given to achieve a perfect result.

If you have a favourite recipe that states 'use 225 g/8 oz self-raising flour', you can substitute 225 g/8 oz plain flour sifted with 2 level teaspoons baking powder.

Most baking powders start to react when blended with moist ingredients, such as when the cake is thoroughly mixed and put into the tin. That is why it is better to cook the cake as soon as possible after preparation. Freezing prevents the baking powder reacting.

In American recipes you will read the term 'double action baking powder'. This is because their raising agent acts in two stages. It only begins to react when mixed with moist ingredients, most of the reaction takes place when subjected to heat.

Bicarbonate of Soda (known as baking soda in USA) used with Cream of Tartar: Use 2 parts cream of tartar to 1 part bicarbonate of soda. Measure the quantity recommended in the recipe very carefully. Always sift the raising agents very thoroughly with the flour, for if bicarbonate of soda is not efficiently sifted with the flour any tiny lumps do not blend with the acid cream of tartar and you have a very unpleasant bitter taste in the recipe.

This combination of raising agents can be used in Scones, see pages 182, 183 and 218.

Bicarbonate of Soda without Cream of Tartar: The raising agent is used by itself in recipes where another ingredient provides the acidity needed, e.g. in a Gingerbread, see page 110, where black treacle or golden syrup are used.

In the Eggless Fruit Cake on page 51 where vinegar (an acid) helps to lighten the mixture.

In Irish Soda Bread, page 194, if sour milk is used. The milk becomes acid when sour.

In all these recipes plain flour with the recommended amount of bicarbonate of soda is better than self-raising flour, or plain flour and baking powder.

Never use bicarbonate of soda by itself unless recommended to do so, for the mixture would have an unpleasant flavour and be unduly dark in colour.

FATS

There is an almost bewildering selection of fats on the market, most of these are suitable to use in baking, providing you appreciate how they vary and their effect in various recipes.

Butter

This is available as a salted or unsalted fat. Butter gives a rich and pleasant flavour to biscuits, cakes and pastry. It is a hard fat and cannot be used for creaming or rubbing in straight from the refrigerator, so remove some time before required and leave at room temperature.

Use butter for making rich biscuits, special cakes and in pastry. You may like to mix butter with cooking fat for pastry. Choose unsalted butter for butter icings. Butter gives a very good flavour to a Victoria Sandwich and similar mixtures and the light sponge type of cake keeps well.

Cooking Fats

Aerated compound white fats produced from edible oils. The fats are soft and therefore easy to cream or rub-in. They have a good flavour.

Use in making pastry and some cakes; the fat gives a very light texture to short-crust pastry.

Dripping

When there were fewer fats available for baking, clarified dripping was used in some family cakes. Dripping loses its very definite 'meaty' taste when well-clarified.

To clarify dripping, see instructions on page 118.

There is a recipe for an old fashioned Dripping Cake on page 118.

Lard

This is a very hard fat. It is not suitable for creaming.

Use in shortcrust pastry with butter or margarine or in hot water crust pastry.

Margarines

Produced from edible oils – mostly vegetable oils. They vary considerably in price, flavour and their use in cooking.

Hard Margarine: Used in the same way as butter for which they are an excellent alternative. They should be removed from the refrigerator some time before use, if being used for the creaming or rubbing-in methods.

Soft Margarine: Sold in tubs and are better used straight from the refrigerator; they should not be left at room temperature. Best in one-stage recipes.

Polyunsaturated Margarine: Both soft and a good choice for anyone following a low cholesterol diet; can be used in the same way as ordinary soft margarines.

Use margarines for biscuits, cakes, pastry. It is less good than butter for cake fillings.

Low Fat Spread

Although this is primarily an alternative to butter and margarine for spreading on bread, it can be used in some forms of baking. It reduces the calorie value of the food.

Use in light cakes; do not use for pastry.

Oil

There are many kinds of oil; most are for frying or making salad dressings. Corn oil is particularly good in certain recipes.

Use in various cakes, see page 120, and in Shortcrust pastry.

Fat in Baking

Fat gives a pleasantly moist texture plus a good flavour and prevents the food becoming stale quickly.

Too generous an amount of fat would

make bread and cakes heavy, biscuits and pastry difficult to handle.

SUGARS

Sugar plays an important part in baking, for it not only sweetens cakes, biscuits, scones and other baked goods, but it helps to lighten the mixture, or make it crisp. If you cut down on the sugar in a cake you lose some sweetness and lightness too. If you cut down on sugar in biscuits, some of the crispness is lost.

These are the types of sugars to use in baking and the recipes for which they are most successful.

White Sugars

These are mainly used in light cakes for they give a pleasant colour to the cake, but there is no reason why you cannot use the unrefined brown sugar if you prefer to do so. The cakes will not be as light though.

Caster Sugar: The very fine white sugar. This is ideal for sponges and many light cakes, for the granules dissolve quickly and easily. It can be used for many biscuits, scones and other baked goods.

Granulated Sugar: Coarser than caster sugar, it is not as good in light cakes, but excellent for many biscuits, for family-type 'rubbed-in' mixtures, for scones and bread, and some boiled icings.

Loaf and Preserving Sugars: Not used a great deal for baking, but can be lightly crushed to put on top of buns before baking, see Bath Buns on page 192.

Icing Sugar: Not only the correct sugar for many icings, but it can be used as an ingredient in meringues and some biscuits. Use a hair or nylon sieve to remove lumps, for if you push icing sugar through a metal sieve with a metal spoon it can become greyish in colour. In Australia, an icing sugar mix is available for making frostings.

Brown Sugars

Some are known as unrefined (or natural) sugars and they do give an excellent flavour to many cakes, biscuits and breads. Others are called refined brown sugars and most tend to have a less definite taste than the unrefined sugars (except Demerara).

Unrefined Granulated Sugar: Not particularly well known, slightly darker than ordinary granulated, a pale golden colour. Use as granulated sugar.

Demerara Sugar: There are two kinds, the unrefined type, which is milder in taste than the refined (London) type Demerara. Use in cakes where you want a slightly 'nutty' taste; this sugar dissolves reasonably well, so is quite good for light cakes. The refined type has larger granules, so is better for biscuits that cakes. Other brown sugar can be substituted if necessary.

Light Brown Sugar: A refined moist sugar with fine granules like caster sugar, so dissolves easily in creaming. Use in semi-light cakes or where indicated in the recipe, gives a good colour to the mixture.

Dark Brown Sugar: A refined moist sugar with fine granules like caster sugar. Use in rich cakes; good in some biscuits.

Barbados Sugar: A strongly flavoured natural sugar. Good for Christmas and similar cakes. There is a light and dark variety of Barbados sugar.

Molasses Sugar: A very strong flavoured sugar, use in rich Christmas type cakes or gingerbreads only.

Muscovado Sugar: Use as Barbados sugar.

Note: If these dark brown sugars have hardened in the pack, stand them over a pan of very hot water for a time and they will soften, or put into a food processor to break up into granules once more.

Always keep sugars in a tightly sealed container when removed from the packet.

Other Sweeteners

Honey, golden syrup, black treacle, debitterised molasses together with jam, marmalade and sugar substitute can be used to sweeten mixtures for baking. You will find a number of recipes in which these are used. Always measure or weigh heavy ingredients like syrup and treacle carefully and do not use them as a replacement for sugar, unless advised. (Molasses maybe substituted for black treacle.)

LOW-CALORIE BAKING

Obviously you cannot eat rich cakes or elaborate pastries if you are on a slimming diet, but many baked savoury dishes are quite permissible. Most slimming diets allow a certain amount of bread and home-made bread is so much nicer than the commercial kinds that it is not difficult to eat with the minimum of butter (fats are high in calories).

In each section you will find one or two lower-calorie recipes; in some of these sugar substitute is used with sugar to lower the calorie intake. Anyone on a diabetic diet will be pleased to know that there are recipes that would fit into their diet too, see pages 72 and 74.

EGGS

Eggs are an important ingredient in most cakes, in batters such as Yorkshire Pudding and the ultra light Choux Pastry, see pages 140 and 208.

Do not use absolutely new-laid eggs in baking; they are at their best for this purpose when 48 hours old; on the other hand stale eggs are not as good as fresh ones. If an egg is very new-laid or stale, it does not whisk as well as when fresh, and does not aerate the mixture as it should.

Do not use eggs straight from the refrigerator; whole eggs or egg whites whisk best when at 24°C/75°F, the temperature of a really warm room. Allow to stand at room temperature for at least 30 minutes.

Egg whites can be whisked more rapidly if near a draught from an open window or door. More about this on page 164.

Some recipes mention the size of the eggs required, i.e. 'large eggs', 'small eggs', etc. for it is important in that particular recipe. These are the weights of eggs in shells:

Very large eggs (labelled size 1) weigh over 70 g/nearly 2¾ oz and over

Large eggs (labelled sizes 2 and 3) weigh 60–70 g/2 oz–nearly 2¾ oz

Medium eggs (labelled sizes 4 and 5) weigh 50–55 g/scant 2 oz–2¼ oz

Small eggs (labelled sizes 6 and 7) weigh under 45–50 g/1½ oz–scant 2 oz

A large egg out of its shell has an average liquid content of 3 tablespoons – yolk 1 tablespoon, white nearly 2 tablespoons.

Australian egg sizes: white–80 g, yellow –70 g, blue–60 g, pink–50 g, green–40 g.

LIQUIDS

You will find a variety of liquids used in the recipes throughout this book. Milk is the usual liquid for moistening cakes and scones; water is used in pastry making, for it is lighter.

While fresh milk is admirable you will have a very light, and therefore better, result if you use buttermilk or soured milk in Scones and Soda Bread, see pages 182 and 194. Yogurt is another liquid used in baking; it helps to produce a particularly light texture. Brandy, sherry and rum are used to mix very rich cakes, these give an interesting flavour to the cake. You will also find recipes in which liqueurs, cider and beer are used.

Do not overlook the value of fresh fruit juices such as lemon, orange and apple juice in mixing ingredients for biscuits, cakes and icings.

FLAVOURING MIXTURES

Flavour is added to a bread, cake or biscuit dough in many ways. The ingredients in the basic recipe naturally add flavour, but additional interest is given by the use of spices, essences and other ingredients.

These are described below and on the following pages.

Any flavouring should be chosen carefully and used subtly. Nothing is worse than an overwhelming flavour of spice or essence.

Alcohol

Alcohol is used to flavour many cakes and puddings. When the mixture is subjected to heat you still retain the flavour, but the alcoholic content is destroyed.

Brandy, rum and sherry are the most usual forms of alcohol used as flavourings but liqueurs, such as curaçao, impart a delicious flavour to many puddings.

Essences

These are obtainable in small bottles. Their flavour is very concentrated so the liquid should be used sparingly. If a recipe states 'a few drops' then the easiest way to obtain this quantity is to insert a skewer into the bottle, remove it and let the drops adhering to the skewer fall into the mixture.

Almond Essence: Used in macaroons and marzipan and any mixture where you need to enhance the almond taste.

Fruit Essence: Banana, raspberry, strawberry essences can be used where it is not practical to add the fruit itself, i.e. as in icings. Lemon and orange essence also are obtainable but in most cases the fruit juice could be used.

Peppermint Essence: Used to flavour sweetmeats, such as peppermint creams, or you can use oil of peppermint.

Ratafia Essence: Gives a similar but rather better flavour than almond essence.

Rum Essence: Can be used where neat rum is either not available or not required. See Babas au Rhum, page 193.

Vanilla: The most useful of all essences for it not only gives its own flavour to the food, but it seems to bring out other flavours, chocolate in particular.

Seeds

The dried seeds of caraway, coriander, cumin and poppy plants are used in baking.

One of the favourite 'old-fashioned' cakes is a Seed Cake, see page 89, flavoured with caraway.

Seeds are used to sprinkle on the top of some breads, see page 189, before baking.

Spices

Spices are essential flavourings in many cakes and are especially important in rich fruit cakes. The list below does not cover all spices, simply those important for interesting baked foods. Ground spices are sold in small drums. Keep tightly closed.

Allspice: The dried fruit of the allspice tree. This spice has a flavour rather like a mixture of cinnamon, cloves and nutmeg. Sold as ground spice.

Use in breads, biscuits and cakes.

Cinnamon: The dried bark of a tree. A spice that blends with most other flavours. Sold in stick form or as ground spice.

Use in all forms of baking.

Cloves: The dried closed buds of an evergreen tree. A strongly flavoured spice, so use sparingly. Sold as whole or ground cloves or as oil of cloves.

Use in pies, puddings, especially good with apples.

Coriander: Seed of a small plant. Can be obtained in ground form.

Use in cakes, although it is more often an ingredient in savoury dishes.

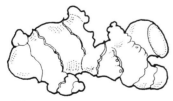

Ginger: The underground stem of a plant. Ginger is obtainable as the green stem, as crystallised or preserved, both of which are used in baking and so is the ground spice.

Invaluable for gingerbreads and other spiced mixtures.

Nutmeg: Dried seed of the fruit from the nutmeg tree. Sold as the whole seed (which must be grated) or the ground spice.

Mace is the dried outer skin of the nutmeg. Sold as blades or ground spice.

Use either nutmeg or mace in cakes, custard tart and other dishes.

Vanilla: A climbing orchid. It may be surprising to find vanilla listed as a spice since to many people it is only known as an essence. Sold as whole pods, the best form. Cut these pods in half, put into jars of sugar, cover and leave. The sugar becomes vanilla flavoured and can be used in baking.

Vanilla sugar is also obtainable from good grocers.

The pod can be infused in a liquid, removed, rinsed, dried and used again.

Interesting Herbs

Although many recipes in this book are for sweet food, and therefore do not require herbs, a large proportion of the baked savoury dishes are enhanced by the clever use of herbs.

The particular herbs recommended are given in each recipe. Use fresh herbs where possible.

If you would use 1 teaspoon chopped fresh herbs reduce the amount to between ¼ and ½ teaspoon if you have to substitute dried herbs.

FRUIT

Fresh, dried and glacé fruits are all used in baking and you will find many recipes using these foods in this book. Nuts are a fruit, but these are described separately.

The method of preparing the fresh fruit is given in individual recipes.

Dried Fruits

Currants, Raisins and Sultanas: These must be cleaned before using in cooking. Many brands of dried fruit are sold ready-cleaned but always inspect the fruit carefully to make sure there are no tiny pieces of stalk in the packet. If the dried fruits are not labelled 'ready-cleaned' then they should be washed in plenty of cold water. Drain well, spread out on flat plates and dry for 48 hours at room temperature.

This is very important, for damp fruit can cause cakes to be heavy. As a speedy emergency measure, you can clean the fruit in flour. Sprinkle a little flour on a clean tablecloth, add the dried fruit and rub vigorously in the flour. This is not as good a method of cleaning as washing, for the fruit tends to be dry in texture but it does save having to leave the dried fruits for 48 hours before using.

Recipes give the kind of dried fruit recommended, but you can substitute others, i.e. use raisins instead of sultanas, although the flavour will be different. Small seedless raisins save chopping and de-seeding the large raisins for cakes and biscuits, although the flavour of the large raisins is stronger.

Dried Dates: Another excellent ingredient in baking. Unless a recipe needs attractive looking dates, buy the cheaper ready-stoned cooking dates rather than the boxed dates with stones.

Dried Apricots, Figs and Prunes: Used less frequently than the more usual dried fruits, but all of these give a delicious taste to various dishes. While these fruits are generally soaked in liquid to make them softer before cooking, you will find that in a few recipes they are used dry.

Glacé or Crystallised Fruits

Glacé Cherries and Similar Fruits: Used in cakes and other recipes as well as for decoration. These fruits are heavy and moist, and therefore you need to follow the recipe most carefully in the amount of liquid used, the type of flour recommended or any other special preparations. Glacé cherries are generally halved or quartered before adding to the mixture. Kitchen scissors do this quickly. A knife is better for chopping the cherries.

Other glacé fruits, such as pineapple, lemon and orange slices are ingredients used in decorating cakes.

Candied Peel: Often called 'crystallised', this is sold ready-chopped nowadays. Very good grocers still sell large pieces of peel which you have to chop yourself; always remove the excess sugar from the peel before chopping.

Angelica: This crystallised stem of a plant can be used as an ingredient in baking, as well as for decoration. It gives an attractive green colour. If the angelica is very 'sugary', rinse in cold water and dry well before cutting into fancy shapes to decorate the food. Do not wash angelica before adding it to a cake mixture.

Fresh fruits

The Rind of Citrus Fruit: These give even more flavour to a cake, biscuit or bread than the juice. Take great care when you grate the rind of lemons or oranges that you use only the top coloured part of the peel. This is known as the 'zest'. Do not include any bitter white pith.

Use the fine side of the grater and rub this against the washed and dried fruit until all the zest is removed.

You extract the maximum flavour from the rind if you are able to cream this with the fat and sugar.

NUTS

The following are the nuts you can use most successfully in baking. Many are sold ready-prepared, either in packets or by weight. You can obtain an excellent variety of nuts from health food stores. The type of nuts and weight referred to in recipes means nuts out of shells.

Almonds
These are sold either in shells, out of shells but with skins on, or with the skins removed, these are known as blanched almonds.

If you want to blanch almonds at home, put the shelled nuts into boiling water for one minute (a longer period over-softens the nuts). Cool sufficiently to handle then pull away the skins. Dry the nuts well before using.

Chopped Almonds: The packet is sometimes labelled 'nibblets' (or 'nibbed' almonds). The nuts are blanched and evenly chopped.

Flaked Almonds: Blanched and cut into wafer thin slices.

Stripped (Slivered) Almonds: Blanched and cut into narrow strips lengthways.

Blanched Ground Almonds: Blanched and finely ground; this is the type sold by most grocers.

Unblanched Ground Almonds: Often called wholenut blanched almonds; it is quite difficult to obtain these. While most people would prefer marzipan made with the blanched ground almonds, the unblanched type give flavour to many cakes and biscuits.

Brazils
These are sold either in shells or out of shells but with the skins on. Some health food stores sell chopped or ground Brazil nuts.

If you want to blanch Brazils at home, put the shelled nuts on to a baking tray and heat for about 10 minutes in a moderate oven, then rub away the skins. Brazils are excellent in a flan, see page 208, or as a cake decoration.

Cashews
Fresh cashew nuts are rarely used in baking but they make an interesting filling, as shown on page 154.

Cobnuts (filberts)
Sold in their shells, can replace hazelnuts, although they are more moist and are better used as cake decoration; do not keep well when once shelled, unless roasted for a time in the oven.

Peanuts
Not a true nut but regarded as one; used in many recipes, buy ready shelled peanuts for baking; salted peanuts give an interesting flavour to scones or biscuits.

Peanut butter is a favourite spread with many people. An excellent ingredient in biscuits and in a filling, see page 153.

Pecans
Sold in shells or ready shelled; use instead of walnuts or in Pecan Pie, see page 208.

Pistachios
Small green nuts that make an attractive decoration on iced cakes. Remove rough outer skin by putting the nuts in boiling water for a short time then dry and chop.

Walnuts
One of the most useful nuts in cooking. Buy ready shelled or ground.

Using Chestnuts
I have not listed chestnuts with the other nuts for they are used rather differently in baking, also you can obtain excellent canned chestnut purée.

If preparing fresh chestnuts, slit the outer skins with a knife, simmer for 10 minutes in water or bake for the same time in a moderate oven. Remove the outer and inner skins while warm, rub through a sieve to make a purée.

Weights and measures

All weights and measures are given in both metric and Imperial amounts in this book. When following a recipe you should use either metric or Imperial, but not muddle the two sets of quantities. The tables on the right and on page 22 show the comparison between metric and Imperial, firstly for weights then for measures.

Metric weights are calculated in grammes (g) and there are 1000 grammes in 1 kilogramme (kg).

Measurements of length are calculated in millimetres (mm) or centimetres (cm).

Measures of liquid are calculated in millilitres, there are 1000 ml in 1 litre which is equivalent to 1.76 pints.

Baking tins are now marked in cm and not in inches, on the right are the measures.

In baking it is essential to have fat, flour and other ingredients strictly in proportion. In quite a number of recipes you will find that, in order to achieve this there seems to be an 'odd' metric amount, let me explain.

In shortcrust pastry and many other recipes you are told to use half fat to flour. As most of the recipes are based upon 8 oz flour, for which the metric conversion is 225 grammes (g), I needed to give the fat in a strictly correct proportion so instead of the accepted 100 g as equal to 4 oz, I have given 110 g which is much nearer half of 225 g. Obviously household scales do not register this extra 10 g easily, but the fact that 110 g is shown in the recipe will remind you that you must be generous with the weight in order to have the right proportion of fat to flour.

Another similar instance is when making shortcrust pastry with 6 oz flour for which the metric equivalent is 175 g; half fat to flour means you need not the usual 75 g to equal 3 oz but 85 g.

SOLIDS

Imperial Ounces	Metric Conversion Grammes	
	Accurate	Accepted
¼	7.9	7
½	14.18	15
1	28.35	25
2	56.7	50
3	85.05	75
4	113.4	100
5	141.75	150
6	170.1	175
7	198.45	200
8	226.8	225
9	255.15	250
10	283.5	300
11	311.85	325
12	340.2	350
13	368.55	375
14	396.90	400
15	425.25	425
16 oz (1 lb)	453.6	450 sometimes given as 500 g or 0.5 kg

MEASUREMENTS

Imperial Inches	Metric Conversion Millimetres and Centimetres	
	Accurate	Accepted
⅛	0.3 cm or 3 mm	2.5 mm
¼	0.6 cm or 6 mm	5 mm
½	1.25 cm	1.5 cm
¾	1.8	2
1	2.54	2.5
2	5.08	5
3	7.62	8
4	10.16	10
5	12.70	13
6	15.24	15
7	17.78	18
8	20.32	20
9	22.86	23
10	25.4	25
11	27.94	28
12	30.48	30.5

LIQUIDS		
Imperial Pints and Fl Oz	**Metric Conversion Millilitres**	
	Accurate	Accepted
1 teaspoon	5	5
1 tablespoon	15	15
¼ pint (5 fl oz)	142	150
½ pint (10 fl oz)	284	300
1 pint (20 fl oz)	568	600

HANDY MEASURES

The spoon measure refers to a level 15 ml spoon or a standard 1 tablespoon.

The cup refers to an accurate 284 ml/½ pint measure (a 10 fl oz cup). The food must not be pressed down in the cup.

Breadcrumbs – Soft
25 g/1 oz = 5 tbsp   65 g/2½ oz = 1 cup

Dried Fruit
25 g/1 oz = 2½ tbsp   200 g/7 oz = 1 cup

Fats
25 g/1 oz = 1⅔ tbsp   300 g/10 oz = 1 cup

It is, however, easier to mark the block of fat into portions. A modern block of fat is now metricated to about 250 g/9 oz.

Flour, Cocoa, Cornflour
25 g/1 oz = 3 tbsp   150 g/5 oz = 1 cup
100 g/4 oz = ⅘ cup   225 g/8 oz = 1⅗ cups

Golden Syrup, Jam, etc.
25 g/1 oz = 1 tbsp   425 g/15 oz = 1 cup

Grated Cheese – Cheddar, etc.
25 g/1 oz = 3 tbsp   150 g/5 oz = 1 cup

Sugar – Caster or Granulated
25 g/1 oz = 1⅔ tbsp   300 g/10 oz = 1 cup
100 g/4 oz = ⅖ cup   225 g/8 oz = ⅘ cup

Sugar – Icing, sifted
25 g/1 oz = 3½ tbsp   100 g/4 oz = ⅘ cup

SPOON MEASURES

Some handy spoon and cup measures follow. It must be stressed that in order to achieve a good result you must use a standard teaspoon or tablespoon. If you look in most homes you will find that teaspoons vary a great deal in size. This really matters when measuring baking powder or other raising agents.

The British teaspoon and tablespoon are the ones designed by the British Standards Institute (B.S.I.) but the modern 5 and 15 ml spoons provide the correct equivalent and it is advisable to buy these and use them in the kitchen.

When measuring a spoonful of liquid make sure the spoon is completely filled.

When measuring a tablespoon of solid food, such as flour, cornflour, etc. then level off the food with a knife, there is an illustration on page 111 under step 1; this shows a teaspoon of bicarbonate of soda being measured. The excess raising agent is removed with a knife, leaving behind an absolutely level measure.

Some people say they find ½ and ¼ spoon measures difficult. For a ½ spoon measure, make a level spoon measure then draw the knife down the centre of the ingredient to indicate clearly the ½ spoon measure; carefully remove food to one side of this line.

For a ¼ spoon measure, make the level, then the ½ measure, of the ingredient as above; then hold the knife horizontally over the ingredient in the spoon, mark the ¼ spoon amount and remove all the food to one side of this line.

Methods of mixing

In all recipes there are certain culinary terms that are used to denote the methods of mixing. It is important to appreciate the meaning of the words used.

Beating: This is the most energetic of the movements used to blend the ingredients. The ingredients for a batter and soft melted mixtures are beaten.

Use a wooden or metal spoon or an electric mixer or food processor.

Boiling: The ingredients in many recipes are combined by heating the sugar with other ingredients. Always stir until the sugar has dissolved, then allow the mixture to boil until it reaches the right temperature. Icings of this type are on page 152.

Use a strong saucepan and a wooden spoon; a sugar thermometer is a great help in checking on the various stages to which the mixture is heated.

Creaming: This method is used throughout Chapter 3 and in many other recipes in this book. Creaming is the word used to describe the method of beating the fat and sugar together for some biscuits, many cakes and butter icings.

Use a wooden spoon or an electric mixer or a food processor.

Cutting In: This describes the way in which fat is incorporated into flour by continual cutting. The method is described in Rough Puff Pastry on page 212.

Use two knives or a mixer or food processor for a very limited period.

Folding: One use of this word describes a light gentle movement illustrated in step 6 on page 127 in which the flour is blended with the whisked eggs and sugar in a sponge.

It also is necessary to fold stiffly whisked egg whites into a cake and folding is one way to incorporate sugar into the whisked egg whites for meringues.

Use a metal spoon or palette (flat-bladed) knife.

If you find this folding movement very difficult, and many energetic people do have problems, then restrict your movements as follows. If you are right-handed hold the spoon or knife in your right hand; hold the right hand wrist with the fore finger and thumb of your left hand. You will find this restricts undue movement and makes you fold correctly.

This term 'folding' is also used to describe the method in which some pastry and yeast doughs are shaped to enclose the fat, see pages 211 and 189.

Kneading: Although this action is carried out after the initial process of combining the ingredients, kneading helps to bind the ingredients together. You knead a bread or biscuit dough and some pastry.

Use the base of the palm of your hand known as 'the heel'. Doughs can be kneaded in a mixer or food processor.

Melting: In this method several of the ingredients, usually the fat and sugar plus golden syrup or treacle, are melted over a gentle heat then beaten with the flour, or other dry ingredients.

This method is described in Chapter 4. It is used for many cakes and biscuits.

After heating the ingredients, beat with a wooden spoon or in a mixer or food processor.

Rubbing In: In this method the fat is rubbed into the dry ingredients. It is described fully in Chapter 2.

This method is used in some biscuits, breads, cakes, pastries and scones.

Use your finger-tips or a mixer or food processor.

Stirring: A movement that is less brisk than beating, but more vigorous than folding. Some less rich cakes, icings and other mixtures are stirred to mix. Use a wooden spoon or a mixer or food processor.

Whisking: Light mixtures such as eggs and sugar are whisked and this process is fully described in Chapter 5. Egg whites are whisked until they stand in peaks. Cream is whisked (although the word 'whipped' is often used) until it is thick. Never over-whisk cream, for if you do it separates into a solid mass like butter and a watery liquid.

Use a hand or electric whisk.

CONSISTENCY OF A MIXTURE

In most recipes in this book it is necessary to produce a particular consistency. The following information indicates the various textures.

Firm Rolling Consistency: This means the mixture should form a firm ball, which leaves the mixing bowl clean.

Shortcrust pastry, flan pastry and many biscuit doughs should be made to a firm rolling consistency that can be rolled out with little, if any, flour required on the pastry board or rolling pin.

Marzipan and Australian fondant icings, pages 148 and 151, are also mixed to this consistency.

Soft Rolling Consistency: This is a slightly softer dough, which tends to leave your fingers a little sticky. You must roll quickly and lightly to avoid using an excess of flour on the pastry board or rolling pin.

Scones and some bread doughs are made to this consistency.

Elastic Dough: A little like a soft rolling consistency, but less soft. The dough can be easily rolled, is not sticky and it can be folded over easily without any sign of breaking. The dough is not short and crumbly. This texture is achieved by the amount of fat and liquid used and is shown in the recipes for Flaky, Puff and Rough Puff pastries on pages 211 and 212.

Sticky Consistency: The mixture should be *just* too soft to roll with your fingers, but sufficiently firm to stand up in peaks in a mixing bowl, see the illustration with Step 5 on page 39.

A good test is to see if a fork or knife can stand upright in the mixture.

This is the correct texture for Rock Cakes, and similar mixtures, see pages 38 to 39.

Dropping Consistency: The mixture only drops from the spoon when given a very hard shake. This is the consistency for most rich fruit cakes.

Soft or Slow Dropping Consistency: The mixture drops from the spoon without a hard shake and within about 3 seconds. The consistency is correct for light cakes, such as a Victoria Sandwich, see page 67.

Very Soft Consistency: The mixture drops from the spoon as soon as this is held suspended over the mixing bowl. This consistency is correct for many very light sponges.

Pouring Consistency: The mixture can be poured from the bowl or the spoon. Cakes made by the melting method are generally of a pouring consistency, so are most batters. The true whisked sponge is made to a thick pouring consistency for a Swiss Roll, see page 127.

The equipment

As with every type of work your 'tools', in this case the equipment used to mix the foods and then cook the prepared mixture, are important.

While it is a mistake to assume you need a vast range of mixing utensils, cake and other tins, there are certain pieces of equipment that are necessary. I have divided the equipment therefore, into two headings, firstly basic needs and secondly the additional utensils you may care to add as your interest in baking increases. Always buy the best quality utensils you can afford and cherish them carefully.

BASIC NEEDS

Boards: You will find a board (generally called a pastry board) extremely useful. Modern pastry boards are made in wood or in laminated finishes. Always wash and dry carefully. Do not use too hot water for cleaning a wooden board and make sure this is adequately dried before putting away. If you can obtain a modern or old-fashioned marble slab to use as a pastry board you will be fortunate, since this helps to keep pastry beautifully cool when rolling it.

A small chopping board is useful and prevents 'scarring' the pastry board when you chop nuts or other foods such as onions, carrots, etc.

Baking Tins and Trays: On page 30 you will find illustrations and descriptions of some of the specialised tins needed for more elaborate cakes, breads and other baked goods.

These are your basic requirements:

1 or 2 flat baking trays, you will find a baking sheet is supplied with most cookers; this is flat without a rim. A typical baking tray is illustrated on this page. You need these for cooking biscuits, scones, and you can bake flat 'slab' cakes in these, ready to cut into smaller pieces for little cakes.

A Swiss roll tin is slightly different, it has a shallow rim; it can be used for baking other foods too. The measurements of the Swiss roll tin correspond to those given in the basic recipe on page 130.

I would buy an **18–20 cm/7–8 inch round cake tin**, for this is a most useful size; a slightly larger one for making special occasion cakes, **a loaf tin**, one to make a 900 g/2 lb loaf (it may be called a 1 kg tin) is probably the most useful. If you intend to batch bake quite a lot of bread then you will need several loaf tins, unless you prefer to make round or other shaped loaves; see page 187. Approximate measurements, as well as capacity, of loaf tins are sometimes given as many shops sell them by measurement rather than the amount of food that can be put in them.

You will need one or more **trays of patty tins** for making small tartlets and

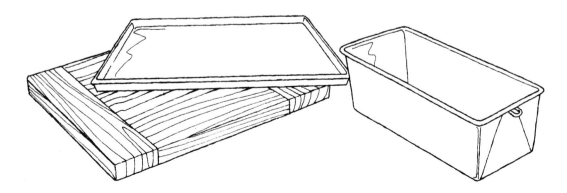

little cakes. The plain type is more useful. More ornamental patty tins are shown on page 30.

Buy **a pair of sandwich tins** for making sponges; I think most people find the 18 cm/7 inch size the most useful; different makers often produce tins that are just below, or just above the 18 cm/7 inches. Note the difference and adjust the baking times by 2–3 minutes; i.e. a tin of 17 cm/6¾ inches diameter means those few minutes extra cooking time, due to the greater depth of mixture; whereas a slightly larger diameter, 18.5 cm/7¼ inches means you should find the sponge takes 2–3 minutes shorter cooking time.

You may be asked if you want sandwich or **cake tins with a loose base**; this makes it easy to remove the cooked sponge or cake, but there are a very few recipes in which I state 'do not use a tin with a loose base'. This is generally because an appreciable amount of liquid is used and this would drip through the cracks between the loose base and tin sides.

Shaped tins (some with loose bases) are described on page 30.

Baking trays and tins are made of metal; if you look after them well no food should stick to the surface; in which case you can continually wipe the trays or tins with soft paper or cloth immediately after use and avoid washing them. If you have to wash them, use warm water only with the minimum amount of detergent, dry the tins with a cloth and then leave them in a warm place for some hours to make absolutely certain they are completely dry before you put them away.

There are many makes of tins that have a silicone (non-stick) finish. These should be washed and dried carefully, or simply wiped as suggested above. Never use abrasive cleaners on these.

Store tins carefully so they keep their good shape.

Bowls and Basins: You will need one or more good-sized mixing bowls and several basins. While plastic is useful there may be occasions when you need to stand a bowl or basin over hot water, so ovenproof glassware is a good choice; some plastic bowls can be subjected to heat over water, but not to the dry heat of an oven. Check carefully therefore on the properties of plastic basins before you buy them, so that you will not be disappointed.

Brushes: You need at least one pastry brush, which you use for coating tins with melted fat or oil before baking. A brush is needed to coat pastry with beaten egg, to 'glaze', i.e. give a shine and for coating food with other forms of glaze too. A good quality pastry brush lasts for years. Wash in a warm mild detergent solution after use, then rinse in cold water and dry well. It is advisable to leave the brush in the warmth of the kitchen before putting it away.

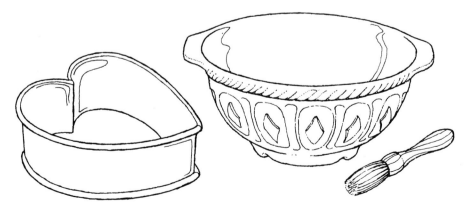

Cutters: You need these to cut rounds or squares of pastry or biscuit dough. Pastry cutters are obtainable in metal or plastic. The metal cutters have a sharper cutting edge. It is traditional to use fluted cutters for sweet items, such as jam tarts, and plain cutters for savoury tarts. If cutting a slightly sticky mixture, always dip the cutting edge in a little flour. Always dry metal cutters well after use, see the advice about drying cake tins. In an emergency, you can use the rim of a cup or glass as a cutter.

Dredgers: If possible have two; one for flour and one for sugar. You need a flour dredger when rolling out pastry, biscuit or yeast doughs; it means you can shake the minimum amount of flour over the surface, whereas if you spoon this you tend to use too much.

A sugar dredger is used to shake sugar over baked sweet pies, sponges and other foods.

Grater: A grater is referred to very frequently in baking recipes, e.g. 'grate the lemon rind', 'grated nutmeg', etc. It is advisable to buy a grater with at least two cutting surfaces or even more for recipes vary. Sometimes you are told to grate the food 'very finely' or 'finely', at other times 'coarsely'.

When grating lemon or other citrus fruit rinds, you will find that the rind tends to stick to the cutting surface. Never try to remove this with a knife, you will damage the cutting surface; use a pastry brush. Grate the food on to or into a container so none is wasted.

Graters vary a great deal in price, the cheaper ones are made of ordinary metal, the more expensive of stainless steel. This means they will not rust when used for acid fruits; the metal ones will not rust if you take great care in cleaning and drying them.

Knives: Obviously you need a sharp knife for chopping foods ready for baking; you also need a flat-bladed knife, known as a palette knife, for blending ingredients; lifting cooked food from the baking tray and many other purposes. I find a fairly firm palette knife fulfils both purposes well but if buying two, choose one that is very flexible so you can 'clean out' mixing bowls and avoid any waste, and one that is firmer.

Measuring Jug: This is another essential aid to baking. You will be told that a teacup is about 150 ml/¼ pint and a breakfast cup about 300 ml/½ pint, but that is too vague for well-proportioned recipes. A proper measure will ensure you use exactly the right amount.

Spoon measures are given separately on page 22.

Rolling Pin: These are obtainable in wood or in ceramic. The latter, of course looks attractive, but is breakable. Do not buy a

rolling pin that is too short in length, for there may be times when you need to roll out a large amount of pastry, or other mixtures. Hold the various makes of rolling pins for a few seconds to gauge whether they feel comfortable; some people like a rolling pin with handles at either end; other people prefer ones without handles.

Wash and dry the rolling pin carefully, leave in a warm place to dry if made of wood before storing.

Scales: Some people say they manage without scales; that may be possible in some forms of cooking, such as when making stews or soups, but correct proportions are so important for baking that you should invest in good scales. There is a choice between the type of scales in which weights are used (these are the easiest to use) and those that register the weight on a gauge.

In each case modern scales have both metric and Imperial weights or measurements.

Both types are illustrated. The gauge type can be obtained to fit on the wall, which is a great help if you are short of space for it is advisable to keep scales readily available. If stored away, you might be tempted to guess weights.

Sieve: Most baking recipes begin with the words 'sift the flour'. This ensures that the flour is smooth and where raising agent, salt, spices or other powdered ingredients are used, it blends the foods together. The illustration shows a typical flour sieve. The words 'sieve the flour' mean exactly the same thing, it is just a case of using which word, 'sift' or 'sieve', you prefer.

You could use a large general purpose sieve, but so often this has a larger diameter than the basin or bowl into which you are sifting the flour, and some is spilled around the basin or bowl.

You will need a sieve for various other ingredients used in recipes in this book such as cooked potato, other vegetables, fruits, etc. While a metal meshed sieve can be used for vegetables, you must use a hair or nylon meshed sieve for fruits, since metal can spoil both the colour and flavour.

Wash and dry sieves very well; if using the sieve just for flour it should only need shaking and wiping well.

Note: Soufflé dishes, pie dishes, flan dishes and rings are all listed under Specialist Equipment.

Spoons: The most important spoons for baking are those with which you measure, described on page 22, and wooden spoons. A wooden spoon enables you to cream, beat or blend most ingredients together. The recipes indicate when you replace this with another implement, such as a palette knife, metal spoon or whisk. Wash and

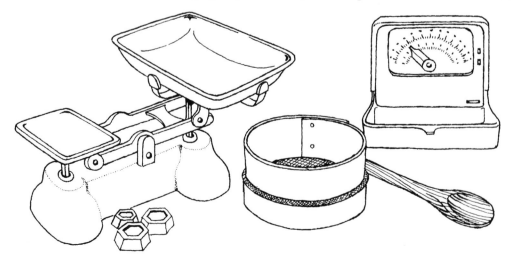

dry wooden spoons very carefully, use warm mild detergent solutions, dry with a cloth, but leave in a warm place before storing.

Whisk: There are many kinds of hand whisks; electric whisks are described on page 128.

A rotary whisk is excellent for speedy whipping of ingredients, but less good for whisking the eggs and sugar in a sponge, see page 127. Take great care in washing this type of whisk that you do not immerse the handle, containing the bearings, in water.

A balloon whisk is good for all forms of whisking.

A flat whisk or coil whisk are the best for whisking the eggs and sugar in a sponge. They do not whip cream or whisk egg whites as rapidly as the rotary or balloon types. They also are excellent for whisking sauces.

These whisks are made of metal, so wash and dry carefully.

Wire Cooling Tray: One of these is essential, for you need to turn most breads and cakes out of the tins while hot, or warm, and allow them to cool with a good circulation of air around. These are sometimes called 'cake racks' but that does not really describe their use, since scones, a few biscuits and many other baked goods are cooled on these. They can be found in various shapes and sizes.

USING AN ELECTRIC MIXER

An electric mixer is invaluable for many of the stages when preparing cakes, bread, biscuits, some kinds of pastry and other baked goods.

It is important however to appreciate the fact that the action of a mixer is very energetic and you must make quite sure that the ingredients used in the recipe are not over-handled.

If your mixer has various speeds, and most of them do, choose the speed that is the most like hand mixing, e.g. when whisking egg whites for meringues by hand one whisks briskly, you can therefore use a high speed with the mixer. When kneading a yeast dough, you do this slowly and deliberately by hand; use a low speed and the special dough hooks provided by most manufacturers.

Special advice on using a mixer is given in every chapter; it follows shortly after the Master Recipe and step-by-step directions. Do read and follow the recommendations, together with any special instructions by the maker of your mixer.

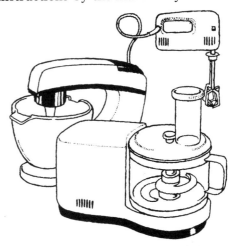

USING A FOOD PROCESSOR

Modern food processors have a very real part to play in preparing the ingredients for cakes, biscuits, bread and some kinds of pastry.

As users of food processors appreciate, this machine is ultra-speedy in mixing and processing foods; this is a great asset but it does mean that every process must be timed to seconds – not minutes.

Special advice on using a food processor is given in every chapter; it follows one or two pages after the Master Recipe and step-by-step directions. Do read and follow the recommendations given, together with any special instructions by the maker of your particular food processor.

SPECIALIST EQUIPMENT

Some of the items given below may well be in your cupboard since they have uses other than for preparing foods for baking.

Apple Corer: For removing cores from apples, hard centres from slices of fresh pineapple. The small round can be used as a cutter for pastry decorations and some biscuits too.

Baking Beans: Plastic, sometimes ceramic, heat-resistant beans useful when baking flans 'blind', see page 207.

Baking Tins: These are some of the interesting tins you can buy:

Assorted shaped patty tins, such as diamonds, hearts, oval and finger shaped, also in small sizes for petits fours.

Boat-shaped patty tins for small pastry cases or light cakes.

Brioche tins vary from small individual fluted tins (also useful for baking light cakes).

Dariole tins, used for Madeleines.

Eclair tins, also useful for sponge fingers, there are also smaller finger tins; used for tiny eclairs, sponge fingers and Langue de Chat biscuits. Larger eclair tins are also available, useful for larger sponge fingers.

Rum Baba tins, individual ring-shaped tins.

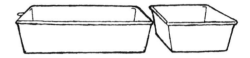

Bread tins in various shapes.

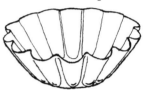

Brioche tins for larger cakes or interesting shaped light cakes.

Shaped cake tins in heart, number, square, oblong, letter and horseshoe shapes.

Raised pie tins that unlock to ease out pies.

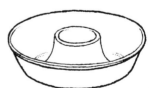

Savarin tins, ring shaped tins that can be used for many recipes, see page 193.

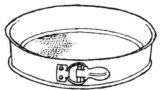

Springform tins that unlock at one side. Ideal for delicate cheesecakes.

Biscuit Cutters: Various shapes, such as animal shapes, figures, stars, etc. enable you to make crisp biscuits in interesting ways for children; also tiny cutters for cocktail sized biscuits and petits fours.

Rich soft biscuit dough can be piped, just as one pipes icing, but you need a special biscuit pipe or former.

Flan Rings: These are made in various sizes, choose a fluted ring for sweet flans, a plain ring for savoury flans.

Small individual flan rings enable you to make perfectly shaped Crumpets, see page 194.

Scissors: Kitchen scissors are excellent for cutting-up many foods.

Shortbread Mould: In wood to shape the biscuit; mould before baking.

Soufflé Dish: Can also be used for microwave 'baking'.

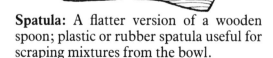

Spatula: A flatter version of a wooden spoon; plastic or rubber spatula useful for scraping mixtures from the bowl.

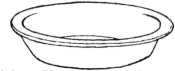

Pie Dishes: Choose various sizes.

Pizza Tin: This large round tin gives an excellent shape to the bread base.

Quiche or Flan Dishes: For baking savoury flans, you can use a flan ring or sandwich tin.

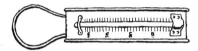

Sugar Thermometer: For cooked icings, see page 152.
Note: Specialist icing equipment is described on page 150.

MODERN 'BAKING' EQUIPMENT

It must look strange to put the word 'baking' in inverted commas, but purists would insist that the only true method of baking is in an oven. They are right of course, but there may be occasions when you can use different equipment for producing a dish that is normally baked in the traditional manner.

Many different kinds of equipment, such as a microwave cooker, a crock-pot (electric casserole), a table cooker and a pressure cooker, save fuel and give good results, if used for the right type of foods and according to instructions.

Modern electric fryers, which are thermostatically controlled, make frying foods, such as doughnuts, very simple and successful.

Throughout this book you will find brief hints on using suitable equipment for the particular kind of mixtures in the section.

Look for this advice under the heading 'Using Modern Equipment'.

Preparing tins for baking

The terms 'grease' or 'grease and flour' are often used to describe the preparation needed before putting the cake, cakes or biscuits on to or into the container.

A little grease may be necessary on a tin when you are baking scones containing oatmeal, syrup, cheese, etc; if baking pastry tartlets in very small tins or the type of pastry that could stick such as choux pastry. Specific instructions for difficult foods like meringues, are given in the recipe.

To grease and flour is the usual preparation when baking cakes. It is advisable to line a tin for very delicate cakes, cakes that are in the oven for a prolonged period or where you are worried that the food might stick to your particular tin.

Silicone treated tins only need greasing where given in the specific Master Recipe.

While you can rub the container with greasy paper to coat it, you obtain a more even finish if you use a pastry brush, see To Grease and Flour below.

It is important to use the right fat for greasing tins, such as butter, cooking fat, good quality margarine, lard or olive oil.

Cheaper margarines and oils used for frying are less good.

TO GREASE AND FLOUR TINS

1. Put a small amount of fat into a pan, heat gently. You can put the fat into a container and stand this in a pan of boiling water to melt. To save wasting any fat, keep the surplus in the container and place this in the refrigerator, ready to use on another occasion.

Dip a pastry brush in the melted fat, brush over the inner surface of the tin to give an even shine. Never use too much.

2. To flour the coated tin, put in a small spoonful of flour. Turn the tin so you get an even coating of flour over the greased surface. Shake the tin hard, then tip out the surplus flour.

When coating small patty tins, a good pinch of flour is enough.

TO LINE TINS

1. *To line the bottom of a tin.* Stand tin on greaseproof or waxed paper or baking parchment. Draw round tin, then cut out paper shape. Put a very little grease on inside tin base to hold paper in position, put in the paper; grease or grease and flour the inside of the tin and paper.

2. *To line the sides and bottom of a round tin.* Make a round as above. Cut a band of double thickness greaseproof or waxed paper or baking parchment 2.5–3.5 cm/1–1½ inches deeper than the depth of the tin and the full length of the circumference of the cake tin. Make cuts at regular 1.5 cm/½ inch intervals to a depth of about 1.5 cm/½ inch. Grease the bottom and sides of the tin in one or two places. Put in the band of paper, with the cut edges at the bottom. These will open and make a snug fit on the tin base. Put round of paper on top, then grease, or grease and flour paper.

3. *To line an oblong tin.*
Method 1: Cut two pieces of greaseproof or waxed paper or baking parchment, one to line the sides and base of the tin and the other to line the ends and base.
Method 2: Cut the paper sufficiently large to completely cover inside and sides of tin, mitring corners.
Line a *square tin* in the same way.

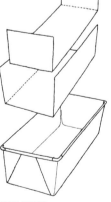

Know about cookers

A perfect control over the oven temperature is more important when baking than any other form of cooking.

If a cake is baked too slowly it becomes over-dry and unpalatable and the low heat may stop the mixture rising correctly. If, on the other hand, the cake is baked too quickly it becomes over-brown, or even burned on the outside before it is cooked in the centre.

It is therefore essential to select the correct cooking temperature, and to check that your particular oven will give this. Ovens vary slightly and while all recipes in this book are tested most carefully, it may be that your oven is a little hotter or cooler than average. Always check oven settings against the manufacturers' advice for YOUR cooker or stove and make any slight adjustment necessary.

Obviously if you consistently find that your oven setting varies a great deal from the setting recommended in various recipes, you should have the cooker checked by the supplier.

PREHEATING THE OVEN

It is advisable to preheat the oven, for most forms of baking as bread, cakes and pastry need to go into an oven which has reached the correct heat recommended in the recipe.

On the other hand if you are using your oven on automatic setting, you could put very rich fruit cakes or economical fruit cakes or shortcrust pastry into a cold oven, providing this is set to begin heating within a relatively short time.

You will spoil light sponges and light cakes, rich pastry (such as puff or flaky pastry), yeast cakes and bread and scones if you try and bake them in an oven that has not been adequately preheated.

POSITION IN THE OVEN

It must be stressed that the oven position is extremely important. The chart below indicates where you should place the various kinds of dishes for baking.

If you have a modern fan-assisted electric oven, you can place the food anywhere in the oven.

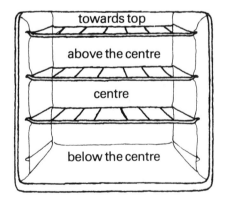

For Swiss rolls

For small cakes, rolls, scones, sponge sandwiches

For loaves of bread, biscuits, large cakes, flans, pies

For very rich cakes, some biscuits. In an electric oven you can put Victoria sandwich here.

The reason for choosing the positions above is to ensure even cooking and the correct speed of cooking.

If you place a large cake above the centre of the cooker, you will find the top of the cake begins to brown too quickly. Biscuits would begin to brown before they are cooked.

If, on the other hand, you put scones or small cakes in the centre of the oven, or below the centre you slow-up the cooking process and the food becomes drier than it should. 33

OVEN TEMPERATURES

The table on the following page shows oven settings and descriptions and how to check your own oven temperature. I have given the various terms used to describe a cool oven which you may find in various recipes, although I say 'cool'.

You will see I have returned to the slightly 'old-fashioned' habit of calling 160°C, 325°F, Gas Mark 3 'very moderate'. Nowadays the word 'very' is generally omitted. I feel this is a pity for it does differentiate between this setting and 180°C, 350°F, Gas Mark 4 which is also described as 'moderate'.

Some cooks term 190°C, 375°F, Gas Mark 5 as 'moderate'; others call it 'moderately hot'.

There can be no confusion in this book about oven temperatures for the description of the heat as well as the recommended setting and position in the oven are given in all recipes together with the cooking time.

The table gives both Celsius (C) and Fahrenheit (F). In addition, the comparable gas setting is given, together with a description of the oven temperature.

If you change from a cooker with Fahrenheit degrees to one with Celsius degrees, you may care to know that the figures given in the table are those marked on the cooker but the accurate conversion from Fahrenheit to Celsius does give slight variations on these, but not enough to cause problems. I have, however, included them for your interest.

Gauging the Heat: The last column in the table tells how you can gauge the heat by a simple test for there may be an occasion when the thermostat on your oven seems to be faulty, or you might find yourself in a strange kitchen where you have to use an unfamiliar cooker, such as one fired by oil or solid fuel.

Use fairly thick good quality writing paper; thin paper is not suitable. If you have no thick paper, test with your hand, as shown under point b) opposite.

If using paper, put into the **centre** of the oven. Do not test towards the top or the bottom of the oven, otherwise you will not obtain an accurate result. The paper should be put directly on to the oven shelf, for if placed on a baking tray the timing would be slightly different.

If using paper, watch carefully and check the timing as you do so, point a) gives you the result you will achieve at different oven temperatures.

If you are using your hand as a test, you must, of course, be very careful that it does not touch any part of the cooker.

Note carefully: These tests should be carried out with a preheated oven. Set the oven to the required electric or gas temperature, allow the normal preheating time then test; you can then make any adjustment after this if necessary.

PLACING CONTAINERS IN THE OVEN

On page 33 you will find advice about the correct oven position of the food.

It also is important that you have good circulation of heat in the oven to ensure even baking, so do not use baking trays that are so large that they need to be placed immediately over the gas burners or touching the sides in an electric oven.

Make sensible use of fuel by baking as many items as possible at one time; naturally you must select those dishes that require the same baking temperature. When the oven is full though check carefully that there is room for heat to circulate.

Opening the Oven Door: You can open the door quite happily when baking biscuits, some breads, pastry (except choux) and scones, but the utmost care must be taken when baking cakes, choux pastry, soufflés. Open the door carefully, try to avoid letting cold air in the oven, inspect the food then close the door quietly.

OVEN TEMPERATURE CHART

Oven description	Degrees C Marked on cooker	Actual	Degrees F Marked on cooker	Gas Mark	How to Test
Very cool	90	93	200	0	a) Paper turns golden after 12 minutes
					b) Hand can be kept in oven without discomfort
Very cool	110	107	225	¼	a) Paper turns golden after 10 minutes
					b) Hand can be kept in oven without discomfort
Very cool	120	121	250	½	a) Paper turns golden after 8 minutes
					b) Hand can be kept in oven without discomfort
Low or slow or cool	140	135	275	1	a) Paper turns golden after 6 minutes
					b) Hand feels pleasantly warm
Low or slow or cool	150	149	300	2	a) Paper turns golden after 5 minutes
					b) Hand feels pleasantly warm
Very moderate	160	163	325	3	a) Paper turns golden brown after 2 minutes
					b) Hand begins to feel hot
Moderate	180	177	350	4	a) Paper turns golden brown after 1½ minutes
					b) Not comfortable for hand
Moderate or moderately hot (see comment on page 34)	190	190	375	5	a) Paper turns golden brown after 1 minute
					b) Hand feels hot the moment it goes in oven
Moderately hot	200	204	400	6	a) Paper turns golden almost at once
					b) Hand held near door feels hot at once
Hot	220	218	425	7	a) Paper turns golden at once
					b) Hand held near door feels hot at once
Very hot	230	232	450	8	a) Blast of hot air on opening door. Do not put paper in, it will burn
					b) Uncomfortable to hold hand near oven
Very hot	240	246	475	9	Impossible to put hand very near the oven

CHAPTER 2

The Rubbing-in Method

I have given this method of mixing the ingredients together, as the first recipe chapter in this book, because rubbing-in is undoubtedly the simplest of all ways of incorporating fat into flour or other dry ingredients.

Rubbing fat into flour is done quickly and easily, so that beginners to cooking should not experience any problems. The rest of the ingredients are simply mixed in with a knife or spoon, as the recipes indicate, or with a mixer or food processor.

Do not imagine that this rubbing-in technique has limited use; it is the basis for many recipes, as the list below shows.

Most of the recipes made by this method are not only simple, but inexpensive too, so they are ideal for economical family fare.

WHAT DOES RUBBING-IN MEAN?

It means that the fat is rubbed by the finger-tips into the flour, or flour and other dry ingredients (such as flour mixed with cornflour or semolina), until the mixture looks like fine breadcrumbs.
It is possible to use a hand or electric mixer or food processor for this purpose.
The other ingredients are then added as the particular recipe.
A good basic recipe is to use exactly half fat to flour as in the Master Recipe on the next page, but proportions for more elaborate cakes vary appreciably.
The rubbing-in method is used for:

Both small and large cakes
Many biscuits and biscuit-type cakes
Various puddings
Crumble puddings
Some pastries, e.g. shortcrust, sweet shortcrust, suet pastry.

Cakes made by the rubbing-in method – Orange Sultana Squares (above, recipe page 54), Apple and Ginger Squares (below, recipe page 51)

ROCK CAKES

This recipe will produce a batch of about 10 small or 1 large cake. There are a number of variations on this recipe and with simple adaptations you can produce many different cakes, see pages 41 to 48.

Baking Utensils: Grease a 35 × 30 cm/14 × 12 inch baking tray or baking sheet; if this is any smaller use two trays or sheets.

Oven Setting: Preheat the oven at moderately hot to hot, 200–220°C, 400–425°F, Gas Mark 6–7. Arrange the shelf just above the centre of the oven. If using two shelves place one just below the centre (with a fan-assisted oven any position can be used).

Cooking Time: 12 minutes.

Makes approximately 10
**225 g/8 oz self-raising flour or plain flour
    with 2 teaspoons baking powder
pinch salt
110 g/4 oz butter or margarine or cooking fat
110 g/4 oz caster or granulated or Demerara
    or moist brown sugar
75–100 g/3–4 oz mixed dried fruit
1 egg
approx. 4 tablespoons milk to mix**

to glaze
½–1 tablespoon caster sugar

CERTAIN SUCCESS

Choice of Ingredients: Use either self-raising flour, or flour with the amount of baking powder given in the Master Recipe above. I list the choice of fat in order of preference for each recipe.
You can use whichever sugar pleases you most in Rock Cakes, or as advised in individual recipes.
The amount of milk given in the Master Recipe is an approximate measure, since different makes of flour vary very slightly in the quantity of liquid they absorb and your choice of fat also determines exactly how much liquid is required; just add enough to make the correct consistency.

Handling the Mixture: While you must rub the fat into the flour efficiently, you should not over-rub, for this would make a too-short texture, which is ideal for a shortbread, but not for small or large cakes or for pastry. Shake the bowl from time to time as you rub in the mixture, to make sure all the fat and flour are blended.

Consistency: The mixture for Rock Cakes should be as shown in steps 5 to 7, or as described in individual recipes.
Remember any mixture where fat is rubbed into flour appears stiffer than one made by the creaming or melting methods.

Preparing Tins: Grease where indicated, except when using a silicone (non-stick) type; here greasing is unnecessary. It rarely is necessary to line tins with greased greaseproof paper for this type of mixture.

Baking: Always preheat the oven at the setting given in the recipe.
If you have not made Rock Cakes before, open the oven door carefully at the end of 5 minutes; the cakes should be pale in colour, soft in texture, but starting to rise and spread. If browning too much, reduce the heat by 10°C, 25°F or 1 Gas Mark. Test after 12 minutes cooking. The cakes should be golden-brown and feel firm to the touch when pressed on the sides.

1 Sift the flour, or flour and baking powder, with the pinch of salt, into a good-sized mixing bowl. Cut the butter, margarine or cooking fat into small pieces with a knife, add to the flour.

2 Lift some of the fat and flour with your finger-tips well above the level of the bowl, so incorporating air into the mixture. Rub this combination of fat and flour with your thumb and forefinger until well blended; do not rub until it becomes over-sticky.

3 Allow the crumbly mixture to drop back into the bowl. Continue like this until all the mixture looks like fine breadcrumbs.

4 Add the sugar and fruit to the rubbed-in mixture, stir with a palette knife to mix with the rubbed-in ingredients. Break the egg into a cup to ascertain that it is fresh, then drop it into the centre of the flour mixture.

5 Stir well to blend the egg with the flour mixture, then add the milk gradually. It is advisable to do this from a spoon, so there is no possibility of using too much liquid, stir as you do so. The mixture should be a sticky consistency that stands in peaks in the bowl.

6 Lift about one tenth of the mixture from the bowl with two metal spoons or two forks (whichever you find more comfortable) and put on to the greased baking tray(s) or sheet(s). Continue like this until all the mixture is used; allow plenty of space between the cakes for they not only rise, but spread out as well.

7 If any of the mounds of cake mixture appear too flat; sweep up in peaks with the tip of a knife. Sprinkle a little caster sugar on the top of each cake to give an attractive shine.

8 Bake for approximately 12–15 minutes. If using two trays you may find the cakes on the lower shelf in the oven take a little longer to cook.

9 Check baking speed, if a little unsure of your own oven, test the cakes after 12 minutes, see opposite.

10 When cooked, remove from the oven, allow to STAND for 5 minutes before removing the buns from the tray(s) or sheet(s). This makes certain that the crisp and short-textured mixture sets and does not break when lifted. Remove each cake on to a wire cooling tray with a palette knife; allow to cool. Serve when freshly cooked.

Using modern equipment

Nowadays many cooks have a mixer and/or a food processor and it is sensible to use labour-saving equipment if this gives a good result.

RUBBING-IN METHOD BY MIXER

The detailed method to follow is given below, with the Master Recipe as an example.

All cakes made by the 'rubbing-in' method can be prepared with a small or large electric mixer, providing the important advice, given below, is followed.

Always consult the manufacturers' handbook as to the maximum amount of mixture that can be dealt with at one time; if you try and mix too great a quantity the result is disappointing.

A MIXER FOR ROCK CAKES

If the machine has a beater, use that or use the whisk(s). Sift the flour, etc, as step 1, previous page, into the bowl. Cut the fat into pieces; if hard allow to soften in the kitchen for a short time (luxury margarine will be sufficiently soft).

Add the fat to the flour; switch on the mixer to the lowest speed and leave running only until the fat is incorporated into the flour. DO NOT OVERBEAT. Add the egg, then add the milk gradually, see step 5, previous page, with the machine in operation. Lastly add the fruit and mix thoroughly. Continue as steps 6–10.
Points to Watch: Use a low speed. Never overbeat the mixture; add the milk gradually.

RUBBING-IN METHOD BY FOOD PROCESSOR

The detailed method to follow is given below, with the Master Recipe as an example.

All cakes made by the 'rubbing-in' method can be prepared with a food processor, providing the important advice, given below, is followed.

Always consult the manufacturers' handbook as to the maximum amount of mixture that can be dealt with at one time; if you try and mix too great a quantity the result is disappointing.

A FOOD PROCESSOR FOR ROCK CAKES

Fix the double-bladed cutting knife and food processor bowl in position. Sift the flour, etc, as step 1, previous page, into the bowl. Cut the fat into pieces; if hard allow to soften for a short time, although a food processor deals with moderately hard fat well (luxury margarines will be sufficiently soft).

Add the fat to the flour, put on the lid and switch on for a few seconds only; DO NOT OVERPROCESS. Remove the food processor lid, add the egg, put on the lid, switch on again and mix for 1–2 seconds only. Add the milk gradually through the feed-tube, with the machine in operation, stop immediately the mixture reaches the right stage, see step 5, previous page. Add the dried fruit to the mixture; this can be done through the feed-tube or by removing the lid, adding the fruit then replacing the lid. Whichever method is used, process for 1–2 seconds only; the cutting knife is so efficient that if the mixture was processed for a longer period the dried fruit would be finely chopped. Continue as steps 6–10, previous page.
Points to Watch: Do not overprocess at any time; do not add too much liquid (one tends to need a few *drops* less than when mixing by hand).

Using your Master Recipe

The Master Recipe on pages 38 and 39 provides a splendid basis for many cakes. Obviously some ingredients are changed and if this makes a difference in the way you prepare the mixture it is covered in the particular recipe.

ECONOMICAL ROCK CAKES

Follow the recipe on pages 38 and 39; but use only 75 g/3 oz butter, margarine or cooking fat and 75 g/3 oz sugar. The amount of dried fruit can be reduced to 50 g/2 oz. Do not omit the egg, since this helps to bind the mixture together; for people who do not want to use eggs there is a version of the cakes called Eggless Rock Cakes.

As less fat is used in the economical recipe, you will need just a few drops more milk to bind the mixture. Bake as the recipe on page 38.

The cakes tend to be firmer and keep a better shape than the standard Rock Cakes, but have a less good flavour.

RICH ROCK CAKES

Follow the recipe on pages 38 and 39, but increase the butter, margarine or fat to 150 g/5 oz and the sugar to 150–175 g/5–6 oz. Add an extra 50 g/2 oz dried fruit with 25 g/1 oz finely chopped candied peel. Use only 1 egg with milk to bind. As you have a higher percentage of fat than in the standard Rock Cakes, you will need slightly less milk.

Bake the richer cakes at a slightly lower temperature, i.e. moderately hot, 190–200°C, 375–400°F, Gas Mark 5–6. The buns will take 2–3 minutes longer cooking time.

Do not be disappointed if these tend to spread during cooking and remain less 'rocky'; their flavour is delicious.

EGGLESS ROCK CAKES

Eggs are an important part of cake recipes, but if you want to omit the egg in the recipe these are the adaptations to make. You can use either the Master Recipe on pages 38 and 39 or one of the versions on this page.

Eggs add colour as well as flavour, so I would use 1 tablespoon less flour and add 1 tablespoon custard powder instead; sift this with the flour.

An average egg adds approximately 2 tablespoons liquid to the Rock Cakes, so you will need a little more milk, but add this very sparingly.

Use the higher temperature given in the recipe, i.e. 220°C, 425°F or Gas Mark 7, if making the standard Rock Cakes or the more economical version, and 200°C, 400°F or Gas Mark 6 for the more luxurious version. This sets the outside of the cakes more rapidly; for eggless recipes tend to lose shape more easily.

WHEATMEAL ROCK CAKES

Follow the recipe for Rock Cakes on page 38 but use wheatmeal self-raising flour instead of ordinary flour. If using plain wheatmeal flour add 2 teaspoons baking powder.

Make the Rock Cakes exactly as the recipe on the previous two pages, but since wheatmeal flour absorbs more liquid you will require slightly more milk to bind the mixture.

Bake as for Rock Cakes, but allow 2–3 minutes extra cooking time because of the additional liquid content. Wheatmeal flour can be used in the Economical or Rich Rock Cakes.

41

SMALL CAKES BASED ON THE MASTER RECIPE

Many people are rather inclined to feel that these small, quickly made and economical cakes, are not particularly interesting. In fact if you eat the cakes, or buns as they are often called, when they are fresh they really are delicious.

The following recipes all follow the technique outlined on pages 38 and 39. Sometimes the amount of liquid has been adjusted because of the particular type of mixture.

MINIATURE ROCK CAKES

Makes 18–20

The Master Recipe on page 38 is given as making approximately 10 cakes. I must stress that these are fairly large cakes, suitable for hungry people. If you like to make dainty sized cakes the mixture will make about 18–20. Bake above the centre of a hot oven, 220°C, 425°F, Gas Mark 7 for about 10 minutes; do not overbake these small cakes.

All recipes that follow are based on making generous sized small cakes and the mixture can be used to produce virtually double the quantity of small ones.

APPLE SAUCE BUNS

Makes 10

Follow the Master Recipe for Rock Cakes on pages 38 and 39 or any of the variations on page 41, but use thick unsweetened apple purée to mix the buns instead of milk.
Note: If you bake the cooking apples, skin and discard the cores while hot, then mash the pulp, you then have a very thick apple purée which is ideal for binding the rubbed-in mixture.

ALMOND ROCK CAKES

Makes 14–16

175 g/6 oz self-raising flour or plain flour with 1½ teaspoons baking powder
110 g/4 oz butter or margarine
150 g/5 oz caster sugar
50 g/2 oz ground almonds
1 egg
few drops almond essence
few drops milk

to decorate
1 tablespoon caster sugar
25 g/1 oz flaked blanched almonds

Sift the flour, or flour and baking powder, into a mixing bowl. Rub in the butter or margarine, as in Rock Cakes page 39, add the sugar and ground almonds. Mix the egg and almond essence together (this makes sure the essence is well distributed), stir into the other ingredients. Add just enough milk to make a sticky consistency, as shown in step 5, page 39.

This recipe contains only three-quarters of the amount of flour used in Rock Cakes and the ground almonds add a certain amount of moisture so be careful as you add liquid.

These cakes are nicer if made rather smaller than Rock Cakes, so put 14–16 heaps on lightly greased baking trays. Top with the sugar and chopped nuts and bake above the centre of a moderately hot to hot oven, 200–220°C, 400–425°F, Gas Mark 6–7 for about 12 minutes; they are best if not too crisp.

ALMOND AND APRICOT ROCK CAKES

Prepare the cakes as above; make an indentation in each cake, fill with apricot jam; bake as above.

BANANA BUNS

Makes 10

Omit the dried fruit in the Master Recipe for Rock Cakes on pages 38 and 39 but use the remaining ingredients plus 1 teaspoon grated lemon rind.

Follow steps 1–4 on page 39, add the egg then 2 peeled and sliced ripe bananas. Add 1 tablespoon lemon juice and sufficient milk to mix as step 5. Continue as the Master Recipe.

The lemon rind, bananas and lemon juice can be added to the Economical or Rich Rock Cakes on page 41.

COFFEE WALNUT BUNS

Makes 10

2 teaspoons instant coffee powder
4 tablespoons hot milk
**225 g/8 oz self-raising flour or plain flour
    with 2 teaspoons baking powder**
110 g/4 oz butter or margarine
150 g/5 oz light brown sugar
50 g/2 oz halved walnuts
1 egg

to decorate
1 tablespoon caster sugar
1 tablespoon chopped walnuts

Blend the coffee powder with the milk, allow to cool. Sift the flour, or flour and baking powder, into a mixing bowl. Rub in the butter or margarine, then add the sugar. Chop the walnuts, stir into the rubbed-in mixture then add the egg and coffee-flavoured milk; use enough to make a sticky consistency as shown in step 5, page 39. Put into heaps on a well-greased baking tray, top with the sugar and chopped walnuts. Bake above the centre of a moderately hot to hot oven, 200–220°C, 400–425°F, Gas Mark 6–7 for 12–15 minutes.

CARROT BUNS

Makes 10

**225 g/8 oz self-raising flour or plain flour
    with 2 teaspoons baking powder**
100 g/4 oz butter or margarine
100 g/4 oz caster sugar
2 teaspoons finely grated orange rind
3 tablespoons finely grated raw carrot
1 egg
2 tablespoons orange juice
little milk if necessary

Sift the flour, or flour and baking powder, into a mixing bowl. Rub in the butter or margarine, add the sugar, orange rind and then the grated carrot. Mix very thoroughly at this stage then add the egg, orange juice and sufficient milk to make a stiff consistency as shown on page 39. Put in small heaps on a greased baking tray and bake above the centre of a hot oven, 220°C, 425°F, Gas Mark 7 for approximately 12 minutes.

ICED COFFEE WALNUT BUNS

Makes 10

**ingredients as Coffee Walnut Buns, but
    omit the sugar and chopped nut
    topping**
**Coffee Glacé Icing, page 146, made
    with 175 g/6 oz icing sugar, etc.**
10–12 halved walnuts

Make and bake the buns as the recipe left, allow to cool. Top with the icing, which must be rather stiff since the buns are not flat on top but rather 'rocky'. Place a walnut half in the centre of each bun, allow the icing to set.

43

CHERRY ROCK CAKES

Makes 10–12

75–100 g/3–4 oz glacé cherries
225 g/8 oz self-raising flour or plain flour
    with 2 teaspoons baking powder
110 g/4 oz butter or margarine
110 g/4 oz caster or granulated sugar
1 egg
approx. 3 tablespoons milk to mix

to glaze and decorate
½–1 tablespoon caster sugar
5–6 glacé cherries

Quarter the cherries; mix with 1 table-spoon of the flour and put on one side. Sift the rest of the flour, or flour and baking powder, into a mixing bowl. Rub in the butter or margarine, as described on page 39, add the sugar, then bind with the egg. Add the cherries, mix thoroughly. It is important to add these before the milk. Gradually blend in the milk until the mixture becomes a sticky consistency, as described in step 5 on page 39. Put 10–12 heaps on to a greased baking tray, sprinkle a little sugar on top of each cake. Halve the remaining cherries and press in the centre of each cake.

Bake just above the centre of a moderately hot oven, 200°C, 400°F, Gas Mark 6 for 12–15 minutes until firm to the touch. Glacé cherries give a slightly more sticky mixture than dried fruit, so it is advisable to bake at the lower of the two settings given under the Master Recipe on page 39.

CHOCOLATE BUNS

Makes 10

ingredients as Rock Cakes on page 38,
    but omit 25 g/1 oz flour
25 g/1 oz cocoa powder

Sift the flour, or flour and baking powder, as Rock Cakes on pages 38 and 39. Rub in the fat. Sift the cocoa powder and add to the rubbed-in mixture. (If preferred you can sift the cocoa powder with the flour but if mixing by hand it is more pleasant to add it afterwards.) Continue as Rock Cakes.

CHOCOLATE ORANGE ROCK CAKES

Makes 10

225 g/8 oz self-raising flour or plain flour
    with 2 teaspoons baking powder
75 g/3 oz butter or margarine
100 g/4 oz caster sugar
2 teaspoons finely grated orange rind
100 g/4 oz plain chocolate
1 egg
approx. 4 tablespoons orange juice to
    mix

Sift the flour, or flour and baking powder, into a mixing bowl. Rub in the butter or margarine, as described under Rock Cakes on page 39; add the sugar and orange rind. Cut the chocolate into small pieces (do not grate this), add to the rubbed-in mixture, then add the egg and orange juice to bind. This mixture must be particularly stiff. Put into small portions on a lightly greased baking tray, as described in step 5 on page 39. Do not sprinkle with sugar, as the buns are sufficiently sweet without this.

Bake just above the centre of a moderately hot oven, 200°C, 400°F, Gas Mark 6 for approximately 15 minutes until firm to the touch.
Note: The butter or margarine could be increased by 25 g/1 oz but do not exceed this as the chocolate adds extra fat to the mixture.

75–100 g/3–4 oz dried fruit can be added to the mixture as in the Chocolate Buns above and Rock Cakes, page 38.

COCONUT BUNS

Makes 10

**ingredients as Rock Cakes on page 38,
but use only 175 g/6 oz self-raising
flour or plain flour with 1½
teaspoons baking powder
75 g/3 oz desiccated coconut**

Sift the flour, or flour and baking powder,
and salt into the mixing bowl. Rub in the
fat, as described under Rock Cakes, then
add the sugar and the coconut. Proceed as
for Rock Cakes, pages 38 and 39.
Note: You can omit the dried fruit and top
the cooked buns with a little sieved apricot
or raspberry jam and a sprinkling of desiccated coconut.

DATE AND WALNUT BUNS

Makes about 15

**225 g/8 oz self-raising flour or plain flour
with 2 teaspoons baking powder
110 g/4 oz butter or margarine
150 g/5 oz dates, weight without stones
50 g/2 oz walnuts
110 g/4 oz moist brown sugar
1 egg**

Sift the flour, or flour and baking powder,
into a mixing bowl. Rub in the butter or
margarine. Cut the dates into small pieces
and chop the walnuts, add to the rubbed-
in mixture together with the sugar and
egg. Mix thoroughly. You will find the
sticky dates and the moist sugar help to
bind the mixture. Add only a very little
milk if necessary. The mixture should be
even stiffer than an ordinary Rock Cake.
   Put about 15 small heaps on one or two
well greased baking trays. Bake just above
the centre of a moderately hot oven,
200°C, 400°F, Gas Mark 6 for 12–15
minutes until firm to the touch.

FRESH CHERRY BUNS

Makes 10

**ingredients as Rock Cakes on page 38,
but omit the dried fruit
about 20 ripe cherries**

Prepare the mixture as shown on page 39,
put 10 portions on to the lightly greased
baking tray. Make an indentation in the
centre of each cake with the back of a
lightly floured teaspoon. Stone the cherries, put into the 'holes' on top of the
cakes.
   Bring the sides of the cake mixture
towards the fruit, partially, but not entirely, enclosing this. Sprinkle the cakes with
the sugar, as for Rock Cakes, and bake as
the instructions given on page 39 for 12–
15 minutes.

GINGER JUMBLES

Makes about 15

**ingredients as Date and Walnut Buns,
but omit the dates
100 g/4 oz crystallised ginger
25 g/1 oz glacé cherries**

Cut the ginger and cherries into small
pieces, add to the rubbed-in mixture
together with the sugar and egg and
enough milk to bind. Continue as the Date
and Walnut Buns.

Note: Crystallised pineapple can be used
in place of the crystallised ginger to make
Pineapple Jumbles. Dice the pineapple
and cherries and proceed as Date and
Walnut Buns. When the cakes are cooked
and cold top with Lemon Glacé Icing,
page 146, made with 175 g/6 oz icing
sugar, etc. Decorate with pieces of crystallised pineapple and glacé cherries, halved
or quartered.

GINGER BUNS

Makes 10

ingredients as Rock Cakes on page 38, but omit the dried fruit
1–2 teaspoons ground ginger
75 g/3 oz crystallised ginger

Sift the ground ginger with the flour then proceed as Rock Cakes; but dice the crystallised ginger and add instead of the dried fruit. Bake as Rock Cakes, page 39.

HONEY AND SPICE BUNS

Makes 10

ingredients as Rock Cakes on page 38, but omit 50 g/2 oz sugar
1 teaspoon allspice
3 tablespoons thin honey

Sift the flour, or flour and baking powder, and spice into a mixing bowl. Rub in the fat as described on page 39, then add the sugar and the egg. Mix well, then stir in the honey and fruit. Finally add the milk, approximately 2 tablespoons. Bake as Rock Cakes, page 39.

JAM BUNS

Makes 10

ingredients as Rock Cakes on page 38, but omit the dried fruit
10 teaspoons jam

Prepare the mixture as shown on page 39, put 10 portions on to the lightly greased baking tray. Make an indentation in the centre of each cake with the back of a lightly floured teaspoon. Fill with a teaspoon of jam; apricot or raspberry are some of the best jams to use in cooking.

Bring the sides of the cake mixture towards the jam, partially, but not entirely, enclosing this. Sprinkle the cakes with the sugar, as for Rock Cakes, and bake as the instructions given on page 39 for 12–15 minutes.
Note: Marzipan Buns are prepared as Jam Buns above. Make marzipan with 50 g/2 oz ground almonds, 25 g/1 oz caster sugar, 25 g/1 oz sifted icing sugar, the yolk of a small egg mixed with a few drops almond essence, see page 148; the proportions above make a softer marzipan than usual. Divide the mixture into 10 portions and use in place of jam.

LEMON JUMBLES

Makes 10–12

225 g/8 oz self-raising flour or plain flour with 2 teaspoons baking powder
75 g/3 oz butter or margarine
75 g/3 oz caster sugar
1 teaspoon grated lemon rind
1 egg
2 tablespoons lemon juice
little milk to mix

Sift the flour, or flour and baking powder, into a mixing bowl. Rub in the butter or margarine until the mixture is like fine breadcrumbs. Add the sugar and lemon rind then bind with the egg and lemon juice. Knead lightly then add enough milk to make a soft rolling consistency.

Divide the mixture into 10 or 12 small pieces of equal size; roll each portion into a long strip, then turn until rather like a Catherine wheel firework. Put on to a lightly greased baking tray. Bake in the centre of a moderate oven, 180–190°C, 350–375°F, Gas Mark 4–5 for a good 15 minutes.

Although similar to the Rock Cake mixture, these little cakes should be more crisp on the outside.

LEMON PEEL BUNS

Makes 10

ingredients as Rock Cakes on page 38, but omit the dried fruit
1 teaspoon finely grated lemon rind
75 g/3 oz candied lemon peel

Add the lemon rind with the rubbed-in mixture, then bind with the egg as step 5 on page 39. Chop the candied peel finely, add to the other ingredients before adding the milk to bind. Continue as Rock Cakes. **Note:** You could use a little lemon juice instead of all milk to mix the cakes; for another change top with Lemon Glacé Icing, given on page 146, when the cooked cakes are cold.

ORANGE ROCK CAKES

Makes 10

ingredients as Rock Cakes on page 38
3 teaspoons finely grated orange rind
approx. 4 tablespoons orange juice instead of milk

Add 2 teaspoons orange rind to the rubbed-in mixture then bind with the egg and orange juice. Put 10 portions on to a lightly greased baking tray, as described under the Master Recipe on pages 38 and 39. Mix the caster sugar for the topping with the remaining orange rind, sprinkle over the top of the cakes. Bake just above the centre of a moderately hot to hot oven, 200–220°C, 400–425°F, Gas Mark 6–7 for 12–15 minutes.
Note: These are delicious if the dried fruit is omitted and the plain orange-flavoured cakes topped with Orange Glacé Icing as page 146. Or make Pineapple Orange Buns, omit the dried fruit, push a well-drained canned pineapple cube into each cake before baking.

MARMALADE CAKES

Makes 10

ingredients as Rock Cakes on page 38, but omit 50 g/2 oz sugar
4 tablespoons finely chopped marmalade or jelly-type marmalade

Prepare the mixture as Rock Cakes on page 39 but add the marmalade after the egg and blend thoroughly, then add the milk. You will need rather less than 2 tablespoons of milk. Bake as Rock Cakes.

MOCHA BUNS

Makes 10

ingredients as Rock Cakes on page 38, but omit 15 g/½ oz flour
15 g/½ oz cocoa powder
use strong coffee to mix instead of milk

Sift the flour into a mixing bowl. Rub in the fat. Sift the cocoa powder and add to the mixture (see under Chocolate Buns on page 44); continue as Rock Cakes.

SAFFRON CAKES

Makes 10

ingredients as Rock Cakes on page 38
10 saffron strands

Warm the milk, used in the Rock Cakes, add the saffron strands and allow to stand for about 30 minutes, then strain the liquid. Make the Rock Cakes as the method given on pages 38 and 39 and bind with the saffron-flavoured milk. Bake as before.
Note: You may be able to purchase saffron powder, instead of strands, in which case sift about ½ teaspoon with the flour, or flour and baking powder.

CAKES WITH CEREALS

Cereals vary in texture and flavour; they add food value and fibre to cakes.

BRAN CAKES

Makes 10–12

50 g/2 oz **All-bran**
3 tablespoons milk instead of 1½
    tablespoons milk
ingredients as Harlequin Cakes, but
    omit the cornflakes
1 tablespoon caster sugar

Put the bran into a basin, add the milk; stand for 15 minutes then blend with the ingredients used in Harlequin Cakes. Spoon in heaps on a well greased baking tray; allow room for the cakes to spread. Sprinkle with the sugar; bake as Harlequin Cakes.

HARLEQUIN CAKES

Makes 10–12

100 g/4 oz **self-raising flour** or plain flour
    with 1 teaspoon baking powder
50 g/2 oz **butter** or margarine
50 g/2 oz **sugar**, preferably Demerara
50 g/2 oz **mixed dried fruit**
25 g/1 oz **glacé cherries**
50 g/2 oz **cornflakes**
1 **egg**
approx. 1½ tablespoons **milk**

Sift the flour, or flour and baking powder, into a mixing bowl. Rub in the butter or margarine, then add the sugar and dried fruit. Cut the cherries into small pieces. Lightly crush the cornflakes, do not make them too fine. Add the cherries and cornflakes to the flour mixture. Add the egg and sufficient milk to bind the mixture.

This should be sufficiently firm to handle. Make 10–12 small heaps of the mixture on a lightly greased baking tray, form these heaps into pyramid shapes with your finger-tips.

Bake above the centre of a moderately hot oven, 200°C, 400°F, Gas Mark 6 for 12 minutes or until firm to the touch. These cakes do not rise or spread as much as ordinary Rock Cakes or cakes based upon the Master Recipe; they do cook rather quickly, so check the baking carefully.

FRUIT OATIES

Makes 10–12

ingredients as Harlequin Cakes, but
    omit the cornflakes
50 g/2 oz **rolled oats**
approx. 2½ tablespoons milk instead of
    1½ tablespoons milk
1 tablespoon caster sugar to glaze

Blend the rolled oats with the other ingredients. Allow to stand for 30 minutes; spoon in heaps on a well-greased baking tray; allow room for the cakes to spread. Sprinkle with the sugar; bake as Harlequin Cakes.

MUESLI CAKES

Makes 10–12

ingredients as Harlequin Cakes, but
    omit the cornflakes
50 g/2 oz **muesli-type cereal**

If the cereal has fairly large particles, these should be lightly crushed to make it easier to blend the cereal with the other ingredients. Blend the muesli cereal with the other ingredients and proceed as Harlequin Cakes.

LARGE CAKES BY THE RUBBED-IN METHOD

The Luncheon Cake that follows is similar to Rock Cakes on page 38, with the exception of the amount of liquid.

When making large, instead of small, cakes from the basic recipe you need extra liquid to compensate for the longer cooking period. You must of course use a lower cooking temperature but never cook these economical cakes too slowly, otherwise they will be ultra-dry.

The Luncheon Cake, below, has similar ingredients to the Rock Cakes on page 39, except for the increased amount of liquid. This is necessary because of the longer and slower baking time. The method of mixing is as page 39; except for the consistency of the mixture.

LUNCHEON CAKE

Makes a 16.5–18 cm/6½–7 inch cake

**225 g/8 oz self-raising flour or plain flour
    with 2 teaspoons baking powder**
pinch salt
**110 g/4 oz butter or margarine or
    cooking fat**
**110 g/4 oz caster or granulated or
    Demerara or moist brown sugar**
75–100 g/3–4 oz mixed dried fruit
1 egg
approx. 6½ tablespoons milk to mix

to glaze
½–1 tablespoon caster sugar

Grease and flour a 16.5–18 cm/6½–7 inch cake tin; and method of mixing as for Rock Cakes (the Master Recipe) but you need sufficient milk to make a sticky rather than a stiff consistency. You will have to remove the mixture from the spoon with a palette knife as it is still too stiff to fall easily. Spoon into the prepared tin; sprinkle the sugar over the top and bake in the centre of a moderate oven, 180°C, 350°F, Gas Mark 4 for approximately 1 hour 10 minutes. The cake is cooked when it has shrunk away from the sides of the tin and is firm to the touch. Turn out on to a wire cooling tray.

LUNCHEON LOAF

Makes 1 loaf

ingredients as Luncheon Cake

Grease and flour a 900 g/2 lb loaf tin and put in the mixture. Top with the sugar and bake for approximately 1 hour at the temperature given in the Luncheon Cake recipe.

ECONOMICAL LUNCHEON CAKE

The ingredients can be reduced as given under Economical Rock Cakes on page 41. Use 7–7½ tablespoons liquid to mix and bake for about 1 hour 5 minutes as temperature above.

RICH LUNCHEON CAKE

Do not increase the fat in a rubbed-in mixture too much, since it is better to make a creamed mixture if you are using a high proportion of fat. You can however use 150 g/5 oz fat in the Luncheon Cake; the sugar can be increased to 150–175 g/5–6 oz and the dried fruit to 150–175 g/5–6 oz. Bake this cake in the centre of a moderate oven, 180°C, 350°F, Gas Mark 4 for 30 minutes, then reduce the heat to very moderate, 160°C, 325°F, Gas Mark 3 for a further 45 minutes or until firm to the touch.

ECONOMICAL LARGE CAKES

These simple large cakes are all based upon the Master Recipe, for Rock Cakes but, like the Luncheon Cake on the previous page, they must have a softer texture and slower baking temperature.

The cakes should be cooked in a 16.5–18 cm/6½–7 inch round cake tin or they could be cooked as the Luncheon Loaf, also on the previous page. Follow the baking time in either of these recipes unless stated to the contrary.

The recipes refer to the basic Luncheon Cake, not the more economical or rich versions.

Almond Cake: Follow the directions for Almond Rock Cakes on page 42 but use 2 tablespoons milk.

Apple Sauce Cake: Follow directions for Luncheon Cake, use 5 tablespoons thick unsweetened apple purée instead of milk.

Carrot Cake: Follow the directions for Carrot Buns on page 43 but use 3 tablespoons milk.

Chocolate Sultana Cake: Ingredients as the Luncheon Cake, but use all sultanas instead of mixed dried fruit plus 100 g/4 oz plain chocolate.

Mix the ingredients for the cake; cut the chocolate into small pieces, stir into the cake mixture. Bake as Luncheon Cake or Loaf; you will find the chocolate remains in small firm pieces.

Cider Cake: Ingredients as Luncheon Cake or the economical or richer versions on the previous page but use sweet cider, instead of milk to mix the ingredients.

Coffee Walnut Cake: Follow the directions for Coffee Walnut Buns on page 43 but use 6 tablespoons hot milk. Top with Coffee Glacé Icing, see page 146.

Date and Walnut Cake: Follow the directions for Date and Walnut Buns on page 45 but use 4 tablespoons milk to mix.

Economical Cherry Cake: Follow the directions for Cherry Rock Cakes on page 44 but use 5 tablespoons milk and only 2–3 halved cherries to decorate the top of the cake before baking.

Economical Coconut Cake: Follow the directions for Luncheon Cake but use only 175 g/6 oz self-raising flour, or plain flour with 1½ teaspoons baking powder, plus 75 g/3 oz desiccated coconut.

Economical Lemon Cake: Ingredients as Luncheon Cake but omit the dried fruit. Add 1–2 teaspoons grated lemon rind and 75 g/3 oz chopped candied peel. Mix with 2 tablespoons lemon juice and 4 tablespoons milk. The cake can be iced with Lemon Glacé Icing, see page 146.

Economical Seed Cake: Omit the dried fruit from the Luncheon Cake, blend 2 teaspoons caraway seeds with the cake mixture. Top with the sugar and another ½–1 teaspoon seeds. Bake as the Luncheon Cake or Loaf.

Ginger Cherry Cake: Follow the directions for the Luncheon Cake but omit the dried fruit and use 100 g/4 oz crystallised ginger and 25 g/1 oz diced cherries. Mix with 4 tablespoons milk. For a more pronounced flavour sift 1–2 teaspoons ground ginger with the flour.

Treacle and Raisin Loaf: Use 100 g/4 oz seedless raisins instead of the mixed dried fruit in the Luncheon Cake. Blend in the egg, 2 tablespoons black treacle and only 3 tablespoons milk. Bake for 1 hour at the temperature given for the Luncheon Cake, but reduce the heat after 35–40 minutes if the cake is getting too brown.

APPLE AND GINGER SQUARES

Illustrated in colour on page 37

Makes a 20 cm/8 inch square cake

450 g/1 lb cooking apples
225 g/8 oz self-raising flour or plain flour
    with 2 teaspoons baking powder
1 teaspoon ground ginger
175 g/6 oz butter or margarine
175 g/6 oz light Muscovado or brown
    sugar
1 tablespoon honey
3 eggs

Line a 20 cm/8 inch cake tin. Peel, core and chop the apples. Sift the flour, or flour and baking powder, and ginger into a mixing bowl. Rub in the butter or margarine, add the sugar, honey, eggs and apples. Put into the prepared tin.

Bake in the centre of a moderate oven, 180°C, 350°F, Gas Mark 4 for 1 hour 10 minutes. Turn out. Cut into squares and serve warm or cold with whipped cream.

VINEGAR CAKE

It may be surprising to learn that vinegar can be used to lighten a cake instead of using an egg.

Follow the recipe for Luncheon Cake on page 49 but omit the egg.

Mix 1½ tablespoons brown malt vinegar with the 6½ tablespoons milk in the Luncheon Cake recipe, blend the dry ingredients with the vinegar and milk. Bake as Luncheon Cake.

The same quantity of vinegar can be used in any of the recipes based upon Luncheon Cake on page 50. The vinegar does not give any unpleasant taste to the mixture.

Cakes made without egg and with vinegar tend to be somewhat fragile when hot so allow to cool for about 10 minutes in the cake tin, then turn out.

EGGLESS LARGE FRUIT CAKE

The advice given on page 41 about making small eggless cakes or the variations applies to making a large cake.

Follow the recipe for Luncheon Cake on page 49 or the variations on the same page; omit the egg and use an extra 2 tablespoons milk. The other recipes on this page give excellent eggless recipes.

'BOILED' FRUIT CAKE

Makes a 20 cm/8 inch cake

300 ml/½ pint moderately strong tea
300 g/10 oz self-raising flour or plain
    flour with 2½ teaspoons baking
    powder
½ teaspoon bicarbonate of soda
pinch salt
1 teaspoon mixed spice
85 g/3 oz butter or margarine or cooking
    fat
100 g/4 oz moist brown sugar
100–175 g/4–6 oz mixed dried fruit

Grease and flour, or line, a 20 cm/8 inch cake tin. Due to the high liquid content this cake is inclined to stick so lining the base of the tin is advisable.

The tea used should be made the usual strength, allowed to stand for a few minutes then strained most carefully. The tea should not be allowed to become 'stewed' in flavour.

Sift the dried ingredients. Pour the 300 ml/½ pint tea into a pan, add the butter, margarine or cooking fat and the sugar. Heat until the fat and sugar have just melted then add the dried fruit. Boil for 1 minute only; allow to cool then pour over the dry ingredients and beat well. Spoon into the prepared tin and bake in the centre of a moderate oven, 190°C, 375°F, Gas Mark 5 for 1 hour or until firm.

51

STREUSEL APPLE CAKE

Makes a 20 cm/8 inch cake

for the base
**225 g/8 oz self-raising flour or plain flour
    with 2 teaspoons baking powder
½–1 teaspoon ground cinnamon
110 g/4 oz butter or margarine
75 g/3 oz granulated sugar
1 egg
225 g/8 oz cooking apples, weight when
    peeled and cored
approx. 4 tablespoons milk**

for the topping
**50 g/2 oz plain flour
¼ teaspoon ground cinnamon
25 g/1 oz butter
50 g/2 oz granulated sugar
25 g/1 oz walnuts**

Line the bottom of a 20 cm/8 inch cake tin with a round of greaseproof paper, grease and flour the paper and tin. Sift the flour, or flour and baking powder, and the cinnamon into a mixing bowl. Rub in the butter or margarine, add the sugar and egg. Cut the apples into small dice, blend with the cake mixture then enough milk to make a stiff consistency. Spoon into the prepared tin, smooth flat.

Sift the 50 g/2 oz flour and cinnamon, rub in the butter add the sugar. Chop the walnuts, mix with the other streusel ingredients. Sprinkle on top of the cake, press gently with a palette knife. Bake in the centre of a moderate oven, 180°C, 350°F, Gas Mark 4 for 45 minutes.

DUTCH APPLE CAKE

Makes a 20 cm/8 inch cake

**ingredients as the base of the Streusel
    Apple Cake**

for the topping
**25 g/1 oz butter
50 g/2 oz granulated sugar
½ teaspoon ground cinnamon**

Make the cake mixture as the Streusel Apple Cake but do not blend the apples with the mixture. Spoon into the cake tin. Slice the apples very thinly, arrange on top of the cake mixture.

Melt the butter, spoon over the apples; blend the sugar and cinnamon, sprinkle over the buttered apple slices. Bake as the Streusel Apple Cake but for 40 minutes.

APRICOT TORTA

Makes a 20 cm/8 inch cake

**ingredients as base of Streusel Apple
    Cake, but use 3 tablespoons milk
1 tablespoon lemon juice
12 soaked and cooked dried apricots**

for the topping
**25 g/1 oz butter
1 teaspoon grated lemon rind
50 g/2 oz granulated sugar
1–2 tablespoons lemon juice**

Make the cake mixture as the Streusel Apple Cake but use the 3 tablespoons milk and 1 tablespoon lemon juice to mix. Spoon the cake mixture into the tin.

Drain the cooked apricots well, arrange on top of the cake mixture. Melt the butter, blend with the lemon rind, spoon over the top of the cake, add the sugar. Bake as Streusel Apple Cake for 35 minutes; sprinkle the lemon juice evenly over the cake (the amount depends upon personal taste); return to the oven for 5–10 minutes. **Note:** An interesting topping is given to the cake if 25–50 g/1–2 oz whole glacé cherries and 25 g/1 oz whole blanched almonds are arranged between the dried apricots on top of the cake before adding the butter, lemon rind and sugar.

PLUM TORTA

Fresh plums can be used instead of the soaked prunes given in the recipe below. Choose 12 large firm plums; halve, stone and arrange with the cut side downwards. Add the topping as given in the Pruna Torta, then bake as directions given. Delicious served with cream cheese.

PRUNA TORTA

Makes a 20 cm/8 inch cake

ingredients as the base of the Streusel Apple Cake on page 52, but omit the apples
12 soaked and stoned prunes

for the topping
as Dutch Apple Cake plus 1 teaspoon finely grated lemon rind

Spoon the cake mixture into the cake tin. Drain the soaked prunes well, arrange on top of the cake mixture. Add the topping (the lemon rind should be mixed with the butter). Bake as the Streusel Apple Cake but for approximately 40 minutes.

Note: The type of prunes that do not need soaking are ideal for this.

APRICOT AND HONEY SQUARES

Makes 16

for the filling
175 g/6 oz dried apricots
300 ml/½ pint water
2 tablespoons lemon juice
2 tablespoons honey
25 g/1 oz butter

ingredients for oatmeal layers as in the Date and Walnut Squares

Grease a 20 cm/8 inch square tin. Cut the apricots into small pieces. Soak in the water and lemon juice for 3–4 hours then tip into a saucepan. Add the honey and butter. Cover the pan and simmer gently for 45 minutes, but which time the excess liquid should have been absorbed and the apricots reasonably soft. Allow to cool then proceed as Date and Walnut Squares.

DATE AND WALNUT SQUARES

Makes 18

for the filling
225 g/8 oz dates, weight without stones
2 tablespoons water
2 tablespoons orange juice
2 tablespoons golden syrup
25 g/1 oz butter

for oatmeal layers
175 g/6 oz butter or margarine
225 g/8 oz plain flour
110 g/4 oz rolled oats
110 g/4 oz Demerara sugar
110 g/4 oz walnuts

Grease a 20 cm/8 inch square cake tin. Prepare the filling so it becomes cold. Chop the dates, put into a saucepan with the water, orange juice, golden syrup and butter. Heat in an open pan until the dates form a soft paste-like mixture; cool.

Rub the butter or margarine into the flour, then add the rolled oats and sugar. Chop the walnuts finely, mix with the flour and rolled oats mixture, sprinkle half the crumb mixture into the prepared tin, then flatten with your knuckles. Top with the date paste, then with the rest of the crumbs. Bake in the centre of a very moderate to moderate oven, 160–180°C, 325–350°F, Gas Mark 3–4 for 40–45 minutes until pale golden and crisp. Cool for about 5 minutes, mark in sections, then cool for 10 minutes and lift carefully from the tin.

ORANGE SULTANA SQUARES

Illustrated in colour on page 37

Makes a 20 cm/8 inch square cake

Muscovado sugar gives both colour and flavour to this simple cake.

Grease and flour, or line, a 20 cm/8 inch square tin. Sift 350 g/12 oz self-raising flour, or plain flour with 3 teaspoons baking powder, with ½ teaspoon ground cinnamon. Rub in 175 g/6 oz butter or margarine; add 175 g/6 oz light Muscovado sugar, 175 g/6 oz sultanas, 2 eggs and 4 tablespoons orange juice.

Bake as the Mocha Loaf for 1 hour. Cool and cut into squares.

MOCHA LOAF

Makes a 900 g/2 lb loaf-shaped cake

25 g/1 oz cornflour
175 g/6 oz self-raising flour or plain flour with 1½ teaspoons baking powder
150 g/5 oz butter or margarine
25 g/1 oz cocoa powder
150 g/5 oz caster sugar
2 eggs
4 tablespoons strong coffee

to decorate
100 g/4 oz plain chocolate
1 tablespoon strong coffee
50 g/2 oz icing sugar
25 g/1 oz flaked blanched almonds

Grease and flour, or line, a 900 g/2 lb loaf tin. Sift the cornflour and flour, or flour and baking powder, into a mixing bowl. Rub in the butter or margarine. Sift the cocoa powder, add to the rubbed-in mixture with the sugar. Beat in the eggs and the coffee. Spoon into the prepared tin and bake in the centre of a moderate oven, 180°C, 350°F, Gas Mark 4 for 1 hour. Turn out of the tin and allow to cool.

Break the chocolate into pieces; put into a basin with the coffee and melt over a pan of hot water, cool slightly. Sift the icing sugar, blend with the melted chocolate. Spread over the top of the cake; sprinkle with the almonds.

FRUITY SQUARES

Makes 16

175 g/6 oz self-raising flour or plain flour with 1½ teaspoons baking powder
85 g/3 oz butter or margarine
85 g/3 oz Demerara sugar
175 g/6 oz dates, weight without stones
50 g/2 oz walnuts
25 g/1 oz blanched almonds
50 g/2 oz glacé cherries
50 g/2 oz candied peel
1 egg

for the topping
15–25 g/½–1 oz icing sugar

Grease and flour, or line, a 20 cm/8 inch square tin. Due to the high content of fruit, etc. lining the base of the tin is advisable. Sift the flour, or flour and baking powder, into a mixing bowl. Rub in the butter or margarine and add the sugar. Chop the dates, nuts, cherries and peel, add to the rubbed-in mixture. Bind with the egg. The mixture will be very stiff, but do not add any milk. Spoon into the prepared tin, press flat on top.

Bake in the centre of a moderately hot oven, 190–200°C, 375–400°F, Gas Mark 5–6 for 30–35 minutes or until just firm to the touch. If browning too quickly reduce the heat after 20 minutes. Do not overcook; this mixture should be slightly sticky. Mark the shallow cake into squares and remove from the tin while warm. Allow to cool, then sift the icing sugar over.
Note: Use wholemeal or wheatmeal flour with 2 tablespoons milk as well as the egg.

COBBLER

The term 'Cobbler' is given to an economical topping, which is cooked over fruit, or can be placed over a savoury base. The mixture is really very like the dough used for sweet or savoury scones, so any of the scone recipes on pages 182, 183 and 218 would be suitable; these would be prepared and cooked as the example below.

A Cherry Cobbler is one of my favourite recipes so I have given this as a basic dish, but you can use any of the combinations of fruit suggested on page 56.

CHERRY COBBLER

Serves 4–6

550–675 g/1¼–1½ lb Morello or dessert
    cherries
150 ml/¼ pint water
50–100 g/2–4 oz sugar (depending upon
    the sweetness of the fruit)

for the Cobbler topping
175 g/6 oz self-raising flour or plain flour
    with 1½ teaspoons baking powder
good pinch salt
40 g/1½ oz butter or margarine
1–2 tablespoons sugar
milk to mix

Stone the cherries with a cherry stoner or a bent end of a new hairpin; do this over the dish, so no juice is wasted. Put the fruit into a 900 ml/2 pint pie dish or ovenproof container. Add the water and sugar, cover with foil; cook in the centre of a moderate oven, 180°C, 350°F, Gas Mark 4 for 20 minutes.

Meanwhile make the Cobbler mixture. Sift the flour, or flour and baking powder, and salt into a mixing bowl. Rub in the butter or margarine, add the sugar and enough milk to make a soft rolling consistency.

Roll out to just under 1.5 cm/½ inch in thickness; cut into rounds or triangles.

Remove the dish from the oven; raise the oven temperature to hot, 220°C, 425°F, Gas Mark 7. Place the scone shapes on the hot fruit; do not cover the dish. Return to the centre of the hot oven, bake for 15 minutes.

Note: To give a more interesting appearance to the Cobbler, top with a little sugar before baking, or with a little milk or cream and chopped nuts.

BROWN AND WHITE COBBLER

Serves 4–6

half the amount of the Cobbler mixture,
    using wheatmeal flour
half the amount of the Cobbler mixture,
    using white flour

Make up the two batches of Cobbler mixture, roll out separately; cut into an equal number of small rounds. Put on to the prepared fruit, bake as the basic Cobbler.

PINWHEEL CHERRY COBBLER

Serves 4–6

ingredients as Cherry Cobbler
25 g/1 oz butter
50 g/2 oz Demerara sugar
25–50 g/1–2 oz walnuts

Prepare the basic Cobbler topping; roll out just under 5 mm/¼ inch in thickness.

Soften the 25 g/1 oz butter, spread over the dough; sprinkle with the sugar. Chop the nuts and add to the butter and sugar mixture. Roll up the dough, just like a Swiss roll, then cut into 6–8 slices. Arrange on top of the hot fruit and bake as the basic Cobbler.

CRUMBLE MIXTURES

Suggestions for the favourite crumble topping on fruit are given below.

Do not imagine that this is the only crumble topping you can make, there are many others; each with a definite character. The crumble mixture can be adapted to top sweet or savoury ingredients.

Remember that the base for any crumble – whether sweet or savoury, fruit or another mixture – must have the minimum of liquid. If the mixture is too moist it bubbles up and spoils the topping.

You should use plain flour, but it does not matter greatly if you only have self-raising flour.

Do not be over-generous with the amount of fat; too much prevents the mixture being crumbly.

I use a rather generous amount of sugar in a sweet crumble as this helps to crisp the mixture. You can use less in the fruit base. This can be granulated, Demerara or other brown sugar.

Only pre-cook firm fruit. Soft berry fruits, such as raspberries, or forced greenhouse grown rhubarb will be adequately cooked by the time the crumble is ready. Do not bake too quickly, otherwise the top burns before the mixture is crisp enough. On the other hand, do not bake too slowly because if you do the base, under the crumble, becomes over-cooked.

BASIC FRUIT CRUMBLE

Serves 4–6

550–675 g/1¼–1½ lb fruit, weight when peeled and cored or stoned
2–4 tablespoons liquid
sugar or honey or syrup to taste

for the crumble
85 g/3 oz butter or margarine
175 g/6 oz flour
100 g/4 oz granulated or Demerara or soft brown sugar

Prepare the fruit, put into a 900 ml/2 pint pie dish. If the fruit is hard then add the liquid, which can be water or orange juice or lemon juice mixed with a little water. Only use enough liquid to keep firm fruit moist, as it is partially cooked. Add the sugar, honey or syrup.

If the fruit is hard, cover the dish, bake in the centre of a moderate oven, 180°C, 350°F, Gas Mark 4 for about 20 minutes or until beginning to soften.

If the fruit is soft, add the sugar or other sweetening, mix with the fruit.

Rub the butter or margarine into the flour, add the sugar. Sprinkle the crumble mixture over the top, press flat with a palette knife. Bake in the centre of the moderate oven, 180°C, 350°F, Gas Mark 4 for 30 minutes. Serve hot or cold.

INTERESTING FRUIT MIXTURES

Almond and Apricot Crumble: Mix 50 g/2 oz blanched whole or chopped almonds with apricots and use a little ratafia essence or liqueur as part of the liquid for cooking the apricots.

Date and Apple Crumble: Mix about 175 g/6 oz stoned and diced dates with prepared apples; or add the grated rind of 1 lemon and use 1 tablespoon lemon juice as part of the liquid for cooking the apples and dates.

Rhubarb and Orange Crumble: Mix the diced rhubarb with a little grated orange rind and use orange juice for the liquid for cooking fresh garden rhubarb; forced rhubarb needs only 1 tablespoon liquid. Mix 2 teaspoons finely grated orange rind with the sugar in the basic crumble, add to the rubbed-in mixture of flour and fat.

FLAVOURINGS FOR THE BASIC CRUMBLE

The following flavourings are added to the basic sweet crumble on the previous page.

Chocolate Crumble: Ingredients as the Basic Crumble, but omit 25 g/1 oz flour and substitute 25 g/1 oz cocoa powder; sift this with the flour, or sift and add after rubbing in the butter or margarine.

This is particularly good over apricots.

Cinnamon Crumble: Ingredients as the Basic Crumble, but sift 1 teaspoon ground cinnamon with the flour.

This is particularly good over cooked apples.

Coconut Crumble: Ingredients as the Basic Crumble, but omit 25 g/1 oz flour; add 75 g/3 oz desiccated coconut with the sugar.

This is good over any fruit.

Cornflake Crumble: Use only 100 g/4 oz flour in the Basic Crumble, add 75 g/3 oz crushed cornflakes. Take particular care in rubbing the fat into the flour that it does not become over-sticky.

This is good over most fruits.

Orange Crumble: Ingredients as the Basic Crumble, but blend 2 teaspoons finely grated orange rind with the sugar; add to the rubbed-in mixture; by mixing the rind with the sugar you ensure that this is evenly distributed.

Grapefruit or lemon or tangerine rind can be used instead.

This is excellent over most fruits.

Wheatmeal Streusel: Use wheatmeal or wholemeal flour in the Spiced Nut Crumble, increase the coconut to 50 g/2 oz.

This can be used over most fruits.

SPICED NUT CRUMBLE

Serves 4–6

550–675 g/1¼–1½ lb fruit, weight when peeled and cored or stoned
2–4 tablespoons liquid
sugar or honey or syrup to taste

for the crumble
175 g/6 oz flour
½ teaspoon grated nutmeg
½ teaspoon ground cinnamon
85 g/3 oz butter or margarine
25 g/1 oz walnuts
25 g/1 oz blanched almonds
100 g/4 oz Demerara sugar
25 g/1 oz desiccated coconut

Prepare the fruit, as Basic Fruit Crumble on page 56, pre-cook if necessary.

Sift the flour, nutmeg and cinnamon into a mixing bowl. Rub in the butter or margarine. Finely chop the nuts; add the sugar, nuts and coconut to the rubbed-in mixture. Sprinkle over the partially cooked, or raw, fruit and bake in the centre of a moderate oven, 180°C, 350°F, Gas Mark 4 for 30 minutes.

SPICED CRUMB CRUMBLE

Serves 4–6

Follow the recipe for Spiced Nut Crumble but use only 150 g/5 oz flour then blend in 50 g/2 oz coarsely crushed digestive or ginger nut biscuit crumbs. The nuts can be omitted from the recipe.

SPICED GINGER CRUMBLE

Serves 4–6

Follow the recipe for Spiced Nut Crumble but add 1 teaspoon ground ginger.

SAVOURY CRUMBLES

These make a very pleasant change from a savoury pie; although the basic crumble is similar to the sweet version, the fact that sugar is omitted does mean you may need to bake the mixture for a few extra minutes to become crisp and brown.

When preparing sauce mixtures, check these are fairly thick in consistency so they do not 'bubble up' over the crumble.

CHEESE CRUMBLE

Serves 4

for the cheese sauce
50 g/2 oz butter or margarine
50 g/2 oz flour
450 ml/¾ pint milk
100 g/4 oz Cheddar cheese
salt and pepper
pinch mustard powder

450 g/1 lb cooked vegetables

for the crumble
50 g/2 oz Cheddar cheese
200 g/7 oz flour
salt and pepper
pinch mustard powder
75 g/3 oz butter or margarine

Heat the butter or margarine, stir in the flour; cook gently for 2–3 minutes, stirring all the time. Blend in the milk, bring to the boil, stir until thickened. Grate the cheese, add to the very thick sauce together with the seasonings. Dice the vegetables and mix with the hot sauce. Put into a 900 ml/2 pint pie dish.

Grate the cheese for the crumble. Sift the flour and seasonings, rub in the butter or margarine, add the grated cheese. Sprinkle over the vegetable mixture. Bake towards the top of a moderate oven, 180–190°C, 350–375°F, Gas Mark 4–5 for 20 minutes.

LEMON CRUMBLE

Serves 4

450 g/1 lb white fish, cod or fresh haddock, weight without skin and bones
300 ml/½ pint milk
salt and pepper
100 g/4 oz mushrooms
50 g/2 oz butter
25 g/1 oz flour
2 tablespoons chopped parsley

for the crumble
175 g/6 oz flour
garlic salt
cayenne pepper
85 g/3 oz butter or margarine
2 teaspoons finely grated lemon rind
pulp of 1 lemon

to garnish
sprigs of parsley

Poach the fish in the milk for 5–7 minutes, add a very little salt and pepper, drain and dice the fish; keep the milk. Slice the mushrooms. Heat half the butter and fry the mushrooms for 3 minutes. Heat the remaining butter, stir in the flour and cook for 2–3 minutes, gradually blend in the milk left from cooking the fish. Bring to the boil, stir until the sauce is thickened. Add the fish, mushrooms and parsley. The mixture must be thick, but if too much milk evaporates in cooking the fish add a little extra. Put into a 900 ml/2 pint pie dish.

Sift the flour and seasonings into a mixing bowl. Rub in the butter or margarine, add the lemon rind. Sprinkle over the hot fish mixture. Bake in the centre of a moderate oven, 180–190°C, 350–375°F, Gas Mark 4–5 for 30 minutes. Meanwhile dice the lemon pulp, sprinkle on top of the crumble, heat for a further 5 minutes. Garnish with the sprigs of parsley, if liked.

BACON AND ONION CRUMBLE

Serves 4

**ingredients as Paprika and Onion
Crumble
2–3 bacon rashers**

Dice the bacon and fry with the onion until the bacon is crisp then proceed as Paprika and Onion Crumble; if the bacon is rather fat reduce the fat from 85 g/3 oz to 50 g/2 oz.

PAPRIKA AND ONION CRUMBLE

Serves 4

**450 g/1 lb stewing beef
25 g/1 oz flour
salt and pepper
1 teaspoon paprika
50 g/2 oz onion
2 large tomatoes
50 g/2 oz fat
600 ml/1 pint beef stock**

for the crumble
**200 g/7 oz flour
salt and pepper
1 teaspoon paprika
1 onion
85 g/3 oz fat**

to garnish
**tomato slices
chopped parsley**

Dice the beef. Mix the flour, salt, pepper and paprika and coat the beef. Slice the onion and tomatoes. Melt the fat, fry the coated beef for a few minutes, then add the onion and tomatoes and continue cooking for 5 minutes. Gradually blend in the stock. Bring to the boil, stirring well, then cover the pan and simmer for 2 hours or until the beef is tender. Using a perforated spoon, spoon into a 900 ml/2 pint pie dish,

leave any excess sauce to serve with the cooked dish.

Sift the flour, salt, pepper and paprika. Meanwhile chop the onion for the crumble. Heat the fat, fry the onion in the fat until tender. Cool, then blend the onion and all the fat with seasoned flour. Mix well, sprinkle over the beef. Bake in the centre of a very moderate oven, 160°C, 325°F, Gas Mark 3 for 35 minutes. Add the sliced tomatoes just before the end of the cooking time. Garnish.

SAVOURY POTATO COBBLER

Serves 4–6

**100 g/4 oz cooked potatoes
100 g/4 oz self-raising flour with 1
teaspoon baking powder or plain
flour with 2 teaspoons baking
powder
salt and pepper
pinch dry mustard powder
25 g/1 oz butter or margarine
1 egg
milk to mix**

Sieve the potatoes. Sift the flour, baking powder, salt, pepper and mustard into a mixing bowl. Rub in the butter or margarine, add the potatoes and the egg. Mix well, then gradually add just enough milk to make a soft rolling consistency. Roll out until 1.5 cm/½ inch in thickness, cut into 6–8 rounds, squares or triangles.

This particular Cobbler can be put on to any savoury base, such as steak and kidney or those given on page 58 and left. The savoury mixture should be hot and almost cooked. It should not be too moist; for the Cobbler shapes must stay firm in texture. Place the Cobbler topping over the base and bake in the centre of a hot oven, 220°C, 425°F, Gas Mark 7 for 15 minutes. **Note:** Chopped parsley, or other herbs, can be added to the potato and flour mix.

BAKED PUDDINGS

There are many interesting puddings, apart from Cobblers and Crumbles, that are prepared by the easy rubbing-in method. The texture is short and crisp.

APPLE BROWNIE

Serves 4–6

100 g/4 oz self-raising flour or plain flour
    with 1 teaspoon baking powder
50 g/2 oz butter or margarine
100 g/4 oz moist light brown sugar
1 egg
75 g/3 oz walnuts
75 g/3 oz dates, weight without stones
450 g/1 lb dessert apples, choose the
    type that cook well – like a Cox's
    Orange Pippin or Granny Smith

Grease a 23 cm/9 inch round or an oblong ovenproof serving dish, measuring approximately 15 × 23 cm/6 × 9 inches. Sift the flour, or flour and baking powder, into a mixing bowl. Rub in the butter or margarine, add 75 g/3 oz of the sugar and the egg, mix well. Chop the walnuts and dates; peel and core the apples, cut each apple into 8 slices. Stir 50 g/2 oz walnuts, all the dates and apples into the rubbed-in mixture. Although the mixture seems stiff, do not add any liquid. Spoon the mixture into the prepared dish. Top with the remaining sugar and walnuts. Bake in the centre of a moderate oven, 180°C, 350°F, Gas Mark 4 for 45 minutes. Serve hot with cream.

Note: The reason for using dessert apples is the slices become tender, but do not lose their shape.
    If you like to use cooking apples you will have a softer texture, which many people may prefer; obviously the pudding will be less sweet than when using dessert apples.

PEAR CHOCOLATE UPSIDE DOWN PUDDING

Serves 4–6

for the base
25 g/1 oz butter
25 g/1 oz caster sugar
1 small can pear halves

for the topping
175 g/6 oz self-raising flour or plain
    flour with 1½ teaspoons baking
    powder
85 g/3 oz butter or margarine
85 g/3 oz caster sugar
1 egg
4 tablespoons milk
50 g/2 oz plain chocolate

for the sauce
100 g/4 oz plain chocolate
3 tablespoons syrup from canned pears

Grease the sides only of a 20 cm/8 inch ovenproof soufflé dish or cake tin without a loose base. Heat the 25 g/1 oz butter and 25 g/1 oz caster sugar until the butter has melted, pour into the dish or tin. Arrange the pear halves on top; put 3 tablespoons of the can syrup on one side for the chocolate sauce.
    Sift the flour, or flour and baking powder, into a mixing bowl. Rub in the butter or margarine, add the sugar. Stir in the egg and milk. Cut the chocolate into small pieces, stir into the pudding mixture. Spoon over the pears, taking care not to disturb the fruit. Bake in the centre of a moderate oven, 180°C, 350°F, Gas Mark 4 for 50–55 minutes until the pudding is firm to the touch.
    Meanwhile break the 100 g/4 oz chocolate in pieces, put into a basin with the pear syrup. Heat over a pan of hot, but not boiling, water until the chocolate has melted.
    Turn the pudding upside down on to a hot dish, serve with the sauce.

SHORTCAKES

A Shortcake is a pleasing blend of a cake and biscuit texture. The recipes vary appreciably and the one given below is economical and firm in texture whereas the richer and softer types are on page 102.

HAM SHORTCAKES

Shortcakes are not always served as a dessert, you can make a savoury dish.

Follow the recipe for Old-Fashioned Shortcakes, but omit the sugar and sift ¼ teaspoon salt, shake cayenne pepper and a pinch dry mustard powder with the flour. Add 100 g/4 oz finely chopped cooked ham to the rubbed-in mixture before binding with the egg and milk.

Split the cooked Shortcakes and fill with cream cheese.

OLD-FASHIONED STRAWBERRY SHORTCAKES

Makes 12

**225 g/8 oz self-raising flour or plain flour
    with 2 teaspoons baking powder
50 g/2 oz butter or margarine
75 g/3 oz caster sugar
1 egg
milk to mix**

to fill
**150 ml/¼ pint double cream
350 g/12 oz strawberries
25 g/1 oz caster sugar**

Sift the flour, or flour and baking powder, into a mixing bowl. Rub in the butter or margarine, add nearly all the sugar. Blend with the egg and enough milk to make a soft rolling consistency. Roll out to approximately 2 cm/¾ inch in thickness, cut into 12 rounds. Put on to a lightly greased baking tray. Top with the remaining sugar. Bake towards the top of a hot oven, 220°C, 425°F, Gas Mark 7 for about 12 minutes.

Whip the cream. Mash half the strawberries, add the sugar. Split the hot Shortcakes. When cold, fill with the strawberry pulp, sandwich together again. Top with fruit, serve with cream, if liked.

SPICED PEACH SHORTCAKE

Serves 4–6

**ingredients as Old-Fashioned
    Strawberry Shortcakes
1 teaspoon mixed spice
50 g/2 oz walnuts**

to fill and decorate
**150–300 ml/¼–½ pint double cream
4–6 fresh peaches
sugar to taste**

Sift the spice with the flour, then proceed as the Shortcake mixture. Chop the walnuts and add to the rubbed-in mixture with most of the sugar. Bind with the egg and milk, roll out to just 1.5 cm/½ inch in thickness. Cut into two equal sized rounds or squares. Put each round or square on to one or two lightly greased baking trays. Sprinkle one Shortcake with the remaining sugar. Bake just above the centre of a moderately hot oven, 190–200°C, 375–400°F, Gas Mark 5–6 for about 20 minutes until firm and golden. Cool.

Whip the cream. Skin the peaches – to do this, put into very hot water for a few seconds, remove and pull away the skin. Halve, stone and slice the peaches. Spread the Shortcake without the sugar topping with half the cream and half the peaches and a little sugar. Cover with the sugar-topped Shortcake, then with the remaining cream and fruit.

Modern baking methods

In a Microwave Cooker

The common factor in all cakes made by the rubbing-in method is that they should be crisp or firm and golden brown, and an oven is essential for this result.

You can use the microwave for a Crumble or Cobbler though, see pages 56–59 and 55. Cook the fruit base lightly, for it can over-cook more readily in a microwave cooker than an oven. Add the crumble or cobbler topping. Check with the manufacturers' instructions, but I allow 10 minutes on HIGH for a crumble and 5–6 minutes for a cobbler. Turn the dish every few minutes (unless the model has a turntable). Use brown sugar or brown flour to give a more appetising colour or grated cheese on a savoury crumble.

The Upside Down Pudding, page 60, cooks well in a microwave cooker; allow about 9 minutes on HIGH or 12 minutes on the SIMMER, or equivalent setting.

In a Crock-Pot

You will find greater details on cooking cakes under page 104. A crock-pot is very good for the Upside Down Pudding; pre-heat on HIGH for 15 minutes, add 600 ml/1 pint boiling water, put in the pudding; cook for 3 hours on HIGH.

In a Pressure Cooker

See page 104 for more details. When cooking the Upside Down Pudding, allow 15 minutes steaming and 25 minutes at LOW/5 lb pressure.

In a Table Cooker (Electric Frying Pan)

You will find more information about these on page 105. The cooker is quite suitable for mixtures made by 'rubbing-in'. Small Rock Cakes, the Master Recipe on pages 38 and 39, can be cooked on the base of the type of table cooker such as a high-domed electric frying pan.

Storing

Uncooked rubbed-in mixtures store well. Use the basic proportions of flour (or flour and fat given on page 38). Put the crumbs in a polythene container and store in the refrigerator. When required, add sugar and other ingredients for cakes or simply sugar to make a sweet Crumble. You can add seasonings and grated cheese, or other ingredients, for a savoury Crumble.

Cooked cakes, made by the rubbing-in method, tend to become stale fairly quickly. Allow to cool, pack in an airtight tin, use within a few days. The cake(s) can be warmed for a few minutes in the oven.

To prevent a large cake becoming over-brown, as it is reheated, wrap in foil or put inside a roasting bag. When warm and moist again, unwrap and heat until firm on the outside.

Freezing

The uncooked rubbed-in mixture, as previously mentioned, can be stored in the freezer, rather than the refrigerator. It will take only a short time to defrost at room temperature. Always defrost the mixture completely before adding egg and liquid to make a cake or small cakes.

It is better to freeze the sweet or savoury Crumble mixture and the fruit or other base separately. This prevents the Crumble topping becoming softened as the ingredients for the base are defrosted.

As cake(s) made by the rubbed-in method become stale quite quickly, always freeze any left-over on the day of baking.

The cake(s) can be heated gently to defrost and give the pleasantly crisp texture associated with these cakes.

PROBLEM SOLVING

It is very important to appreciate just WHY things go wrong, and how to amend them.

Q. *If, when making Rock Cakes, or similar recipes, I add a little too much liquid, should I then stir in extra flour?*
A. No, if you do that you will have a badly proportioned mixture.
Quick Remedy: Instead of putting small heaps of the mixture on to a flat baking tray, put spoonfuls into greased and floured patty tins; cook as the Master Recipe on page 38 or the variations based upon this. The cakes will not be as crisp and 'rocky' as usual, but very pleasant.

Q. *Is there any remedy for Rock Cakes that have spread badly?*
A. Mark round each cake with a large pastry cutter while the mixture is warm, or gently pull the mixture towards the centre of each cake to give a neater result immediately after cooking.

Make sure it does not happen again by using less liquid in the recipe, see the Master Recipe and comments on page 39. Make quite sure the oven is preheated at the right setting, so the mixture starts to set as soon as possible; too slow cooking often accounts for the mixture spreading.

Q. *The way to test cakes made by the rubbing-in mixture is given as 'check to see if shrunk away from the sides of the tin' and 'press firmly on top, and no impression should be left'. I find the crisp top makes it difficult to do this?*
A. It sounds as if your cakes are baked for slightly too long a period and so are becoming over-crisp; test the cake a few minutes earlier than you have been doing. You could insert a fine skewer or knitting needle into the mixture; it will come out clean, i.e. free from any mixture, if the cake is really well-cooked.

Q. *Cakes based upon the Rock Cake mixture get stale quickly, is there any way of keeping them fresh longer?*
A. Freezing is the only solution; you then can defrost as required.
Quick Remedy: Reheat the cakes for a few minutes in the oven to freshen and crisp on the outside.

Q. *What makes small cakes, like Rock Cakes, dry and hard and not crisp?*
A. Too slow cooking; always preheat the oven thoroughly; too little fat; too much liquid, which means the cakes take too long to brown and cook; the sugar topping was omitted.
Quick Remedy: Melt 15 g/½ oz butter and brush over the cakes, sprinkle with a generous layer of sugar, put into a hot oven for 3–4 minutes only; eat while warm.

Q. *Why is a crumble topping sometimes soggy, rather than crisp?*
A. Because the fruit or savoury base was too moist; see recipes on pages 56 to 59 and advice about adding liquid. Because too much fat was used in the crumble or too little sugar used in a sweet crumble; because the crumble topping was sprinkled over the fruit or savoury base and left too long before cooking. In all cases, the base soaks into the crumble.
Quick Remedy: If the dish in which the crumble was baked is safe to put under a grill (i.e. it is 'flameproof'), sprinkle a sweet crumble with sugar, crisp slowly under the grill with the heat turned to low.

Sprinkle a savoury crumble with breadcrumbs and grated cheese; crisp as above.

If the dish is not suitable for placing under the grill, put the crumble into a hot oven for a very short time so the topping crisps, but allow no time for the moist base to bubble up and soften the new topping.

CHAPTER 3

The Creaming Method

This method of incorporating the ingredients is the basis for the largest group of cakes, ranging from the light sponge-type Victoria Sandwich, which is the Master Recipe, to light small and large cakes and very rich Christmas and Wedding cakes. The list below gives an idea of how many kinds of cakes and puddings are based upon creaming fat and sugar together.

Creaming fat and sugar can be done by hand, home-cooks generally prefer to use a wooden spoon, although in the past professional pastry cooks liked to cream the fat and sugar with their hands.

Modern 'luxury' margarine enables one to make family cakes very quickly, these are on pages 70 and 71. In this case the technique is slightly different from that given under the Master Recipe on the next two pages.

WHAT DOES CREAMING MEAN?

It means that the fat and sugar are beaten together until they reach the consistency of a thick whipped cream. It is possible to use a hand or electric mixer for this purpose and to adapt recipes to use a food processor; detailed information is given on pages 68 and 69.
The other ingredients, such as eggs and flour, are then incorporated into the creamed mixture.
The classic proportions for the Master Recipe uses the same weight of fat, sugar, eggs and flour.
Proportions for other cakes made by this method vary a great deal.
The creaming method is used for:

Both small and large cakes
ranging from the light to the very rich
Many biscuits and biscuit-type cakes
Various puddings
Some types of pastry, e.g. flan (fleur) and biscuit-crust

Cakes made by the creaming method – Victoria Sandwich (recipe page 66), Vanilla Cheesecake (recipe page 98), Madeleines (recipe page 83)

VICTORIA SANDWICH

This recipe produces two sponges that are sandwiched together with jam or other filling. There are many variations and adaptations on the recipe and you can produce a whole range of small and large cakes, see pages 69 to 104.

Baking Utensils: Two prepared 19–20 cm/7½–8 inch sandwich tins, see below.

Oven Setting: Preheat the oven at moderate, 180–190°C, 350–375°F, Gas Mark 4–5. Arrange the shelf just above the centre of the oven; place both tins on the same shelf. In a small cooker, bake one sponge under the other (with a fan-assisted oven use any position).

Cooking Time: Approximately 20 minutes.

Illustrated in colour on page 65

Makes a 19–20 cm/7½–8 inch sponge sandwich
175 g/6 oz margarine or butter
175 g/6 oz caster sugar
3 large eggs★
**175 g/6 oz self-raising flour or plain flour
    with 1½ teaspoons baking powder**

to fill
**4–6 tablespoons jam or lemon curd
home-made cream (see page 76)**

to decorate
1–2 tablespoons caster or icing sugar

★If using smaller eggs add enough water to give desired consistency, see step 3.

CERTAIN SUCCESS

Choice of Ingredients: Use either self-raising flour, or plain flour with the amount of baking powder specified in the recipe. In some recipes plain flour with little, if any, baking powder is given, the reason for this is explained on page 92.
The type of fat and sugar recommended is given in order of preference in individual recipes; margarine makes a lighter Victoria Sandwich, butter a richer one.

Handling the Mixture: Cream the fat and sugar very well; this is to incorporate air into the mixture and dissolve the grains of sugar. Eggs must be beaten gradually into the creamed mixture; if added too quickly the creamed mixture will curdle (separate) which spoils the texture of the sponge or cake. The moment you find the mixture starting to curdle, beat in a little sifted flour before adding more egg. Add flour, see step 4.

Consistency: The consistency of the Master Recipe is easily obtainable as all ingredients have the same weight (i.e. 175 g/6 oz), see step 5.

Preparing Tins: Grease and flour lightly; silicone (non-stick) tins do not need flouring. If you are worried about the sponge sticking, line the base, or base and sides of the tins, with greased greaseproof paper; preparations needed for rich fruit cakes are on page 94.

Baking: Always preheat the oven at the setting given in the recipe. If you have not made a Victoria Sandwich before, open the oven door carefully at the end of 7–8 minutes; the sponges should be pale in colour, soft in texture, but starting to rise. If browning too much reduce the heat by 10°C, 25°F, 1 Gas Mark. Test after 18 minutes, see step 7.

1 Take the margarine or butter out of the refrigerator some time before making the sponge so this softens, or see advice on the next page. Stand the mixing bowl on a folded teacloth, so it will not slip on the working surface as you beat. Put the fat into the bowl; beat for 1 minute.

2 Add the sugar, then cream with the margarine or butter until soft and light in texture and almost white in colour. Steady the bowl by holding this with your left hand as you cream with a wooden spoon held in

your right hand. Beat in a clockwise direction; make quite certain that ALL the fat and sugar are evenly creamed; feel the spoon go right down to the bottom of the bowl.

3 When the fat and sugar are adequately creamed, break the first egg into a cup, add to the creamed mixture; beat in thoroughly. Repeat with the second and third eggs, but read the comments on the page opposite, about the danger of curdling.

4 Sift the flour, or flour and baking powder, into the creamed mixture. Change the wooden

spoon for a large metal spoon; fold the flour gently and carefully into the other ingredients. Folding means flicking and turning in a figure of eight movement.

5 When mixed the sponge should be of a soft or slow dropping consistency, i.e. it needs a hard shake to fall from a spoon. Spoon an equal amount into the tins; for the depth of mixture affects the baking time. Smooth flat on top.

6 Place the tins on the same shelf in the oven, or see comments about baking opposite. The sponges should take approximately 20 minutes cooking time, but check baking progress and test at the end of 18 minutes, see opposite and step 7.

7 To test if cooked press gently, but firmly, in the centre of each sponge; if uncooked your finger will leave an impression; if cooked the impression comes out, see also comments about testing and baking, left.

8 When cooked allow to cool in the tins for 1 minute; this allows the mixture to contract. Turn the first sponge out of the tin on to a folded teacloth on the palm of your hand; then invert it on to the wire cooling tray; so the top side is uppermost; this prevents the wire tray marking top surface of sponge. Repeat with second sponge.

9 When cold sandwich the two sponges with jam or lemon curd or other filling. Top with caster or sifted icing sugar.

Using modern equipment

CREAMING METHOD BY MIXER

Creaming fat and sugar is hard work, when this process is done with a wooden spoon; particularly if you are dealing with a large amount of fat and sugar. It is therefore sensible to use an electric mixer for the purpose.

The result of using an electric mixer for the initial stages of creaming fat and sugar, then adding the eggs is excellent, providing you follow the important advice given under the instructions for making a Victoria Sandwich. This is the Master Recipe for the creaming technique and is given on page 67.

Always consult the manufacturers' handbook as to the maximum amount of fat and sugar that can be creamed at one time. If the recipe contains a large amount, as in a wedding cake, which is beyond the capacity of the particular machine, then use the machine to cream part of the mixture, transfer this to another container, then cream the rest of the mixture with the electric mixer.

If cooks are not entirely pleased with the result of using an electric mixer for this very important form of mixing, it is because they tend to add the eggs too rapidly and/or they allow the mixer to blend the flour into the creamed fat, sugar and eggs too vigorously, or for too long a period. There are homely cakes, made by the creaming method, where this does not matter, but for a sponge, such as the Victoria Sandwich, a careful folding movement, when adding the flour, is an essential part of success.

To remove the mixture from the mixer bowl, first take out the beater or the whisk(s). Tap sharply against the sides of the mixer bowl, so any cake or sponge mixture drops back into the bowl, and is not wasted. If a stiff mixture, you will need to remove it from the beater or whisk(s) with the help of a plastic spatula or flat bladed knife. Do this carefully, for if you damage the wires of the whisk you will not get such a good action on subsequent occasions. Use the plastic spatula, or the utensil provided by the manufacturer, to clean out the mixer bowl.

A MIXER FOR A VICTORIA SANDWICH

If the machine has a beater, use that or use the whisk(s). If the fat is hard then do not soften by melting this; you can either cut it into pieces, put into the bowl and leave at room temperature until slightly softened or you can warm the mixing bowl by standing this in a bowl of warm water. The mixer does not deal well with hard fat. Luxury margarine will not need presoftening.

Add the sugar to the fat in the bowl, switch to the lowest speed and allow the mixer to run until the fat and sugar are adequately creamed. You can increase the speed slightly when the fat and sugar mixture is nearly ready, but if you use too fast a speed the mixture is thrown to the sides of the bowl.

Add the first egg, as step 3; switch on to low speed and beat thoroughly into the creamed mixture; do not add the second or third eggs until you are satisfied the first egg has been incorporated. The mixture can curdle when using a machine in exactly the same way as when mixing by hand.

Sift the flour, or flour and baking powder, as step 4, previous page. I like to add the flour by hand, in exactly the same way as described in step 4; but if you are in a hurry you can switch to low speed and incorporate the flour using the machine. Never allow the machine to overbeat the flour into the creamed mixture.

When the ingredients are mixed proceed as steps 5–9, previous page.

Points to Watch: Add eggs carefully; add flour gently; never overmix.

CREAMING METHOD BY FOOD PROCESSOR

The Victoria Sandwich, which is the Master Recipe, in this section, shows the correct way of using a food processor for the creaming method of making cakes, see on the right.

You will find a processor is perfectly adequate for the majority of sponges and cakes, made by this technique; although the texture is never quite as light as when prepared by hand or in a mixer.

Always consult the manufacturers' handbook as to the maximum amount of mixture that can be dealt with at one time; for the processor cannot mix too great a quantity. If you want to make a large cake then put half or a quarter of the quantities of fat, sugar, eggs and flour into the bowl; process this, remove into another container, then continue in this way, until all the cake is prepared. All you need to do then is to gently blend each batch together by hand.

There are many fruit cakes made by the creaming method; be very careful when adding fruit, glacé cherries etc. to the cake mixture, process for 1–2 seconds only to blend the fruit with the cake mixture. The double-bladed cutting knife is so efficient that it would chop the fruit finely if the processor was used for a longer period. In fact you can use the processor for chopping glacé cherries into halves or smaller portions; this will take only a very few seconds, so watch carefully, and switch off the moment the cherries are the right size.

To remove the mixture from the processor bowl, remove the lid, if any mixture should have splashed upwards to this then remove and add to the ingredients in the processor bowl. Lift out the double-bladed cutting knife very carefully (remember this is very sharp). Remove any mixture with the spatula provided by the manufacturer. Scrape out the sponge or cake mixture with the same spatula.

A FOOD PROCESSOR FOR A VICTORIA SANDWICH

A food processor does not aerate the ingredients when creaming fat and sugar, as happens when you cream by hand or with an electric mixer.

It is, however, possible to make a reasonable Victoria Sandwich if you follow the method given on page 70, i.e. use luxury margarine and put all the ingredients into the bowl together. If you want to use ordinary margarine or butter, you must leave this in the food processor bowl at room temperature until it becomes softer, then add all the ingredients.

Use the double-bladed cutting knife, fix the lid and switch on for about 25 seconds or until the mixture is well-blended.

It must be stressed, however, that the processor method is not quite as good for this classic sponge-type cake, as when using a mixer or creaming by hand, since the aeration of the mixture is so important. When the ingredients are mixed proceed as steps 5–9, which are on page 67.

Points to Watch: Never overprocess the mixture; this gives a sticky and far from light result.

CREAMING IN MIXERS AND PROCESSORS

The advice on page 68 and on this page will enable you to make the best use of either a mixer or food processor.

If you are used to making cakes by the creaming method by hand, you will be delighted with the ease and speed of using modern equipment, but please do read the advice in your handbook and on these pages.

ONE-STAGE SPONGES AND CAKES

Modern soft-type margarines, often referred to as 'luxury' or 'tub-type', enable you to produce acceptable sponges, or any of the adaptations based upon the Victoria Sandwich mixture, in a very short time. You can use this method for many other cakes too.

You can also select one of the soft polyunsaturated margarines if you want to reduce the cholesterol content of foods; although you must check that you are allowed cakes using eggs.

Low-calorie spread (like margarine) can be used to make a one-stage sponge or cake. Obviously if you are slimming seriously you must limit your intake of cake.

Kosher soft margarine can be used.

If butter or hard margarines are allowed to become very soft, you could use these instead of the soft margarine.

There are certain points to remember when making one-stage sponges and cakes from soft margarine:

a) Do not allow the fat to stand at room temperature, take it straight from the refrigerator; it will be quite soft enough to blend with other ingredients.

b) Do not overbeat the mixture. Put all the ingredients into the mixing bowl, beat for 2 minutes only. Overbeating does not improve the mixture. If using an electric mixer then 1 minute is quite sufficient time to combine the ingredients. In a food processor allow a few seconds only.

c) The mixture does not rise as well as when the cake or sponge is made by the traditional method. When creaming fat and sugar together for a prolonged period you introduce an appreciable amount of air; you do not do this when using the one-stage process. This means that the sponge or cake does not rise as much as usual. In many cakes this will not matter and you can use the normal amount of baking powder, or use self-raising flour. If you are used to a very light Victoria Sandwich, made by the traditional method, you will probably be disappointed with the result unless you use extra raising agent. You will see the amount suggested in the recipe that follows. Do not exceed this, otherwise you will taste the baking powder. By using such a generous amount of raising agent you will find that the sponge tends to become stale more readily, so do not keep it for too long a period.

d) A Victoria Sandwich made by the one-stage method is better baked at a slightly lower temperature than that given in the Master Recipe, page 66.

There are many suggestions for adapting the Master Recipe, from page 74 onwards. The One-Stage method of mixing can be followed for all of these and for other cakes in this section providing soft margarine is used and the advice given on this page is carefully followed.

ONE-STAGE VICTORIA SANDWICH

Makes a 19–20 cm/7½–8 inch sponge sandwich

You need the same proportions as the Master Recipe, i.e. 175 g/6 oz soft margarine, 175 g/6 oz caster sugar, 3 large eggs, 175 g/6 oz self-raising flour, or plain flour with baking powder. If you decide to add extra baking powder, sift 1 LEVEL teaspoon with self-raising flour, or 2½ LEVEL teaspoons (instead of the usual 1½ LEVEL teaspoons) with plain flour.

Put the ingredients into the bowl, beat as directed in point b. Divide the mixture between the two prepared sandwich tins, bake just above the centre of a very moderate oven, 160°C, 325°F, Gas Mark 3 for 25–30 minutes or until firm to the touch. Turn out, cool then fill and top with sugar as directed on page 67.

ECONOMICAL VICTORIA SANDWICH

Makes a 16.5–19 cm/6½–7½ inch sponge sandwich

85–110 g/3–4 oz margarine or butter
85–110 g/3–4 oz caster sugar
2 large eggs
175 g/6 oz self-raising flour or plain flour
    with 1½ teaspoons baking powder
milk or milk and water to mix, see
    method

to fill and decorate
see Master Recipe, page 66

Although this adaptation of the classic Victoria Sandwich uses appreciably less fat and sugar than the Master Recipe on page 66, you should still produce a beautifully light sponge, if you follow the advice given on pages 66 and 67. If you are using the smaller amounts of fat and sugar, and still require a thick sponge, then use the smaller sized sandwich tins. If using the larger amount of fat and sugar then choose the bigger tins, although you will not have such a thick sponge as when the classic proportions are used.

The economical sponge does not keep moist for as long as the 'true' Victoria recipe, due to the lower fat content.

Cream together the margarine or butter with the sugar until soft and light. Gradually beat in the eggs, see points 1–3 on page 67. Sift the flour, or flour and baking powder, then fold half into the creamed mixture. You should then gently fold in 2 tablespoons milk, or milk and water. Fold in the remaining flour, then enough milk, or milk and water, to give a soft dropping consistency. This is clearly indicated in step 5 on page 67.

As you will appreciate due to the fact that you are using less fat and 2 instead of 3 eggs, you need liquid to blend the mixture. The amount varies slightly for flours absorb different amounts. Generally speaking you will need 5 tablespoons if using only 85 g/3 oz fat and about 3½ tablespoons if using 110 g/4 oz. Milk gives a richer flavour.

Divide the mixture between the prepared tins, see pages 66 and 67. Bake just above the centre of a moderate oven, 180–190°C, 350–375°F, Gas Mark 4–5 for 15–20 minutes or until firm to the touch. Turn out, cool, sandwich and top as page 67.

ONE-STAGE ECONOMICAL VICTORIA SANDWICH

Makes a 16.5–19 cm/6½–7½ inch sponge sandwich

Before making, read about one-stage sponges and cakes on the previous page.

Follow the proportions of fat, sugar, eggs, sifted flour or flour and baking powder, in the recipe with one exception. If you decide to use extra raising agent, sift 1 LEVEL teaspoon baking powder with the self-raising flour, or 2½ LEVEL teaspoons baking powder (instead of the usual 1½ LEVEL teaspoons baking powder) with plain flour. Put all these ingredients into the mixing bowl, or bowl of a mixer or food processor. DO NOT add all the liquid at this stage, add just 2 tablespoons; you can adjust the consistency at the end of the mixing time.

Beat for 2 minutes by hand, or allow 1 minute in a mixer or a few seconds in a food processor; gradually add the extra liquid, until the mixture makes a soft dropping consistency.

Sponges made with soft margarine are better baked at a slightly lower setting than when using traditional fats and methods of mixing. Bake just above the centre of a very moderate oven, 160°C, 325°F, Gas Mark 3 for 20–25 minutes. Turn out, cool, then fill and top as directed in the Master Recipe on page 67.

71

WHEATMEAL VICTORIA SANDWICH

While wholemeal flour is not satisfactory for light cakes made by the creaming method, wheatmeal flour gives a very good result.

Follow the proportions and method of mixing given under the Master Recipe for the classic Victoria Sandwich on pages 66 and 67. You can also use wheatmeal flour to make a more economical version as on page 71 or for the one-stage method of mixing on page 70.

When making the Master Recipe on page 66, in which the same weight of fat, sugar, eggs and flour are used you still need to add 1–2 tablespoons water, to produce the soft or slow dropping consistency seen on page 67, step 5. This is because wheatmeal flour, like wholemeal flour, absorbs more liquid. Fold the water into the mixture gently and carefully after adding all the flour.

When making the Economical Victoria Sandwich on page 71, increase the amount of liquid by 1–2 tablespoons.

Bake the wheatmeal sponge as directed, although it may take a little longer.

Any of the recipes based upon the Victoria Sandwich can be made with wheatmeal flour. Always check the consistency most carefully to give the best result. This also applies when making any of the cakes in this section.

Where lemon, orange or other flavourings are used, you probably find you need extra to give a definite flavour to a sponge or cake made with wheatmeal flour.

LOWER CALORIE CAKES AND SPONGES

You can reduce the calories in many recipes if you omit half the sugar. To compensate for this add sugar substitute, which contains virtually no calories, instead. Allow 6–8 crushed saccharine tablets or 1½–2 teaspoons sweetening powder for each 25 g/1 oz sugar omitted.

In this section the crushed saccharine or sweetening powder should be creamed with the fat and smaller amounts of sugar.

In other sections blend the crushed saccharine tablets or powder with the sugar. You can appreciate the fact though that sugar not only sweetens a cake or sponge it adds bulk and lightness too, so when you omit some of the sugar the result cannot be as good.

Sweetening for diabetic cakes is to be found on page 74.

EGGLESS 'SPONGE'

Makes a 16.5–18 cm/6½–7 inch sponge sandwich

75 g/3 oz margarine or butter
75–100 g/3–4 oz caster sugar
1 LEVEL tablespoon golden syrup
175 g/6 oz self-raising flour with 1 teaspoon baking powder or plain flour with 2½ teaspoons baking powder
150 ml/¼ pint milk

Grease and flour, or line, two 16.5–18 cm/6½–7 inch sandwich tins. Cream together the margarine or butter, sugar and golden syrup until soft and light. Sift the flour and baking powder. Fold the flour and milk alternately into the creamed mixture. Divide the mixture between the prepared tins. Bake above the centre of a moderate oven, 180–190°C, 350–375°F, Gas Mark 4–5 for approximately 18 minutes or until firm to the touch. Cool for 2–3 minutes in the tins, then turn out on to a wire tray.

This mixture makes a surprisingly light sponge-type cake. Fill and top as the Master Recipe on pages 66 and 67 or as the suggestions on page 74.

VARIOUS SIZED BUTTER SPONGES

The Master Recipe on pages 66 and 67 produces a medium sized Victoria Sandwich (also called a Butter Sponge) of 19–20 cm/7½–8 inches in diameter. This assumes the sponge was baked in tins measuring at least 3 cm/1¼ inches in depth. There are some very shallow sandwich tins, if you only have these then choose tins that are slightly larger in diameter. If, on the other hand, you have very deep sandwich tins you could use those that are slightly smaller in diameter, to accommodate the amount of mixture.

The size of the tin is generally measured at the base. You will find some tins slope slightly, becoming larger at the top.

There may be many occasions when you do not want two sponges but one light sponge cake, made from the same basic recipe as the Victoria Sandwich.

This sponge is generally known as a 'Butter Sponge' to differentiate between this and the whisked type of sponge. You do not, of course, have to use butter in the ingredients, you can use margarine instead. When you bake the mixture in one, instead of two tins, you must use a lower temperature and bake for an appreciably longer time. A slight range of tin sizes is given in each case, so you can adapt the mixture to the utensils you have available; remember a mixture in a tin that is smaller in diameter, so giving a greater depth of mixture, takes a little longer cooking time.

In each case follow the method of preparing the tins and the mixture given on pages 66 and 67.

Sponge sandwiches are baked just above the centre of a moderate oven, 180–190°C, 350–375°F, Gas Mark 4–5 unless stated to the contrary. A sponge cake is baked in the centre of a very moderate oven, 160°C, 325°F, Gas Mark 3 unless stated to the contrary.

To make two 15–18 cm/6–7 inch sponge sandwiches or one 15–18 cm/6–7 inch sponge cake:

Use 110 g/4 oz margarine or butter, 110 g/4 oz caster sugar, 2 large eggs, 110 g/4 oz self-raising flour or plain flour with 1 teaspoon baking powder.
Bake the sandwiches for 15–18 minutes. Bake the sponge cake for 35–40 minutes.

To make two 19–20 cm/7½–8 inch sponge sandwiches or one 19–20 cm/7½–8 inch sponge cake:

Follow the Master Recipe pages 66 and 67. Bake the sandwiches for 20 minutes. Bake the sponge cake for 45–50 minutes.

To make two 21.5–23 cm/8½–9 inch sponge sandwiches or one 21.5–23 cm/8½–9 inch sponge cake:

Use 225 g/8 oz margarine or butter, 225 g/8 oz caster sugar, 4 large eggs, 225 g/8 oz self-raising flour or plain flour with 2 teaspoons baking powder.
Bake the sandwiches for 25–30 minutes, check after 20 minutes, lower heat if necessary. Bake the sponge cake for 50–60 minutes, check after 30 minutes, reduce heat if necessary.

To make two 24–25 cm/9½–10 inch sponge sandwiches or one 24–25 cm/9½–10 inch sponge cake:

Use 300 g/10 oz margarine or butter, 300 g/10 oz caster sugar, 5 large eggs, 300 g/10 oz self-raising flour or plain flour with 2½ teaspoons baking powder.
Bake the sandwiches above the centre of a very moderate to moderate oven, 160–180°C, 325–350°F, Gas Mark 3–4 for 35–40 minutes. Check after 25 minutes, reduce heat if necessary. Bake the sponge cake for 1 hour–1 hour 10 minutes.

Always check that sponges baked in larger sized tins, as immediately above, do not become over-brown too quickly; reduce heat quite early if necessary.

BAKING FOR DIABETIC DIETS

An alternative to sugar in cooking is Sorbitol; it is good in baking for it gives bulk, as well as a sweet flavour. Substitute 25 g/1 oz Sorbitol for 25 g/1 oz sugar. The sweetening power of Sorbitol is two thirds that of sugar; so to recompense for this you may also like to add a few crushed saccharine tablets or a little sugar substitute powder to the Sorbitol to produce a more acceptable flavour.

In my opinion the best uses of Sorbitol in baking are in simple cakes, scones, teabreads and biscuits including macaroons, but not in whisked sponges or meringues. In this creaming section the Sorbitol should be beaten with the fat in the same way as sugar. In other sections use as sugar.

There are three important points to appreciate when using Sorbitol:
a) 25 g/1 oz produces 100 calories, so it is not a true slimming aid.
b) No more than 25 g/1 oz Sorbitol should be eaten in any form during a day.
c) Cakes made with Sorbitol tend to become stale quickly, so bake only small amounts, or freeze any leftover.

Some diabetics need to measure their intake of fat, as well as protein, in that case you would be wise to follow the economical recipes, that are lower in fat.

SIMPLE LAYER SPONGES

The following layer cakes are all based on the Victoria Sandwich on page 66, i.e. the plain sponge made with 3 eggs, etc.

The amount of filling given in each recipe assumes that each of the sponges is cut horizontally, so giving four layers in all.

If you require a less rich cake then halve the amount of filling and do not slice the layers, simply sandwich the two sponges together.

Apricot Layer Sponge: Make twice the amount of Jam Filling on page 153 using apricot jam. Sandwich the layers with this. Top the sponge with Jam Glaze made as page 154, again using sieved apricot jam. Whip 150 ml/¼ pint double cream or make Almond Butter Icing with 50 g/2 oz butter etc. as page 147. Pipe butter icing or whipped cream round top edge.

Banana Cream Sponge: Mash 4 bananas with 25 g/1 oz sugar and 1 tablespoon lemon juice. Whip with 150 ml/¼ pint cream, blend half with the bananas. Spread the layers of sponge with apricot jam then the banana cream mixture. Top the sponge with whipped cream and decorate with grated chocolate.

Chocolate Layer Sponge: Make four times the amount of Chocolate Butter Icing on page 147. Use just over half to sandwich the layers of sponge together, then top the cake with some of the remaining icing. Pipe a neat border around the sponge with the last of the chocolate icing.

Chocolate Cream Sponge: Whip 300 ml/½ pint cream until firm. Blend just over half of this with 50–75 g/2–3 oz grated plain chocolate. Sandwich the layers together with a little apricot jam and the chocolate-flavoured cream. Top the sponge with whipped cream and decorate with grated chocolate.

Coconut Layer Sponge: Make four times the amount of Coconut Butter Icing on page 147. Sandwich and top the layers of sponge with this. Decorate the top of the sponge with halved glacé cherries.

Coffee Layer Sponge: Make four times the amount of Coffee Butter Icing on page 147. Use just over half to sandwich the layers of sponge together, then top the cake with some of the remaining coffee icing. Pipe a neat border around the edge of the sponge with coffee icing.

FLAVOURINGS FOR A VICTORIA SANDWICH

The Master Recipe on pages 66 and 67 is an excellent basis for a variety of flavours. You could add the extra flavouring to the basic mixture then cook it as one sponge-type cake, see page 73, or you could bake as the Victoria Sandwich on pages 66 and 67, fill with a suitable flavoured jam and top the sandwich with sugar as in the Master Recipe.

You can turn the sponge into an exciting gâteau with the addition of a filling and icing. All these ideas are covered under the various recipes.

The amount of flavouring given in the various recipes on this and the next page are based upon those used in the Master Recipe using 175 g/6 oz butter or margarine, 175 g/6 oz caster sugar, 3 large eggs and 175 g/6 oz self-raising flour, or plain flour with 1½ teaspoons baking powder. You will therefore need to reduce or increase these in proportion if making the smaller or larger sponges on page 73.

For details and cooking times for one 19–20 cm/7½–8 inch cake or the Master Recipe see pages 73 and 66. The flavourings could also be used in the One-Stage Sponge on page 70 or the Economical Victoria Sandwich on page 71.

RICH ALMOND SPONGE

Makes a 20 cm/8 inch sponge sandwich

175 g/6 oz butter or margarine
175 g/6 oz caster sugar
¼ teaspoon almond essence
3 large eggs
150 g/5 oz self-raising flour or plain flour
    with ½ teaspoon baking powder
50 g/2 oz ground almonds
1 tablespoon water

for the topping
25 g/1 oz flaked almonds

for the filling
50 g/2 oz icing sugar
50 g/2 oz ground almonds
few drops almond essence
1 egg yolk
2 tablespoons apricot jam

Grease and flour, or line, two 20 cm/8 inch sandwich tins. Cream together the butter or margarine and sugar with the almond essence. Gradually beat in the eggs as described on page 67, then sift the flour, or flour and baking powder, with the ground almonds. Fold gently and carefully into the creamed mixture together with the water. Divide between the prepared tins. Top one sponge with the almonds.

Bake just above the centre of a moderate oven, 180°C, 350°F, Gas Mark 4 for approximately 20 minutes or until firm to the touch. Turn out carefully and allow to cool.

Sift the icing sugar into a basin, add the ground almonds, almond essence and egg yolk, mix together. Spread the sponge without the almond topping with the jam and then with the soft marzipan. Put the second sponge on top.

ALMOND SPONGE

Makes a 19–20 cm/7½–8 inch cake or sponge sandwich

Follow the Master Recipe on pages 66 and 67 but add ¼ teaspoon almond essence to the butter or margarine and sugar when creaming these. Either put into a single prepared 19–20 cm/7½–8 inch cake tin or into two prepared tins of the same diameter. Top the cake, or one of the sponges, with approximately 25 g/1 oz blanched flaked almonds. Bake as for a sponge cake on page 73 or the sponge sandwiches as page 66. When the sponge sandwiches are cold, put together with apricot jam.

75

...OLATE SPONGE

Makes a 19–20 cm/7½–8 inch cake or sponge sandwich

Ingredients as the Victoria Sandwich on page 66 but omit 25 g/1 oz flour and substitute 25 g/1 oz cocoa powder. Sift the cocoa with the flour, or flour and baking powder. Proceed as the Master Recipe on pages 66 and 67. Either put into a single prepared 19–20 cm/7½–8 inch cake tin or into two prepared sandwich tins of the same diameter. Bake as for a sponge cake on page 73 or the sponge sandwiches on page 66. When the sponge sandwiches are cold, they can be sandwiched together with apricot jam or with Chocolate Butter Icing. You need the quantity as the recipe on page 147.

Top the sponge with a little sifted icing sugar or with 100–150 g/4–5 oz melted plain chocolate.

CHOCOLATE SPONGE GÂTEAU

Makes a 19–20 cm/7½–8 inch gâteau

ingredients as Victoria Sandwich on page 66, but omit 25 g/1 oz flour
25 g/1 oz cocoa powder

for the filling and coating
175 g/6 oz butter or margarine
¼ teaspoon vanilla essence
175 g/6 oz icing sugar
50 g/2 oz sweetened chocolate powder
1 tablespoon milk
5 tablespoons apricot jam
50–75 g/2–3 oz plain chocolate

Grease and flour, or line, two 19–20 cm/ 7½–8 inch sandwich tins. Cream together the 175 g/6 oz margarine or butter and 175 g/6 oz caster sugar as in the Victoria Sandwich on page 66. Gradually beat in the 3 large eggs. Sift the 150 g/5 oz self-raising flour, or plain flour and 1¼ teaspoons baking powder, with the 25 g/1 oz cocoa powder and fold into the creamed mixture. Divide the mixture between the prepared tins and bake just above the centre of a moderate oven, 180°C, 350°F, Gas Mark 4 for approximately 20 minutes or until firm to the touch. Turn out carefully and allow to cool.

Cream together the butter or margarine and vanilla essence until soft. Sift the icing sugar and chocolate powder into the butter or margarine, add the milk and beat until smooth. Spread one sponge with 2 tablespoons apricot jam then with about a quarter of the chocolate butter icing. Place the second sponge on top. Coat the sides and top of the sponge with the remaining jam then the chocolate butter icing. Grate the chocolate and press against the butter icing on the sides and top of the sponge. Use all the chocolate to give a generous coating.

HOME-MADE CREAM

Makes approximately 300 ml/½ pint

This makes an ideal filling and topping. It is easily prepared, more economical than dairy cream and tastes excellent; it is shown in the photograph on page 65.

Pour 150 ml/¼ pint milk into a saucepan. Sprinkle 1 teaspoon gelatine on top of the *cold* milk; add 100 g/4 oz *unsalted* butter (cut into small pieces). Heat gently, stirring all the time, until the butter and gelatine have dissolved. DO NOT allow the mixture to become more than luke-warm. Add ½ teaspoon sugar and 1–2 drops of vanilla essence (optional). Pour into a bowl; chill for at least 3 hours then put through a cream-maker or into a liquidizer or food processor and whisk on full speed for 30 seconds. Chill briefly then whip.

CARAMEL COFFEE GÂTEAU

Serves 6

ingredients as Victoria Sandwich on pages 66 and 67

for the filling and topping
350 g/12 oz icing sugar
175 g/6 oz butter
1 tablespoon coffee essence or 1½ teaspoons instant coffee and 1 tablespoon warm milk
225 g/8 oz granulated sugar
8 tablespoons water
2 tablespoons blanched almonds

Make the Victoria Sandwich as pages 66 and 67, bake in two tins as instructed and allow to cool.

Sift the icing sugar and blend with the butter; beat until soft and white. Gradually add the coffee essence, or blend the instant coffee powder with the warm milk, cool and add to the creamed butter and sugar.

Sandwich the two cakes with about one-third of the mixture; cover the remaining coffee icing until ready to use, so it does not become too dry.

Put the granulated sugar and water into a strong saucepan; stir until the sugar melts then allow to boil, without stirring, until the mixture turns a golden brown. Pour on to a large flat tin to give a thin layer; spread with a knife if necessary. When nearly set, mark 6–8 triangles in the caramel with an oiled knife; leave until firm and set. Top the cake with another third of the coffee butter icing, then arrange the triangles of caramel on top of this, so they stand upright. Chop the almonds and scatter between the caramel triangles. Use the remaining third of the icing to pipe a border around the cake edge. **Note:** Any caramel left can be crushed. You could use it instead of the almonds in the recipe above, or store it in a covered tin to use on a future occasion.

Caramel-topped Cakes: The sugar topping, which has been boiled to become a caramel, will become sticky if exposed to the air for too long, so serve freshly made. It is better not frozen.

CHOCOLATE ORANGE SPONGE

Makes a 16.5–18 cm/6½–7 inch sponge sandwich

50 g/2 oz All-Bran
150 ml/¼ pint orange juice
100 g/4 oz butter or margarine
100 g/4 oz caster sugar
1 teaspoon grated orange rind
2 large eggs
100 g/4 oz self-raising flour or plain flour with 1 teaspoon baking powder
3 tablespoons jelly-type orange marmalade
150 ml/¼ pint double cream
75 g/3 oz plain chocolate

Grease and flour, or line, two 16.5–18 cm/6½–7 inch sandwich tins. Put the bran into a basin, add the orange juice and allow to stand for 30 minutes. Cream together the butter or margarine, sugar and orange rind until soft and light. Gradually beat in the eggs. Sift the flour, or flour and baking powder, into the mixture then add the soaked bran with any orange juice left. Fold gently and carefully into the creamed mixture. Divide the mixture between the prepared tins and bake just above the centre of a moderate oven, 180°C, 350°F, Gas Mark 4 for approximately 25 minutes or until firm to the touch. Turn the sponges out of the tins and allow to cool.

Cover one sponge with the marmalade; whip the cream, spread a little over the marmalade, top with the second sponge.

Melt the chocolate in a basin over hot water; spread over the top of the sponge and decorate with the remaining cream.

COFFEE SPONGE GÂTEAU

Makes a 19–20 cm/7½–8 inch sponge sandwich

There are two ways of flavouring a sponge mixture with coffee. You can use concentrated coffee essence. This is particularly good as it is very concentrated, so giving a good flavour. It also is slightly sweetened.

If you have no coffee essence then use instant coffee powder, blended with a little boiling or hot liquid.

175 g/6 oz margarine or butter
175 g/6 oz caster sugar
3 very small eggs
1 tablespoon coffee essence or 1½
    teaspoons instant coffee powder
    with 2 tablespoons water or milk
175 g/6 oz self-raising flour or plain flour
    with 1½ teaspoons baking powder

for the filling and coating
175 g/6 oz butter or margarine
225 g/8 oz icing sugar
1 tablespoon coffee essence or 1
    teaspoon instant coffee powder
    with 1½ tablespoons milk
75 g/3 oz walnuts

Grease and flour, or line, two 19–20 cm/ 7½–8 inch sandwich tins. Cream together the margarine or butter and caster sugar. Gradually beat in the eggs. If using coffee essence, beat this gradually into the creamed mixture. If using instant coffee powder heat the water or milk, dissolve the coffee powder in this; allow to become cold then beat gradually into the creamed mixture. The coffee essence or liquid is very strong, so take care the creamed mixture does not curdle; if it shows signs of doing this read the advice on page 67, step 5. Sift the flour, or flour and baking powder, fold into creamed ingredients.

Divide the mixture between the prepared tins and bake just above the centre of a moderate oven, 180°C, 350°F, Gas Mark 4 for approximately 20 minutes or until firm to the touch. Turn out carefully and allow to cool.

Cream the butter or margarine until soft. Sift the icing sugar into the butter or margarine and beat well, then gradually blend in the coffee essence. If using instant coffee powder heat the milk, dissolve the powder in this, cool, then beat gradually into the creamed mixture.

Sandwich the sponges with a little coffee-flavoured icing then coat the sides and top of the sponge with the remainder. Chop the walnuts and press against the icing on the sides and top of the sponge.

COFFEE WALNUT LAYER CAKE

Illustrated in colour on the jacket
Makes a 19–20 cm/7½–8 inch layer cake

**ingredients as Coffee Sponge Gâteau,
    but use medium eggs and only ½
    tablespoon coffee essence**
25 g/1 oz walnuts

for the filling
ingredients as Coffee Sponge Gâteau

for the icing
**American Frosting based on 2 egg
    whites as page 152**
few walnut halves

Prepare the sandwich tins as in Coffee Sponge Gâteau. Cream together the butter or margarine and sugar until soft and light. Gradually beat in the eggs and then the coffee essence. Sift the flour, or flour and baking powder, chop the walnuts very finely. Fold the flour and walnuts into the creamed mixture. Bake as the Coffee Sponge Gâteau.

Split each sponge horizontally to give four layers. Make the filling and use all of this to sandwich the layers together. Prepare the frosting, spread over the top and sides of the cake. Top with walnut halves.

DATE AND WALNUT LAYER CAKE

Makes a 20–23 cm/8–9 inch layer cake

110 g/4 oz butter or margarine
110 g/4 oz light brown sugar
3 large eggs
225 g/8 oz self-raising flour or plain flour
    with 2 teaspoons baking powder
½–1 teaspoon ground cinnamon
1 tablespoon cocoa powder
5 tablespoons milk
110 g/4 oz dates, weight without stones
110 g/4 oz walnuts

for the filling
50 g/2 oz butter
50 g/2 oz light brown sugar
2 tablespoons single cream
225 g/8 oz dates, weight without stones

In this particular recipe it is advisable to line the base of the two 20–23 cm/8–9 inch sandwich tins with rounds of greased greaseproof paper unless using 'non-stick' tins, grease and flour the sides of the tins.

Cream together the butter or margarine and sugar until soft and light. Gradually beat in the eggs. Sift the flour or flour and baking powder, cinnamon and cocoa, fold into the creamed ingredients with the milk. Finely chop the dates and walnuts. Blend with the other ingredients. Divide between the prepared tins and bake just above the centre of a moderate oven, 180°C, 350°F, Gas Mark 4 for 25 minutes or until firm to the touch. Cool for 2–3 minutes in the tins then turn out carefully and remove the paper from the bottom of the sponges. Put on a wire cooling tray and allow to cool.

Put the ingredients for the filling into a saucepan and stir over a very low heat until the butter and sugar have melted and the mixture forms a thick purée. Allow to cool and sandwich the cakes together with the mixture.

LEMON SPONGE

Makes a 19–20 cm/7½–8 inch cake or sponge sandwich

ingredients as Victoria Sandwich on
    page 66, but use 3 small eggs
1–1½ teaspoons very finely grated
    lemon rind
1 tablespoon lemon juice

Add the lemon rind to the margarine or butter and sugar and cream until soft and light. Gradually beat in the eggs, then sift the flour, or flour and baking powder, into the creamed mixture and fold in gently and carefully. Lastly add the lemon juice. Bake as for the sponge cake on page 73 or the sponge sandwiches on page 66.

When the sponge sandwiches are cold, put together with lemon curd or lemon marmalade. Top the sponge with caster or sifted icing sugar as the Master Recipe on pages 66 and 67.

RING CAKES AND SPONGES

If you want a slightly different appearance to a sponge, or indeed any kind of cake, bake the mixture in a ring shaped tin.

Obviously you will need a tin that is somewhat larger in diameter for you have a fairly narrow ring instead of a complete sponge or cake. If you take the Lemon Sponge above as an example, you would bake that in a 19–20 cm/7½–8 inch cake tin, you then need a 21.5–24 cm/8½–9½ inch ring tin. Grease and flour the tin well, put in the mixture.

If you consult page 73 you will find that the quantity of sponge baked in a 19–20 cm/7½–8 inch tin requires 45–50 minutes cooking. I always deduct about 25% of the total cooking time so that means the ring cake needs 34–38 minutes cooking time.

SPONGE SLAB

It is often extremely useful to bake the Victoria Sandwich, pages 66 and 67, or any of the other recipes based upon this, pages 75–79, in an oblong tin. This enables you to cut the sponge into small shapes. You can adapt the sponge as the suggestions on the right or use it as an alternative to the Genoese Pastry for fancy cakes as pages 132 and 133. You need an oblong shape to make the Battenburg Cake on page 81.

If using a shallow rimmed Swiss roll tin, you *must* line it with a large piece of greased greaseproof paper, so the edges stand well above the rim of the tin and so support the sponge as it cooks; even with a deeper tin it makes it easier to remove the sponge if the tin is lined with greased greaseproof paper. Cut the corners of the paper carefully, so you have a neat shape, see page 32.

Do not overcook a sponge slab; the mixture is spread over a large area and is relatively shallow, even in the deeper tin.

To make a shallow sponge approximately 25 × 18 cm/10 × 7 inches or a deeper sponge at least 2.5 cm/1 inch in depth and about 20 × 15 cm/8 × 6 inches: Use 110 g/4 oz margarine or butter, 110 g/4 oz caster sugar, 2 large eggs, 110 g/4 oz self-raising flour or plain flour with 1 teaspoon baking powder.

Bake above the centre of a moderate oven, 180°C, 350°F, Gas Mark 4. Allow approximately 15–18 minutes for the shallow sponge and 20–23 minutes for the deeper sponge.

To make a shallow sponge approximately 30.5 × 20 cm/12 × 8 inches or a deeper sponge at least 2.5 cm/1 inch in depth and about 25–28 × 18 cm/10–11 × 7 inches:

Use the Master Recipe, i.e. 175 g/6 oz margarine or butter, 175 g/6 oz caster sugar, 3 large eggs, 175 g/6 oz self-raising flour or plain flour with 1½ teaspoons baking powder.

Bake above the centre of a moderate oven, 180°C, 350°F, Gas Mark 4. Allow about 18–20 minutes for shallow sponge and 25–30 minutes for the deeper one.

To make a really large slab, use an average-sized meat tin measuring about 33 × 25 cm/13 × 10 inches:

Use 300 g/10 oz margarine or butter, 300 g/10 oz caster sugar, 5 large eggs, 300 g/10 oz self-raising flour or plain flour with 2½ teaspoons baking powder.

Bake in the centre of a moderate oven, 180°C, 350°F, Gas Mark 4 for approximately 1–1¼ hours for you have a really deep cake. Check after 40 minutes and reduce heat slightly if necessary.

TRAY BAKES

This term is used to describe a mixture cooked in a baking tray. Almond Slices on page 202 are a good example. The method of baking a Victoria Sandwich mixture on this page is ideal if you want to make lots of small cakes for a children's party. Decorate the slab with Glacé or Butter Icing, as pages 146 and 147. If planning a party for tiny children, top the icing with small jellied sweetmeats, 'Smarties' or 'hundreds and thousands' and cut into bite-sized pieces – much quicker than making individual cakes.

Spread the cold sponge with sieved apricot jam, then with a lightly set fruit-flavoured jelly. Allow the jelly to become quite stiff, then cut the sponge into the required shapes with a warm knife.

Spread the top of the sponge with raspberry jam, coat with desiccated coconut and decorate with glacé cherries.

BATTENBURG CAKE

Makes a cake 20–30.5 cm/8–12 inches long

**ingredients as Victoria Sandwich on
pages 66–67, either using
110 g/4 oz fat, sugar and flour with
2 large eggs or 175 g/6 oz fat, sugar
and flour with 3 large eggs
colouring or flavouring, see method**

to coat and decorate
**apricot jam
Marzipan, see method and page 148
few glacé cherries
small piece angelica**

Use the correct sized deeper tin for the smaller or larger sponge, measurements on page 80, for you need four fingers of sponge at least 2.5 cm/1 inch in depth. Grease and flour, or line, the tin. Make a long narrow strip of greaseproof paper, the length of the tin, grease this on both sides, place down the centre of the tin, it will separate the white and coloured sponge during baking.

Make the sponge as pages 66 and 67, spread half down the tin. Either tint the sponge remaining in the bowl with a few drops pink or green food colouring, or add 1½–2 teaspoons sifted cocoa powder plus 2 teaspoons milk, or 1½–2 teaspoons coffee essence with 1½–2 teaspoons extra flour. Put the mixture the other side of the paper. Bake as the timings given on page 80. Allow to cool and cut into two long white and two long coloured strips. Join these together with sieved apricot jam, with white and coloured strips alternately. Spread the top of the cake with jam.

Make the marzipan and roll out to an oblong sufficiently large to completely cover the cake, except the short ends. The amount of marzipan depends a little on the thickness desired, but you need: 110–175 g/4–6 oz ground almonds etc. for the smaller cake and 175–225 g/6–8 oz ground almonds etc. for the larger cake, recipe on page 148.

Invert the cake, with the jam top downwards on to the marzipan; spread all the surfaces, except the short ends, with more jam. Wrap the marzipan around the cake; seal the join. Flute the top long edges of the marzipan. Halve the cherries, make leaves of angelica, press these on top.

LAMINGTONS

Makes 16

**ingredients as Victoria Sandwich on
page 66, using 175 g/6 oz butter etc.**

for the icing and coating
**225 g/8 oz icing sugar
25 g/1 oz cocoa powder or 50 g/2 oz
sweetened chocolate powder
approx. 2 tablespoons water
few drops vanilla essence
15 g/½ oz butter
75 g/3 oz desiccated coconut**

Grease and flour, or line, a 20–23 cm/8–9 inch square tin. Prepare the sponge mixture as page 66. Spoon into the tin and bake just above the centre of a moderately hot oven 180°C, 350°F, Gas Mark 4 for approximately 20–25 minutes. Turn out and allow to cool then cut into 16 equal sized squares.

Sift the icing sugar with the cocoa powder or chocolate powder. Put into a saucepan with the water, vanilla essence and butter, and stir over a very low heat until a flowing consistency. Put the coconut on a sheet of greaseproof paper.

Insert a fine skewer in the first square of sponge; dip in the warm icing until evenly, but thinly, coated. Drop into the coconut and turn round in this until evenly coated. Repeat this process with all the squares of sponge. Allow to stand for several hours until the icing has hardened.

LIGHT SMALL CAKES

Many small cakes are made by the creaming method. The small cakes on this and the next page are based on the Master Recipe, pages 66 and 67, and others that follow on subsequent pages are slight adaptations.

I like to bake small cakes fairly quickly so they do not become dry, which can happen with prolonged slower cooking; you must, of course, make quite certain that the outsides of the cakes do not become overbrown before the mixture is set in the centre.

Preparing Patty Tins: These should be lightly greased and floured. If using 'non-stick' tins there is no need to grease or flour. When removing the cooked cakes from the oven allow to stand for ½ minute then ease out of the tins. You can use a small flat-bladed knife with ordinary tins, but not with 'non-stick' tins; tap the base of the tins sharply.

The variation in the numbers of cakes that can be made in each recipe depends upon the depth of the patty tins.

EASTER NESTS

Makes 12–18

ingredients as Cup Cakes

to decorate
**Chocolate Butter Icing, made with
    75 g/3 oz butter, etc. as page 147
little chocolate vermicelli
approx. 36 small Easter eggs**

Make the Cup Cakes but bake in greased and floured patty tins instead of paper cases. Turn out and allow to cool.

Spread the flat tops with a little butter icing, coat with the chocolate vermicelli and put the eggs in position. Spread or pipe the remaining butter icing around the edge of the cakes to make nest shapes.

CUP CAKES

The Victoria Sandwich, pages 66 and 67, is ideal for Cup Cakes, except the ingredients given would produce about 36 small cakes, which may be too many for the average family, although you can freeze any left. The proportions given below make 20–24 cakes; the reason you can produce more Cup Cakes, compared with other cakes, based upon the same recipe, is that you must not over-fill the paper cases. The cakes rise in baking and you should leave space for the icing, which needs to be supported by the paper cases.

Makes 20–24

**110 g/4 oz margarine or butter
110 g/4 oz caster sugar
2 large eggs
110 g/4 oz self-raising flour or plain flour
    with 1 teaspoon baking powder**

for the topping
**Glacé Icing made with
    225–300 g/8–10 oz icing sugar, as
    page 146**

Put 20–24 small cake paper cases into patty tins; these support the cakes as they rise. A baking tray is less good. Cream together the margarine or butter and sugar, gradually beat in the eggs. Sift the flour, or flour and baking powder, fold gently into the creamed mixture. Spoon the sponge into the paper cases, fill slightly under half. Bake towards the top of a moderately hot oven, 200°C, 400°F, Gas Mark 6 for 10–12 minutes or until firm. Allow to cool.

Make the icing as page 146 to a soft consistency, spoon over the cakes, allow to set.

Note: The sponge mixture can be flavoured as given on pages 76 to 79 and the icing can be flavoured too.

PEANUT BUTTER CUP CAKES

Makes 20–24

50 g/2 oz peanut butter
50 g/2 oz margarine or butter
150 g/5 oz moist light brown sugar
¼ teaspoon vanilla essence
2 large eggs
110 g/4 oz self-raising flour or plain flour
    with 1 teaspoon baking powder
½ tablespoon milk

for the topping
50 g/2 oz plain chocolate
175 g/6 oz icing sugar
50 g/2 oz butter

Cream together the peanut butter, margarine or butter, sugar and essence. Gradually beat in the eggs. Sift the flour, or flour and baking powder, fold into the creamed mixture with the milk. Spoon into 20–24 paper cases as described under Cup Cakes, page 82. Bake towards the top of a moderately hot oven, 200°C, 400°F, Gas Mark 6 for 12 minutes or until firm; cool.

    Break the chocolate into pieces, melt in a basin over hot water. Sift the icing sugar into the chocolate, add the butter, blend well. Spread over the cakes.

MADELEINES

Illustrated in colour on page 65
Makes 12–16

ingredients as Cup Cakes on page 82

to decorate
3–4 tablespoons sieved raspberry jam
50 g/2 oz desiccated coconut
6–8 glacé cherries
pieces of angelica

Grease and flour 12–16 dariole moulds (castle pudding tins). Prepare the sponge mixture and half fill the tins. Bake as Cup Cakes, turn out and allow to cool.

    Warm the jam; put the coconut on to a flat plate, insert a fine skewer into the base of the first cake to support it. Hold the skewer with one hand; dip a flat-bladed knife or pastry brush in the jam and coat the sides and top of each cake then roll in the coconut. Repeat until all the cakes are coated. Halve cherries, press on top with angelica leaves.

MUSHROOM CAKES

Makes 12–18

ingredients as Cup Cakes on page 82

to decorate
**Chocolate Butter Icing, made with
    50 g/2 oz butter, etc. as page 147**
**Marzipan, made with 50 g/2 oz ground
    almonds, etc. as page 148**
little icing sugar

Make the Cup Cakes, but bake in greased and floured patty tins instead of paper cases. Turn out and allow to cool.

    Spread the flat tops with the icing, mark with a fine skewer to look like the tops of a mushroom. Form the marzipan into 12 small 'stalks', press on to the icing. Sift a little icing sugar over the top.

FAIRY CAKES

Makes 12–18

25–40 g/1–1½ oz currants
ingredients as Cup Cakes on page 82

Small fluted patty tins are traditional to use. Grease these well, put in the currants, top with the sponge mixture, then bake as Cup Cakes. Turn the little cakes upside down to serve.

QUEEN CAKES

Makes 12–18

85 g/3 oz margarine or butter
85 g/3 oz caster sugar
2 large eggs
110 g/4 oz self-raising flour or plain flour
    with 1 teaspoon baking powder
50 g/2 oz mixed dried fruit

Cream together the margarine or butter and sugar until soft and light. Gradually beat in the eggs. Sift the flour, or flour and baking powder, fold into the creamed mixture. Add the fruit. Spoon into 12–18 paper cases. Bake towards the top of a moderately hot oven, 200°C, 400°F, Gas Mark 6 for 12–15 minutes or until firm to the touch.

BASKET CAKES

Makes 12–18

ingredients as Queen Cakes, but omit
    the dried fruit

to decorate
150 ml/¼ pint double cream
25 g/1 oz glacé cherries
2 teaspoons caster sugar
25 g/1 oz sultanas
12 long narrow strips angelica
little icing sugar

Make the Queen Cakes but bake in greased and floured patty tins instead of paper cases. Turn out and allow to cool. Make a horizontal cut and remove a thin slice from the top of each cake.

Whip the cream until stiff, chop the cherries, add to the cream together with the sugar and sultanas. Spread over the top of the cakes. Halve the slices removed from the cakes, put one half flat over the filling, tilt the other half to look like a half opened basket. Moisten the angelica in a little warm water then press into position as handles. Sift a little sugar over.

BUTTERFLY CAKES
Illustrated in colour on the jacket

Makes 12–18

ingredients as Queen Cakes, but omit
    dried fruit

to decorate
2–3 tablespoons raspberry or sieved
    apricot jam
150 ml/¼ pint double cream (optional)
2 teaspoons sugar (optional)
little icing sugar

Make and bake the Queen Cakes, allow to cool. Cut a slice from the top of each cake; divide the slices in halves to form the 'wings'. Spread the top of each cake with jam. Whip cream, add sugar, spread or pipe over the jam. Press 'wings' of cake in position. Sift a little icing sugar over.

CHERRY CAKES

Makes 12–18

ingredients as Queen Cakes, but omit
    dried fruit
50 g/2 oz glacé cherries

Make the cake mixture as Queen Cakes; quarter the cherries, add to the cake mixture. Put into greased and floured patty tins, or into paper cases; halve 6–9 extra glacé cherries, press in the centre of each cake. Bake as Queen Cakes.

Batch Baking – Mandarin Glory Gâteau, Walnut Sultana Loaf Cake,
Cherry Coconut Fingers (page 219)

LIGHT LARGE CAKES

The Madeira Cake that follows is a typical cake made by the creaming method. As you will see it is an excellent basic cake, which can be adapted in many ways. A true Madeira Cake is a rich moist cake because a high percentage of butter is used. I have given a more economical version, but this is really not to be compared to the classic recipe.

The term 'Madeira' suggests that wine should be used in the recipe, but that is not the case. In the days when Madeira was drunk more often than today, a slice of the light rich cake was a usual accompaniment. I have however on occasions used dry sherry or dry Madeira wine instead of milk to mix the Madeira Cake on this page and found it makes a delicious alternative.

About 1–2 teaspoons very finely grated lemon rind can be creamed with the butter and sugar.

RICH MADEIRA CAKE

Makes an 18 cm/7 inch cake

175 g/6 oz butter
175–200 g/6–7 oz caster sugar
3 large eggs
225 g/8 oz plain flour with 1 teaspoon
   baking powder, see method, or
   110 g/4 oz plain flour and
   110 g/4 oz self-raising flour
approx. 2 tablespoons milk

to decorate
1 tablespoon caster sugar
piece of candied lemon peel

Grease and flour, or line, an 18 cm/7 inch cake tin. Cream together the butter and sugar until soft and light; the larger amount of sugar helps to give a very light texture. Beat the eggs and gradually add to the creamed butter mixture. Should this

show signs of curdling, see page 67 step 5. Sift the flour and baking powder or both flours together; the small amount of raising agent ensures a cake that is flat on top. Fold the flour into the creamed ingredients, then add enough milk to make a soft dropping consistency. Put into the prepared tin, sprinkle the tablespoon of sugar on top. Bake in the centre of a very moderate oven, 160°C, 325°F, Gas Mark 3 for approximately 1¼–1½ hours. Halfway through the cooking time, place the peel on top of the cake (do not bring it out of the oven). If the cake seems to be getting too brown, lower the heat slightly.

If preferred, the lemon peel can be put on the cake before baking and covered halfway through the baking period with a piece of greaseproof paper or foil to prevent it becoming dry or burned. Test the cake by pressing firmly on top, see step 7 on page 67 in the Master Recipe. Turn the cake out carefully, allow to cool.

Note: You can bake the cake in a 20 cm/8 inch cake tin, allow about 1 hour 10 minutes cooking time.

Use 4 large eggs and omit the milk.

The reason why the cake should not be brought out of the oven when adding the peel is because halfway through the cooking period is a critical time.

LARGE MADEIRA CAKE

Makes a 23 cm/9 inch cake

A large plain cake is often extremely useful to take the place of a fruit cake; it can be iced for special occasions.

Use exactly double the ingredients given in the Madeira Cake, i.e. 350 g/ 12 oz butter etc. Put into a prepared 23 cm/9 inch cake tin and bake in a very moderate oven, 160°C, 325°F, Gas Mark 3 for 1 hour and then in a slow oven, 150°C, 300°F, Gas Mark 2 for approximately 1 further hour or until firm to the touch.

ECONOMICAL MADEIRA CAKE

Makes an 18 cm/7 inch cake

Reduce the amounts of fat and sugar to 110 g/4 oz each and the eggs to two. Use more milk to make a soft dropping consistency. Bake as Rich Madeira Cake on page 86 but allow a slightly shorter cooking time. This does not have the richness of a true Madeira Cake.

RICH ALMOND CAKE

Makes an 18 cm/7 inch cake

ingredients as Madeira Cake on page 86, but use 175 g/6 oz plain flour with 100 g/4 oz ground almonds and only 1 tablespoon milk

Cream a few drops of almond essence with the butter and sugar. Bake in a very moderate oven, 160°C, 325°F, Gas Mark 3 for 1 hour then in a slow oven, 150°C, 300°F, Gas Mark 2 for a further 30–35 minutes or until firm to the touch.

SAND CAKE

Makes a 19–20 cm/7½–8 inch ring cake

In this cake cornflour and rice flour take the place of ordinary flour, producing a cake that has a fine texture but which may be rather dry for some tastes. Traditionally it is baked in a ring tin, which means a shorter cooking time, and the tin is coated with macaroon or ratafia crumbs. This is not essential, but it makes a more interesting looking cake.

for the coating
15 g/½ oz butter
2–3 tablespoons fine macaroon or ratafia crumbs

110 g/4 oz butter or margarine
110 g/4 oz caster sugar
1 teaspoon finely grated lemon rind
2 large eggs
85 g/3 oz cornflour
25 g/1 oz rice flour
1 teaspoon baking powder

Grease a 19–20 cm/7½–8 inch ring tin with the 15 g/½ oz butter and coat with the crumbs, press these into the butter.

Cream together the butter or margarine, sugar and lemon rind. Gradually beat in the eggs. Sift the cornflour, rice flour and baking powder together, fold into the creamed mixture. Spoon into the prepared tin and bake in the centre of a very moderate oven, 160°C, 325°F, Gas Mark 3 for 40–45 minutes until firm. Cool in tin for a few minutes then turn out.

WINDSOR LEMON CAKE

Makes an 18 cm/7 inch cake

225 g/8 oz butter or margarine
225 g/8 oz caster sugar
1 teaspoon grated lemon rind
2 large eggs
100 g/4 oz plain flour
1 teaspoon baking powder
175 g/6 oz ground rice
2 tablespoons lemon juice
milk to mix

Grease and flour, or line, an 18 cm/7 inch cake tin. Cream together the butter or margarine, sugar and lemon rind until soft and light. Gradually beat in the eggs. Sift the flour and baking powder. Fold gently into the creamed mixture with the ground rice, lemon juice and enough milk to make a soft dropping consistency, as illustrated on page 67, step 5. Spoon into the prepared tin and bake in the centre of a very moderate oven, 160°C, 325°F, Gas Mark 3 for 1½–1¾ hours or until firm to the touch.

MAKING CHERRY CAKES

Cherry cakes seem to pose a problem to many cooks, for they find that in the recipe they use the glacé cherries fall to the bottom of the cake as it cooks.

It must be appreciated that glacé cherries are heavy; if they are chopped or quartered there is less possibility of their falling in a cake. When you have a very rich Christmas or wedding cake the cherries are cut in pieces and mixed with the other fruits. Another important point though is that rich cakes containing cherries plus a great weight of dried fruit generally are based on plain flour and are baked slowly.

The use of too much raising agent, which produces an ultra-light cake mixture, is another reason why cherries fall. The cake mixture rises drastically, but cannot carry the weight of the cherries with it. Naturally when little raising agent is used the cake will not rise a great deal, but it will still be light in texture.

Many people advocate rinsing the cherries in cold water first, to get rid of the lovely sticky syrup. I feel this is a great pity for it is the syrup that makes the cherries moist and delicious. The recipe that follows uses flour with very little raising agent, it is baked slowly, and the cake mixture is kept fairly firm to compensate for the moistness of the cherries.

RICH CHERRY CAKE

Makes an 18–20 cm/7–8 inch cake

175 g/6 oz butter or margarine
175 g/6 oz caster sugar
3 large eggs
225 g/8 oz plain flour with 1 teaspoon
    baking powder or 110 g/4 oz plain
    flour and 110 g/4 oz self-raising
    flour
175–225 g/6–8 oz glacé cherries

Grease and flour, or line, an 18–20 cm/7–8 inch cake tin. Cream together the butter or margarine and sugar. Gradually beat in the eggs. Sift the flour and baking powder or both flours together. Halve the cherries and mix with the flour. Fold the flour and cherries gently but thoroughly into the creamed mixture. Spoon into the prepared tin.

Bake in the centre of a slow oven, 150°C, 300°C, Gas Mark 2. Allow approximately 1¾ hours for the cake in the 18 cm/7 inch tin, but barely 1½ hours for the cake in the 20 cm/8 inch tin. Allow to cool for 2–3 minutes then turn out of the tin.

CHERRY CORNFLOUR CAKE

Makes an 18–20 cm/7–8 inch cake

**ingredients as Rich Cherry Cake, but
    omit 50 g/2 oz plain flour and use
    50 g/2 oz cornflour**

Make and bake as Rich Cherry Cake. The inclusion of cornflour makes a firm and fine textured cake. This cake has a very pleasant flavour if the grated rind of 1 lemon is creamed with the butter or margarine and sugar.

CHERRY ALMOND CAKE

Makes an 18–20 cm/7–8 inch cake

**ingredients as Rich Cherry Cake, but
    omit 50 g/2 oz self-raising flour and
    add 75 g/3 oz ground almonds**

Make and bake as Rich Cherry Cake, but allow an extra 5 minutes cooking time.

This cake can be topped with 25–50 g/1–2 oz blanched almonds and a few glacé cherries before baking.

RICH SEED CAKE

Makes an 18 cm/7 inch cake

**ingredients as Madeira Cake on page
    86, but omit the candied peel
    topping
2–3 teaspoons caraway seeds**

Make the Madeira Cake but add most of
the caraway seeds. Put into the prepared
tin. Top with caster sugar, as the Madeira
Cake, and the remaining seeds. Bake as
Madeira Cake.

CHERRY ALMOND LOAF

Makes a 900 g/2 lb loaf-shaped cake

**ingredients as Marzipan Nut Loaf, but
omit the milk (to make a firmer
mixture), the cashew nuts and walnuts
and use just the 50 g/2 oz blanched
almonds. Cut 75 g/3 oz glacé cherries
into quarters, mix with a little of the
flour and the chopped blanched
almonds**

Make the cake as the Marzipan Nut Loaf,
spoon the mixture into the prepared tin.
Top with 3–4 glacé cherries and a few
whole blanched almonds. Bake as Marzipan Nut Loaf.

NUT LOAF

Makes a 900 g/2 lb loaf-shaped cake

**ingredients as Marzipan Nut Loaf, but
    omit the topping**

Spoon the mixture into the prepared tin,
sprinkle lightly with caster sugar. Arrange
a few nuts on top, brush these with any egg
white that remains in the egg shells. Bake
as Marzipan Nut Loaf.

MARZIPAN NUT LOAF

Makes a 900 g/2 lb loaf-shaped cake

**175 g/6 oz butter or margarine
175 g/6 oz caster sugar
few drops almond essence
3 medium eggs
225 g/8 oz self-raising flour or plain flour
    with 2 teaspoons baking powder
25 g/1 oz ground almonds
2 tablespoons milk
50 g/2 oz blanched almonds
25 g/1 oz cashew nuts
25 g/1 oz walnuts**

for the topping
**1½ tablespoons apricot jam
75 g/3 oz icing sugar
75 g/3 oz ground almonds
few drops almond essence
1 egg white
50 g/2 oz mixed nuts**

Grease and flour, or line, a 900 g/2 lb loaf
tin. Cream together the butter or margarine, sugar and almond essence until soft
and light. Gradually beat in the eggs. Sift
the flour, or flour and baking powder, and
ground almonds. Fold into the creamed
mixture with the milk. Chop the nuts, add
to the cake mixture. Spoon into the prepared tin and bake in the centre of a very
moderate oven, 160°C, 325°F, Gas Mark 3
for 1¼ hours or until firm to the touch.
Turn out and allow to cool.

Warm and sieve the jam. Spread over
the top of the loaf. Sift the icing sugar into
a basin, add the ground almonds, almond
essence and enough egg white to bind.
Roll out on a sugared board to an oblong
shape to fit the top of the loaf. Press over
the jam. Press the nuts on top, to form a
neat design. Brush the marzipan and nuts
with a little of the remaining egg white.

Put the loaf under the grill, preheated
on low; and heat very gently for a few
minutes to glaze the top of the loaf.

GENOA CAKE

Makes a 20 cm/8 inch cake

175 g/6 oz butter or margarine
175 g/6 oz caster sugar
1 teaspoon grated lemon rind
4 large eggs
225 g/8 oz flour, preferably plain with 1
    teaspoon baking powder, see
    Madeira Cake on page 86
50 g/2 oz mixed candied peel
225 g/8 oz mixed dried fruit
1 tablespoon caster sugar to sprinkle

Grease and flour, or line, a 20 cm/8 inch cake tin. Cream together the butter or margarine, sugar and lemon rind until soft and light. Beat the eggs and add gradually to the creamed mixture; see comments on page 67 step 5 about preventing the mixture from curdling. Sift the flour and baking powder, chop the peel. Stir the flour, peel and fruit into the creamed mixture. Spoon into the tin. Sprinkle the tablespoon of sugar on top.

Bake in the centre of a very moderate oven, 160°C, 325°F, Gas Mark 3 for approximately 1½ hours or until firm to the touch, reduce the heat slightly after 1¼ hours if the cake is overbrowning.
Note: This cake can be baked in an 18 cm/7 inch cake tin; bake for 1¾ hours. Allow 1 hour at 160°C, 325°F, Gas Mark 3 then reduce the heat to 150°C, 300°F, Gas Mark 2 for the remaining time.

RAISIN CAKE

Makes an 18–20 cm/7–8 inch cake

**ingredients as Genoa Cake, but omit
    the mixed fruit and peel and use
    300 g/10 oz seedless chopped raisins**

Bake as Genoa Cake, timing the cooking according to the size of tin used.

DUNDEE CAKE

Illustrated in colour on the jacket
Makes a 20 cm/8 inch cake

175 g/6 oz butter or margarine
175 g/6 oz caster sugar
3 large eggs
225 g/8 oz plain flour with 1 teaspoon
    baking powder or use 110 g/4 oz
    plain and 110 g/4 oz self-raising
    flour
25 g/1 oz ground almonds
2 tablespoons dry sherry or milk
50 g/2 oz glacé cherries
50 g/2 oz candied peel
450 g/1 lb mixed dried fruit

to decorate
25–50 g/1–2 oz blanched whole or flaked
    almonds

Grease and flour, or line, a 20 cm/8 inch cake tin. Cream together the butter or margarine and sugar until soft and light. Gradually beat in the eggs, save the shells. Sift the flour and baking powder or two kinds of flour (this amount of raising agent gives a light cake, that rises absolutely flat and still ensures that the fruit is evenly distributed). Fold the flour and ground almonds into the creamed mixture, then add the sherry or milk. Quarter the glacé cherries, chop the peel, add to the fruit and stir into the cake mixture.

Spoon into the tin, smooth flat on top. Place the almonds in position on top of the cake in a neat design and brush these with remains of egg white from egg shells.

Bake in the centre of a very moderate oven, 160°C, 325°F, Gas Mark 3 for 30 minutes, then reduce the heat to slow, 150°C, 300°F, Gas Mark 2 for a further 1½ hours or until the cake is firm to the touch and has shrunk from the sides of the tin. Turn out on to a wire cooling tray.
Note: The One-Stage method of mixing can be used in this cake, if soft margarine is used. Bake as above.

CITRUS LOAF

Makes a 675 g/1½ lb loaf-shaped cake

100 g/4 oz butter or margarine
1 tablespoon lime marmalade
75 g/3 oz caster sugar
1 teaspoon finely grated lemon rind
1 teaspoon finely grated orange rind
2 eggs
175 g/6 oz self-raising flour or plain flour
with 1½ teaspoons baking powder
1 tablespoon grapefruit or lemon juice

for the topping
1 orange
50 g/2 oz walnuts
75 g/3 oz light brown sugar

Grease and flour, or line, a 675–900 g/1½–2 lb loaf tin. Cream together the butter or margarine, marmalade, sugar, lemon and orange rinds until soft and light. Gradually beat in the eggs. Sift the flour, or flour and baking powder, and fold into the creamed ingredients together with the fruit juice. Spoon into the prepared tin and bake in the centre of a moderate oven, 180°C, 350°F, Gas Mark 4 for 50–55 minutes until firm to the touch. Remove from the tin and allow to cool on a wire cooling tray.

Meanwhile grate the rind and squeeze out the juice of the orange, chop the walnuts and blend with the sugar. Place a plate under the wire cooling tray so any topping is not wasted. Spoon the topping carefully over the top of the loaf. If any spills on to the plate, remove with a spoon then put over the loaf. Leave for at least an hour before serving so the topping moistens the cake.

GOLDEN COCONUT CAKE

Makes a 20 cm/8 inch cake

175 g/6 oz butter or margarine
175 g/6 oz caster sugar
3 large eggs
225 g/8 oz self-raising flour or plain flour
with 2 teaspoons baking powder
50 g/2 oz desiccated coconut
100 g/4 oz sultanas
100 g/4 oz mixed candied peel
100 g/4 oz glacé cherries
175 g/6 oz walnuts or Brazil nuts
approx. 2 tablespoons milk

Grease and flour, or line, a 20 cm/8 inch cake tin. Cream together the butter or margarine and sugar until soft and light. Gradually beat in the eggs. Sift the flour, or flour and baking powder, fold into the creamed mixture with the coconut and sultanas. Chop the peel, cherries and nuts, blend with the other ingredients and stir in enough milk to give a slow dropping consistency. Spoon into the prepared tin and bake in the centre of a very moderate oven, 160°C, 325°F, Gas Mark 3 for 1¼ hours, then reduce the heat to 150°C, 300°F, Gas Mark 2 for another 45 minutes.

LEMON RICE CAKE

Makes an 18 cm/7 inch cake

This recipe is mixed and baked as the Rich Madeira Cake on page 86. The rice flour gives a fine crumbly texture.

Cream together 175 g/6 oz butter or magarine, 175 g/6 oz caster sugar and the finely grated rind of 2 large lemons. Gradually beat in 3 large eggs. Sift in 175 g/6 oz plain flour, 25 g/1 oz rice flour and 1½ teaspoons baking powder. Continue as the Madeira Cake.

91

SIMNEL CAKE

A Simnel Cake is a traditional recipe; originally it was the cake made by maids to take home to their mothers on Mothering Sunday. Nowadays though it has become a celebration cake for Easter. The characteristics of this cake is that a layer of marzipan is placed in the middle of the cake mixture before baking and another layer on the top of the cake after it is cooked.

Dundee cake is an excellent basis for a Simnel Cake. Use recipe for Dundee Cake mixture on page 90; you do not require the almonds for the topping. In addition make marzipan with 225 g/8 oz ground almonds, 110 g/4 oz caster sugar, 110 g/4 oz sifted icing sugar, a few drops almond essence and 2 egg yolks (this gives thin layers of marzipan). If you want a very generous topping of marzipan, use rather more than this, see recipe page 148.

Take just about half of the marzipan, roll it out to a round at least 5 mm/¼ inch smaller than the diameter of the cake tin; this makes certain the marzipan does not stick to the sides of the tin.

Prepare the tin as page 90. Put half the cake mixture in the tin, add the round of marzipan, then the rest of the cake mixture. Bake as the Dundee Cake, but in view of the moist marzipan layer, allow about 15–20 minutes extra cooking time. Allow the cake to cool.

Brush the top with a little sieved apricot jam then put on a round of marzipan. Form 11 small balls of marzipan, put round edge of the cake. Brush the marzipan with a little egg white, put under a grill, set at low heat, for a few minutes to glaze the marzipan. Decorate with miniature Easter eggs and chickens. The centre of the cake can be covered with a round of Glacé or Royal icing if desired, see recipes pages 146 and 149, but do not coat the marzipan completely.

RICH FRUIT CAKES

A rich fruit cake is not difficult to make or cook.

A successful recipe should have a high percentage of fat, sugar and fruit in proportion to the amount of flour used.

The mixture is darkened by using spices, treacle and moist brown sugar. Do not exceed the recommended amount of treacle, for the flavour would be too strong and would dominate the cake. Moist brown sugars are described on page 15. You can use sugar marked 'dark brown' or 'moist dark brown' or choose Barbados or Muscovado sugar for a very definite taste. As pointed out on page 15, Molasses sugar is very strongly flavoured, it has a definite taste of black treacle, so you may care to use partly this sugar and partly another less strongly flavoured brown sugar in a rich fruit cake.

Over-beating should be avoided in rich fruit cakes, for you must not over-aerate the mixture; if you do you could find the actual cake mixture rises too well, it cannot carry the substantial weight of fruit, which then falls to the bottom of the cake. It is for this reason also that one uses plain flour, with no baking powder, in a rich fruit cake.

Protect the tin with paper, see pages 32 and 93, time the cooking carefully and check the speed of baking as given under the recipe on page 93. Always test the cake when you think it is cooked; full information is given under the Rich Dark Christmas Cake on page 93.

Rich fruit cakes need several weeks storage to mature after cooking, this means you cannot make the cake at the last minute. If you have to produce a Christmas cake with only a week or two to spare then I would suggest you make the Last Minute Christmas Cake or the Dark Dundee Cake, both on page 94.

RICH DARK CHRISTMAS CAKE

Makes a 23 cm/9 inch round or 20 cm/8 inch square cake

350 g/12 oz plain flour
1 teaspoon ground cinnamon
1 teaspoon mixed spice
100 g/4 oz mixed candied peel
50–100 g/2–4 oz blanched almonds
100 g/4 oz glacé cherries
900 g/2 lb mixed dried fruit, preferably
    450 g/1 lb currants, 225 g/8 oz
    sultanas, 225 g/8 oz seedless
    raisins
5 large eggs
2 tablespoons sweet sherry or brandy or
    rum or milk
300 g/10 oz butter
300 g/10 oz dark moist brown sugar
1 LEVEL tablespoon black treacle or
    molasses or golden syrup
1 teaspoon finely grated lemon rind
1 teaspoon finely grated orange rind

Line the base and sides of a 20 or 23 cm/8 or 9 inch cake tin with greased greaseproof paper, see page 32. It is also a good idea to put a layer of brown paper under the greaseproof paper on the base of the tin and to tie a band of double thickness brown paper around the outside of the tin; this should stand above the tip of the tin to protect the top of the cake as it cooks.

Sift the flour and spices. Chop the peel and almonds, quarter the cherries; mix with the dried fruit. Blend the eggs with the sherry, brandy, rum or milk.

Cream together the butter, sugar, treacle or golden syrup and fruit rinds until soft and light. Do not over beat, as this type of cake does not need as much aerating as light cakes. Gradually blend in the beaten eggs and liquid then the sifted dry ingredients (check the mixture does not curdle, see page 66). Stir in all the fruit mixture, blend thoroughly, then spoon into the prepared tin. Press the top of the mixture with damp knuckles, this helps to prevent this becoming over-crisp.

Put into the centre of a very moderate oven, 160°C, 325°F, Gas Mark 3. I use this temperature for the first part of the baking time as I find it sets the outside early in the cooking period and gives an exceptionally moist inside. Bake at this temperature for 1½ hours, then reduce the heat to 140–150°C, 275–300°F, Gas Mark 1–2 and bake for a further 2 hours. Baking times for rich fruit cakes like this vary considerably according to your particular oven, so check carefully during baking, particularly if this is the first time you have baked a rich cake, see below.

To Test the Cake: First press firmly on top, then check to see if the cake has shrunk away from the sides of the tin. If it has then remove from the oven and listen very carefully. A rich fruit cake that is not quite cooked gives a definite faint humming noise, in which case return the cake to the oven, test again 10 minutes later.

Cool the cake in the baking tin, this keeps it moist and prevents it breaking. Turn out carefully, wrap in foil; store in an airtight tin. Leave the greaseproof paper on the cake until moistening it with alcohol as below or covering with marzipan and icing as page 148–149.

To Moisten the Cake: Use a fine steel knitting needle or skewer, make a number of small holes on top of the cake, spoon over sherry, brandy or rum. You can turn the cake upside down and repeat on the bottom. Do this the day after baking, repeat once or twice more at weekly intervals if desired.

To Check your Oven during Baking: At the end of the third of the cooking time (i.e. just over an hour) the cake should have changed colour very slightly. If darkening, then reduce the heat at once. At end of second third of cooking time (i.e. just over 2 hours) the cake should have darkened but top still feel soft. For smaller and larger cakes, see page 97.

ECONOMICAL CHRISTMAS CAKES

Some families do not enjoy a very rich Christmas cake, so instead you can substitute a less rich and extravagant cake and cover this with marzipan and icing. The Dundee Cake or Genoa Cake on page 90 would be excellent alternatives. The Dundee Cake could be made a week before Christmas, but the more economical Genoa Cake should be prepared only a few days beforehand. You could of course freeze either of these cakes so they could be baked up to 3 months beforehand, wrapped and frozen, then unwrapped, defrosted and iced.

The Marzipan Nut Loaf, page 89, or the cakes on page 91 would make interesting changes. I would also recommend the cakes made by the rubbing-in method on page 49.

LAST MINUTE CHRISTMAS CAKE

Makes a 23 cm/9 inch round or 20 cm/8 inch square cake

This is based upon the recipe on page 93, which is adapted to produce a rich cake that needs just a week or two to mature. The secret lies in marinating the fruit. Prepare the tin as page 93.

Put the currants, raisins and sultanas into a basin with the grated orange and lemon rinds. Pour over 6 tablespoons sherry, brandy or rum; press the fruit down, cover the basin, leave for 24 hours.

Cream together 225 g/8 oz butter and 225 g/8 oz moist brown sugar, omit the treacle or syrup. Gradually beat in the 5 eggs. Sift the flour and spices; chop the cherries, blend with the flour. This makes sure they are kept well distributed in the cake. Blend the flour, spices and cherries with the creamed mixture. Add the chopped peel and chopped almonds and finally the moistened fruit. Put into the prepared tin and bake as the recipe on page 93.

LIGHT COLOURED CHRISTMAS CAKE

It makes a pleasant change to have a rich cake that is light in colour and has different kinds of fruit.

Follow the proportions on page 93 or any of the sizes in the table on page 96 but make the following adaptations.

Use caster in place of brown sugar.

Omit the spices.

Use golden syrup but no black treacle.

Omit the currants and raisins in the cake on page 93; use 450 g/1 lb instead of 225 g/8 oz light sultanas with an extra 50 g/2 oz chopped glacé cherries, 175 g/6 oz diced crystallised pineapple, 175 g/6 oz finely chopped dried apricots and 50 g/2 oz chopped angelica.

These alterations give the same proportions of fruit as in the cake on page 93. Any cake can be adapted in the same way, i.e., double the amount of sultanas and replace currants and raisins with extra glacé cherries, crystallised pineapple, dried apricots and angelica.

DARK DUNDEE CAKE

The Dundee Cake on page 90 makes an excellent Christmas Cake for those families who prefer a less rich cake. It can be made in exactly the same way as the recipe given on page 90, except that the topping of almonds can be omitted if you intend to cover the cake with marzipan and icing.

If, however, you prefer a dark looking cake then substitute moist dark brown sugar for the sugar used in the recipe. Do not, however, add any black treacle or syrup to the other ingredients; ½–1 teaspoon ground cinnamon can be sifted with the flours, or flour and baking powder.

WHEATMEAL FRUIT CAKES

Wheatmeal flour can be used to make any of the fruit cakes on the next pages. You must however add extra liquid to prevent the cake becoming over-dry. Do not use wholemeal flour in these rich fruit cakes, this excellent flour would give a disappointing result. In both the Rich Dark Christmas Cake and the Dundee Cake on pages 93 and 90, 2 tablespoons liquid are given as the amount to use with white flour. Increase this to 3½ tablespoons if using wheatmeal flour in these particular recipes.

Wheatmeal flour is heavier than white flour, so while plain flour, without raising agent, can still be used in the rich cakes it is better to use all self-raising flour or plain flour with 2 teaspoons baking powder in the Dundee Cake.

SIZES OF RICH CAKES

The average sized tin is given in each case; as you will see from page 93, a 20 cm/8 inch square cake tin takes the same amount of mixture as a 23 cm/9 inch round cake tin.

Cake tins vary in their depth as well as their diameter so it is important to check on this point. The cakes have been tested in tins of average depth, i.e. 8 cm/3 inches. If the cake tin you use is more shallow than this then use a cake tin which is approximately 2.5 cm/1 inch larger in diameter. If you do this you will need to decrease the baking time, see right.

This is however one point to appreciate when putting the cake mixture into the tin. The vigour with which you press down the mixture makes an appreciable difference to the amount of space it fills. I believe in filling cake tins gently when making light cakes but pressing down firmly with a rich cake mixture. This helps to make a cake that slices beautifully.

Remember if you cook the mixture in a tin larger than the one recommended you have a cake that is bigger in diameter but smaller in depth and you should *decrease* the total baking time by 25–30 minutes in the slow oven.

If you decide to use a tin that is smaller than the one recommended you increase the depth of mixture and should therefore *increase* the total baking time by 25–30 minutes in the slow oven. Obviously you must make certain that the mixture will fit into the smaller tin.

VARIOUS SIZED CHRISTMAS CAKES

The table on page 96 shows you the various sizes of Christmas cakes together with the ingredients required and the approximate baking time. I have begun with a 10 cm/4 inch round or 8 cm/3 inch square cake since these small cakes make an excellent present for anyone living alone. You could make this up at the same time as you prepare your own cake, simply adding on the extra ingredients.

To get all the information into the table there are certain abbreviations made, these are:

t = teaspoon
T = tablespoon
R = a round cake tin
S = a square cake tin
A = baking temperature at very moderate 160°C, 325°F, Gas Mark 3
B = baking temperature at slow 140–150°C, 275–300°F, Gas Mark 1–2

For further details consult the information and recipe given fully on page 93. I have simply used sherry under the list of ingredients, but you can use any of the alternatives on page 93.

To Keep Fruit Cakes Flat on Top

A rich fruit cake should be flat on top when it is baked. This is achieved by using a well-balanced recipe based on plain flour and one which is sufficiently moist in texture; by using the correct sized cake tin (if a tin is too full the mixture is inclined to 'peak' in the centre as it cooks).

It is important to spread the mixture flat before putting the cake in the oven. If making one of the less rich fruit cakes, it is a good idea to gently move the mixture away from the very centre so making a very shallow hollow.

WEDDING CAKES

The recipe on page 93 is sufficiently rich to make a very good Wedding Cake, but if you prefer a slightly richer one keep the amounts of other ingredients as the recipe, but increase the amount of dried fruit, glacé cherries and almonds by 25%. This means that in the recipe on page 93 you would use 1.12 kg/2½ lb mixed dried fruit, 150 g/5 oz glacé cherries and up to 150 g/5 oz blanched almonds. The baking time would only be about 25 minutes longer at the lower setting. Other sized cakes

CAKE TIN SIZES	cm/inch R 10/4 S 8/3	cm/inch R 13/5 S 10/4	cm/inch R 15/6 S 13/5	cm/inch R 18/7 S 15/6	cm/inch R 20/8 S 18/7
plain flour	65 g/2½ oz	85 g/3 oz	130 g/4½ oz	175 g/6 oz	225 g/8 oz
ground cinnamon	pinch	¼ t	scant ½ t	½ t	¾ t
mixed spice	pinch	¼ t	scant ½ t	½ t	¾ t
candied peel	25 g/1 oz	40 g/1½ oz	40 g/1½ oz	50 g/2 oz	75 g/3 oz
blanched almonds	25 g/1 oz	40 g/1½ oz	40 g/1½ oz	50 g/2 oz	75 g/3 oz
glacé cherries	25 g/1 oz	40 g/1½ oz	40 g/1½ oz	50 g/2 oz	75 g/3 oz
currants	75 g/3 oz	150 g/5 oz	175 g/6 oz	225 g/8 oz	350 g/12 oz
raisins	40 g/1½ oz	50 g/2 oz	85 g/3 oz	110 g/4 oz	175 g/6 oz
sultanas	40 g/1½ oz	50 g/2 oz	85 g/3 oz	110 g/4 oz	175 g/6 oz
eggs	2 small	2 medium	3 small	3 medium	5 medium
sherry	¼ T	½ T	¾ T	1 T	1½ T
butter	50 g/2 oz	85 g/3 oz	110 g/4 oz	150 g/5 oz	180 g/6½ oz
brown sugar	50 g/2 oz	85 g/3 oz	110 g/4 oz	150 g/5 oz	180 g/6½ oz
treacle or syrup	1 t	1¼ t	1½ t	½ T	¾ T
lemon rind	scant ¼ t	¼ t	¼ t	½ t	¾ t
orange rind	scant ¼ t	¼ t	¼ t	½ t	¾ t
APPROXIMATE A	½ hour	¾ hour	1 hour	1¼ hours	1½ hours
BAKING TIME B	¾ hour	1 hour	1¼ hours	1½ hours	1¾ hours
ICING NEEDED					
Marzipan*	110 g/4 oz	150 g/5 oz	175 g/6 oz	225 g/8 oz	350 g/12 oz
Royal Icing** or Australian Icing	350 g/12 oz	450 g/1 lb	550 g/1 lb 4 oz	675 g/1 lb 8 oz	800 g/1 lb 12 oz

*This refers to the ground almonds only (you need other ingredients as page 148), and gives a moderately thick layer which could be slightly reduced.

would have 25% increases, see the table.

Do allow at least 6 weeks for the cake to mature, soaking it with alcohol as suggested on page 93.

If you want a wedding cake with several tiers, you must allow at least 5 cm/2 inches differential in the diameter of the tiers. You could mix the total amount required for the two or three tiers at one time, if you have a bowl sufficiently large and bake the cakes separately. The uncooked mixture will not spoil by being kept waiting for 24 hours but cover the mixing bowl with foil, so the cake mixture does not dry out.

Amount of Cake to Allow

The servings of wedding cake are small; if you take the total weight of the cake (excluding the icing) you can easily gauge the number of portions it will give; allow about 50 g/2 oz per person.

As an example the cake on page 93 has a total weight of about 2.4 kg/5½ lb so would give over 40 × 50 g/2 oz portions.

CAKE TIN SIZES	cm/inch R 23/9 S 20/8	cm/inch R 25/10 S 23/9	cm/inch R 28/11 S 25/10	cm/inch R 30.5/12 S 28/11	cm/inch R 33/13 S 30.5/12
plain flour	350 g/12 oz	450 g/1 lb	560 g/1 lb 4 oz	775 g/1 lb 9 oz	850 g/1 lb 14 oz
ground cinnamon	1 t	1¼ t	1½ t	2 t	2¼ t
mixed spice	1 t	1¼ t	1½ t	2 t	2¼ t
candied peel	100 g/4 oz	175 g/6 oz	225 g/8 oz	300 g/10 oz	375 g/13 oz
blanched almonds	75 g/3 oz	100 g/4 oz	150 g/5 oz	200 g/7 oz	275 g/10 oz
glacé cherries	100 g/4 oz	150 g/5 oz	200 g/7 oz	300 g/10 oz	350 g/12 oz
currants	450 g/1 lb	560 g/1 lb 4 oz	775 g/1 lb 9 oz	850 g/1 lb 14 oz	1.12 kg/2 lb 8 oz
raisins	225 g/8 oz	300 g/10 oz	375 g/13 oz	475 g/1 lb 1 oz	600 g/1 lb 5 oz
sultanas	225 g/8 oz	300 g/10 oz	375 g/13 oz	475 g/1 lb 1 oz	600 g/1 lb 5 oz
eggs	6 medium	8 medium	10 medium	12 medium	15 medium
sherry	2 T	2½ T	3¼ T	4 T	5 T
butter	300 g/10 oz	400 g/14 oz	500 g/1 lb 2 oz	650 g/1 lb 7 oz	800 g/1 lb 12 oz
brown sugar	300 g/10 oz	400 g/14 oz	500 g/1 lb 2 oz	650 g/1 lb 7 oz	800 g/1 lb 12 oz
treacle or syrup	1 T	1¼ T	1½ T	2 T	2½ T
lemon rind	1 t	1¼ t	1½ t	2 t	2½ t
orange rind	1 t	1¼ t	1½ t	2 t	2½ t
APPROXIMATE A	1½ hours	1½ hours	1½ hours	1¾ hours	1¾ hours
BAKING TIME B	2 hours	2¾ hours	3½ hours	4¼ hours	4¾ hours

ICING NEEDED

Marzipan★	400 g/14 oz	450 g/1 lb	550 g/1 lb 4 oz	675 g/1 lb 8 oz	800 g/1 lb 12 oz
Royal Icing★★ or Australian Icing	900 g/2 lb	1 kg/2 lb 4 oz	1.2 kg/2 lb 8 oz	1.35 kg/3 lb	1.6 kg/3 lb 8 oz

★★Icing enough for one coat and a little piping or coating and a little moulding. Amount refers to sugar in icings, pages 149 and 151.

CHEESECAKES

A Cheesecake is one of the most popular dishes for a special dessert. The Vanilla Cheesecake below is a good basic recipe, it can be topped with seasonal fruit or adapted by adding 50 g/2 oz dried fruit such as sultanas – if doing this, add 25 g/1 oz cornflour to the other ingredients.

Cooked Cheesecakes are made by the creaming method. On page 99 are two uncooked cheesecakes, set by gelatine.

VANILLA CHEESECAKE

Illustrated in colour on page 65

Serves 6–8

for the biscuit crumb crust
175 g/6 oz digestive wheatmeal biscuits
50 g/2 oz butter
50 g/2 oz caster sugar

for the filling
75 g/3 oz butter
75 g/3 oz caster sugar
½ teaspoon vanilla essence
3 eggs
450 g/1 lb cream or curd cheese
3 tablespoons double cream

Choose a 20–23 cm/8–9 inch springform tin or a cake tin with a loose base. Brush the inside with a very little melted butter. Crush the biscuits. Melt the 50 g/2 oz butter, add to the biscuit crumbs with the sugar. Press the biscuit crumb mixture on to the base and sides of the tin.

Cream together the 75 g/3 oz butter, sugar and vanilla essence. Separate the whites from the yolks of the eggs; beat the yolks into the creamed mixture, then add the cheese and cream, blend thoroughly. Whisk the egg whites until stiff, fold into the cheese mixture. Spoon over the biscuit crumb base. Bake in the centre of a slow oven, 150°C, 300°F, Gas Mark 2 for 1–1¼

hours until just firm. Cool in the oven with the door left open; when quite cold, remove from the tin. Top with whipped cream and fruit of your choice.

COFFEE RAISIN CHEESECAKE

Serves 6–8

**biscuit crumb crust as Vanilla
    Cheesecake**

for the filling
100 g/4 oz seedless raisins
3 tablespoons Tia Maria or similar
2 teaspoons instant coffee powder
2 tablespoons boiling water
75 g/3 oz light brown sugar
450 g/1 lb cottage cheese
3 tablespoons double cream
3 eggs

to decorate
raisins (see method)
150 ml/¼ pint double cream
25 g/1 oz walnut halves

Butter the tin and prepare the biscuit crumb crust as in the Vanilla Cheesecake.

Put the raisins into a basin, add the coffee liqueur. Blend the coffee powder with the boiling water, add to the raisins together with sugar. Leave 30 minutes.

Sieve the cheese and blend with the unwhipped cream. Separate the eggs and stir the yolks into the cream and cheese mixture, together with two-thirds of the raisins and liquid in which they were soaked. Finally whisk the egg whites until stiff, fold into the cheese mixture. Spoon over the biscuit crumb base. Bake in the centre of a slow oven, 150°C, 300°F, Gas Mark 2 for 1–1¼ hours until firm to touch.

Allow to cool in the tin, then remove on to a serving dish. Spoon the remaining raisins and any liquid left from soaking these on top of the cheesecake. Whip the cream, pipe or spoon around the edge of the cheesecake and top with the nuts.

CITRUS CHEESECAKE

Serves 6–8

for the biscuit crumb crust
50 g/2 oz butter
50 g/2 oz caster sugar
grated rind of 1 orange
grated rind of 1 lemon
150 g/5 oz digestive wheatmeal biscuits

for the topping
1 medium can mandarin oranges
15 g/½ oz gelatine
3 tablespoons orange juice
1 tablespoon lemon juice
grated rind 1 orange
grated rind 1 lemon
2 eggs
75 g/3 oz caster sugar
450 g/1 lb cream or curd cheese
150 ml/¼ pint double cream

to decorate
1 teaspoon arrowroot
syrup from mandarin oranges
3 tablespoons apricot jam
150 ml/¼ pint double cream

Butter a 20–23 cm/8–9 inch springform tin or cake tin with a loose base.

Cream together the butter, sugar and fruit rinds until very soft. Crush the biscuits; add to the butter mixture. Press into the base only of the tin. Bake in the centre of a moderate oven, 180°C, 350°F, Gas Mark 4 for 10 minutes, allow to cool. This stage could be omitted, but gives a crisper base.

Drain the syrup from the mandarin oranges; save 6 tablespoons and half the oranges for decoration. Chop the remaining oranges. Soften the gelatine in the orange juice, dissolve over a pan of hot, but not boiling, water. Add the lemon juice and fruit rinds. Separate the eggs, beat the yolks and sugar until light. Add the orange gelatine mixture, allow to cool; blend with the cheese and chopped oranges. Whip the cream and the egg whites in separate bowls until stiff, fold the cream and then the egg whites into the cheese mixture. Spoon on to the biscuit base, leave to set.

Remove the cheesecake from the tin on to a serving plate; top with the oranges. Blend the arrowroot and orange syrup. Sieve the jam, stir the jam and arrowroot mixture over a low heat until thickened. Cool and then brush over the top of the cheesecake. Whip the remaining cream, pipe round the cake.

LEMON CHEESECAKE

Serves 6

for the biscuit crumb crust
150 g/5 oz digestive wheatmeal biscuits
50 g/2 oz butter
25 g/1 oz Demerara sugar

for the filling
2 tablespoons water
15 g/½ oz gelatine
3 eggs
100 g/4 oz caster sugar
6 tablespoons lemon juice
450 g/1 lb curd cheese
150 ml/¼ pint soured cream

Crush the biscuits; melt the butter, blend with the biscuit crumbs and sugar. Press into a 20 cm/8 inch cake tin (with a loose base) and chill well.

Put the water into a basin, sprinkle the gelatine on top. Stand over a saucepan of hot, but not boiling, water and allow the gelatine to dissolve. Separate the eggs, put the yolks and sugar into a mixing bowl with the lemon juice and whisk over hot water until thickened. Add the melted gelatine, cool and blend in the cheese and soured cream.

Whisk the egg whites until stiff, fold into the cheese mixture; spoon over the biscuit crumb crust and allow to set.

HOT LEMON AND ORANGE CHEESECAKE

Serves 6–8

**biscuit crumb crust as Vanilla
    Cheesecake on page 98**

for the filling
350 g/12 oz cream cheese
3 eggs
2 tablespoons flour
75 g/3 oz caster sugar
2 tablespoons single cream
2 teaspoons grated lemon rind
2 teaspoons grated orange rind
2 teaspoons lemon juice
2 teaspoons orange juice
1 small can mandarin oranges

for the topping
6 tablespoons mandarin orange syrup
1 teaspoon arrowroot
25 g/1 oz sugar

Butter the tin and prepare the biscuit crumb crust as in the Vanilla Cheesecake.

Put the cheese into a mixing bowl. Separate the eggs, add the yolks to the cheese together with the flour, sugar, cream, fruit rinds and juice. Open the can of mandarin oranges; drain carefully put the syrup on one side. Chop half the mandarin orange segments, add to the cheese mixture. Finally whisk the egg whites until stiff, fold into the other ingredients for the cheesecake and spoon over the biscuit crumb base.

Bake in the centre of a slow oven, 150°C, 300°F, Gas Mark 2 for 1 hour or until firm to the touch. Carefully remove from the tin on to a serving dish.

Blend 6 tablespoons of the syrup from the can with the arrowroot, put into a saucepan with the sugar and stir until thickened and clear. Arrange remaining orange segments on top of hot cheesecake. Top with glaze; serve with cream.

COFFEE GÂTEAU

Serves 6–8

**one 20 cm/8 inch Butter Sponge as page
    73, made with 3 eggs etc.**

for the filling and coating
300 ml/½ pint very strong cold coffee
3 tablespoons Tia Maria
150 g/5 oz butter
225 g/8 oz icing sugar
1 egg
50 g/2 oz flaked blanched almonds
150 ml/¼ pint double cream

Cut the cake horizontally into four layers. Line the base of a 20 cm/8 inch cake tin without a loose base or a soufflé dish with greaseproof paper.

Place a round of sponge in the tin or dish. Blend the coffee with 1 tablespoon Tia Maria. Cream the butter, sift the icing sugar into the butter, beat until light. Separate the egg, add the yolk to the creamed mixture; gradually beat in another tablespoon Tia Maria and 2 tablespoons of the liquid coffee. Put half the mixture on one side for coating the cake, cover with damp paper to save it getting hard; use the remainder for the filling.

Moisten the round of sponge in the tin or dish with a quarter of the coffee; spread with a third of the filling. Repeat this process with the second and third rounds of sponge. Add the last round of sponge and just moisten this with rest of coffee.

Put a round of greaseproof paper, a plate and light weight on the sponge. Leave for 24 hours. Pour away any coffee that may have risen over the plate. Turn the gâteau on to a serving plate, spread the sides with the remaining butter mixture, coat with the almonds.

Whisk the egg white until stiff in one basin and the cream in a second basin, blend together with the remaining Tia Maria. Spread over top of the cake. Chill.

UPSIDE DOWN PUDDINGS

The light Victoria Sandwich mixture on pages 66 and 67 is an excellent basis for an Upside Down Pudding providing the base is not too moist.

If you have a recipe with a very syrupy base you are well advised to use a slightly less delicate sponge. Both kinds of creamed mixtures are given in the recipes that follow.

APRICOT UPSIDE DOWN PUDDING

Serves 4

for the base
25 g/1 oz butter
50 g/2 oz sugar
8–12 fresh apricots
8–12 fresh or canned cherries
8–12 blanched almonds

for the pudding
110 g/4 oz butter or margarine
110 g/4 oz caster sugar
2 eggs
110 g/4 oz self-raising flour or plain flour
 with 1 teaspoon baking powder

Grease the sides of an 18–20 cm/7–8 inch soufflé dish or cake tin without a loose base and spread the butter on the base. Add the sugar then arrange the fruits and nuts in a neat pattern.

Cream together the butter or margarine and sugar. Gradually beat in the eggs. Sift the flour, or flour and baking powder, fold into the creamed mixture. Spread over the top of the fruits. Bake in the centre of a moderate oven, 180°C, 350°F, Gas Mark 4 for 40–45 minutes or until firm to the touch. Turn upside down on to a heated serving dish. Serve hot or cold with cream or ice cream.

PEAR UPSIDE DOWN PUDDING

Serves 4

for the base
25 g/1 oz butter
25 g/1 oz Demerara sugar
2 tablespoons golden syrup
1 tablespoon lemon juice
4 firm ripe dessert pears

for the pudding
75 g/3 oz butter or margarine
75 g/3 oz caster sugar
1 teaspoon grated lemon rind
2 eggs
150 g/5 oz self-raising flour or plain flour
 with 1½ teaspoons baking powder

Grease the sides of a 20–23 cm/8–9 inch soufflé dish or cake tin without a loose base, do not grease the bottom. Melt the butter, sugar and golden syrup for the base of the pudding; add the lemon juice. Peel, halve and core the pears; turn in the melted mixture, so they will keep a pleasant colour in cooking. Arrange the halved pears in a neat design on the base of the dish or tin; add the syrup mixture.

Cream together the butter or margarine, caster sugar and lemon rind. Gradually beat in the eggs. Sift the flour, or flour and baking powder, fold into the creamed mixture. Do not add any extra liquid. Spoon the mixture carefully over the pears and syrup. Bake in the centre of a moderate oven, 180°C, 350°F, Gas Mark 4 for 50–55 minutes or until firm to the touch. Turn upside down on to a heated serving dish. Serve hot with cream or custard.

Harvest Upside Down Pudding: Make the base and pudding as the Pear Upside Down Pudding but omit 1 egg and add 225 g/8 oz diced cooking apples instead. Cook as the Pear Upside Down Pudding but allow an extra 10 minutes cooking time, reduce the heat slightly after 45 minutes if necessary.

SHORTCAKES

A shortcake is, as the name implies, a combination of cake and biscuit. The recipes range from the scone-like mixture on page 61 to richer recipes. Fill and top a shortcake just before serving.

LIGHT SHORTCAKE

Make the Victoria Sandwich on pages 66 and 67 but use only 2 instead of 3 eggs. This produces a firm crisp texture. Bake as page 66, turn out very carefully.

APPLE SHORTCAKE

Serves 4–6

110 g/4 oz butter or margarine
110 g/4 oz caster sugar
110 g/4 oz plain flour
50 g/2 oz semolina

for the filling
3 tablespoons redcurrant or apple jelly
300 ml/½ pint thick sweetened apple
    purée
150 ml/¼ pint double cream

Grease and flour two 18 cm/7 inch sandwich tins. Cream together the butter or margarine and sugar until soft and light. Add the flour and semolina. Knead the mixture well, put half into each prepared tin, press flat with your finger-tips. Bake in the centre of a moderate oven, 180°C, 350°F, Gas Mark 4 for 25 minutes or until firm.

Allow to stand for 5 minutes in the tins for the mixture is very brittle when freshly baked. Remove from the tins, allow to cool. Place one shortcake on a serving plate, spread with the jelly and apple purée. Whip the cream. Spoon 3 tablespoons over the apple. Place the second

shortcake on top, decorate with cream.
Note: Fresh whole raspberries or sliced strawberries could be used in place of apple purée.

STRAWBERRY SHORTCAKE
Illustrated in colour on the jacket

Serves 6

100 g/4 oz butter or margarine
100 g/4 oz caster sugar
few drops vanilla essence
2 large eggs
175 g/6 oz self-raising flour or plain flour
    with 1½ teaspoons baking powder

for the filling and topping
450 g/1 lb ripe strawberries
1 tablespoon caster sugar
300 ml/½ pint double cream

Grease and flour, or line, two 18 cm/7 inch sandwich tins. Cream together the butter or margarine, sugar and vanilla essence until soft and light. Gradually beat in the eggs. Sift the flour, or flour and baking powder, and fold into the creamed ingredients; it will produce a sticky consistency, but do not add any liquid. Divide the mixture between the prepared tins and smooth flat with a palette knife. Bake the shortcakes just above the centre of a moderate oven, 180°C, 350°F, Gas Mark 4 for nearly 25 minutes or until pale golden and very firm to the touch; the cakes should feel firmer than a Victoria Sandwich.

Allow to cool for 3–4 minutes in the tins, for these shortcakes are brittle when hot, then turn out as described under Victoria Sandwich on page 67. Cool.

Hull the strawberries. Halve or slice approximately half, spread over one shortcake, sprinkle with sugar. Whip the cream, spread some over the fruit. Put on the second shortcake. Top with the remaining cream and strawberries.

ORANGE ALMOND GÂTEAU

Makes a 19–20 cm/7½–8 inch cake

175 g/6 oz butter or margarine
175 g/6 oz caster sugar
2 teaspoons finely grated orange rind
3 large eggs
175 g/6 oz self-raising flour or plain
    flour with 1½ teaspoons baking
    powder

for the filling and decoration
100 g/4 oz icing sugar
100 g/4 oz ground almonds
½ teaspoon grated orange rind
2½ tablespoons orange juice
few drops orange food colouring
small piece angelica

for the icing
75 g/3 oz plain chocolate
1 tablespoon orange juice
few drops olive oil
150 g/5 oz icing sugar
2 tablespoons apricot jam

Grease and flour, or line, two 19–20 cm/ 7½–8 inch sandwich tins. Cream together the butter or margarine, sugar and orange rind until soft and light in the same manner as the Master Recipe pages 66 and 67. Gradually beat in the eggs. Sift the flour, or flour and baking powder, and fold into the creamed mixture. Divide the mixture between the prepared tins and bake just above the centre of a moderate oven, 180–190°C, 350–375°F, Gas Mark 4–5 for approximately 20 minutes or until firm to the touch. Cool for 1–2 minutes in the tins then turn out and allow to cool.

Sift the icing sugar, blend with the ground almonds and grated orange rind and half the orange juice. Colour the marzipan with a few drops of orange colouring, take out a quarter of the mixture and form into 6–8 tiny oranges for decoration. Cut the angelica into leaf shapes.

Blend the rest of the orange juice with the remaining three-quarters of the marzipan mixture, to give a soft spreading consistency. Slice each sponge horizontally to give four layers. Sandwich together with the soft marzipan.

Break the chocolate in pieces, put into a basin with the orange juice and oil. Place over a pan of hot water, leave until the chocolate has melted. Allow to cool then sift the icing sugar into the mixture and blend thoroughly. Sieve the apricot jam, spread over the top of the sponge. Top with the chocolate icing, decorate with the marzipan oranges and angelica.

TIPSY CAKE

A Tipsy Cake is an excellent, if rather extra-vagant, alternative to a sherry trifle. A Victoria Sandwich (Butter Sponge) is an ideal choice for it is sufficiently firm to keep its shape even when soaked with sherry.

Bake the required size in one deep tin. You will find quantities of ingredients and baking times on page 73. Allow a sponge made with 3 large eggs for 6–8 portions.

In addition to the sponge you need:
several different flavoured jams
a good amount of sherry
flaked or chopped blanched almonds
double or whipping cream
glacé or Maraschino cherries and
    leaves of angelica to decorate

Split the cake to give four layers. Put the first layer on the serving dish, spread with jam, then soak carefully in sherry, top with a sprinkling of the almonds. Continue like this, using a different flavoured jam for each layer. When you put on the top layer, only soak in sherry.

Whip the cream, spread over the cake and decorate with the cherries, leaves of angelica and more almonds.

Prepare the Tipsy Cake several hours before serving, but do not freeze.

Modern baking methods

In a Microwave Cooker

Opinions vary as to the success of baking a Victoria Sandwich, or similar sponge-type cake, in a microwave cooker. While I think a sponge pudding cooked in a microwave is extremely good, I do find the cake is a little too much like a pudding to compare with a baked sponge. There may however be occasions when the oven is in use or you are in a hurry and prefer to use the microwave cooker. Models vary and in some cookers you are advised to add a little extra water to the basic mixture, (i.e. up to 2 tablespoons) to the mixture made with 3 large eggs, etc. given on pages 66 and 67. Check this point carefully with the manufacturers' instructions.

I would choose to make a coffee or chocolate flavoured sponge cake, rather than a plain one; although this has a better colour if you use natural granulated sugar instead of caster sugar but, as you will appreciate, the texture will not be as fine. Obviously you can decorate the cold sponge to give colour. Serve the cake when fresh, for it does tend to become stale more quickly than when baked.

The rich fruit cakes in this book are not designed for microwave cooking; you are advised to use those microwave recipes specially created.

Microwave cookers vary, some models you are advised to 'bake' on HIGH in others on the SIMMER, or equivalent setting; check this point carefully with your instruction book.

As an example of cooking time the Master Recipe on pages 66 and 67, if baked in one container, takes 6½–7 minutes on HIGH or 12–15 minutes on SIMMER. Allow about 9 minutes on HIGH or 15–16 minutes on SIMMER for the Upside Down Puddings on page 101.

Never use metal tins in the microwave cooker, shallow or deep ceramic soufflé dishes or round casseroles are excellent. You can buy ceramic loaf shapes too. The mixture rises more drastically in a microwave cooker than when baked in an oven. It is wise therefore to use a container about 2.5 cm/1 inch wider in diameter than that given in the recipe, to make sure the mixture does not rise above the level of the dish.

If you stand the container on an upturned saucer you have better results in cooking cakes and cake-type puddings. Never over-cook cakes in a microwave cooker. The mixture may appear very soft on top, but it continues to cook as it cools. Test by inserting a very fine skewer. If this comes out clean and free from any mixture the cake is cooked, it will become firm as it cools.

In a Crock-Pot

The various sponge mixtures can be cooked in the crock-pot, although they are not unlike a pudding in appearance, but if eaten when fresh and decorated they are very edible.

I would not use ordinary cake tins, for many have a loose base, which is not satisfactory, also it does not do the tin any good to be in contact with water and you must use liquid in the crock-pot container.

First preheat the crock-pot on HIGH for 15 minutes. Add 600 ml/1 pint boiling water. Make the cake, put it into the soufflé dish, or other container. Do not cover, for the top will become firm, so it is more like a proper cake. Place into the crock-pot, put on the lid.

You allow about 3 times the cooking time given in the recipe on the HIGH position, or about 2½ hours, whichever is the greater. Test the cake in the usual way.

In a Pressure Cooker

While sponge puddings are excellent in a pressure cooker I would not try and cook these particular cakes, but you can cook the Upside Down Puddings on page 101.

Put the mixture into a suitable sized container; you may have to use a basin, rather than a wider container, to fit into the pressure cooker. Cover the top of the container. Place the rack (trivet) in the cooker, then stand the pudding on this. Add 900 ml/1½ pints boiling water. Fix the lid, but allow the cooker to steam without pressure for 15 minutes, this is important, for if you cook under pressure from the beginning the baking powder in the mixture will fail to activate and you will have a heavy sponge. Close the pressure valve, bring up to LOW/5 lb pressure and cook for 25 minutes. Allow the pressure to drop at room temperature.

In a Table Cooker (Electric Frying Pan)
I use this term to describe the small cookers that have evolved from a table frying pan. Modern table cookers are thermostatically controlled; it is possible to do a limited amount of baking in these. Set to maximum heat, preheat the cooker as directed by the manufacturer. Use the rack, if directed to do so and place it into the cooker. Put the creamed mixture into a suitable sized tin or container. Place the lid on top of the cooker – when baking make certain the vent is fully open and the lid fits snugly. The baking time is very similar to that given in recipes for oven baking, but check for the first few times you use the cooker for this purpose, but do not lift the lid to inspect the cake(s) until over half the baking time has elapsed.

You can bake on the base of the cooker, this is useful for scones and for small firm cakes or for a mixture sufficiently large to cover the base.

Grease the base well, add the mixture, as though putting it into a cake tin. In this case you will find that with most cookers you are advised to preheat at a more moderate temperature and obviously you do not use the rack. Test the cakes in the usual manner. The cakes tend to have less colour than when cooked in an oven so they are better if iced or decorated.

Storing

Uncooked creamed mixtures store well for 24 hours if you place them in the refrigerator. Cover the container so the mixture will not dry out in any way.

Cooked cakes made by the creaming method vary in the time they can be kept. The Master Recipe Victoria Sandwich on pages 66 and 67 will keep well for several days if put into an airtight tin when it is cold. The large fruit cakes such as the Rich Dundee will keep beautifully for some weeks, again if stored in an airtight tin. The information about the Christmas Cake and Wedding Cake indicates that these not only store well but improve with being stored, for they mature in flavour particularly if soaked periodically with alcohol. Always put them into an airtight container or wrap them fairly tightly in foil.

Freezing

An uncooked creamed mixture can be stored in the freezer for several weeks. This could be useful if you have no time to bake the mixture but really it is probably more helpful to bake the sponges or plain cakes, allow them to cool and then freeze them. The Victoria Sandwich Master Recipe freezes beautifully for up to 3 months and so do any cakes based on this. If the cake is iced you may well find that fairly dry crisp icings crack in freezing, that is why you will find a section of icings marked for freezing on page 154. You do not need to freeze either rich Christmas or Wedding Cakes unless your storage conditions are very poor, i.e. hot and damp. The cakes do not mature in flavour in the same way if put into a freezer rather than in an airtight container.

PROBLEM SOLVING

Creaming is the method by which so many different cakes are made. There are a good diversity of recipes in the preceeding pages and, although the method of mixing is similar, the results give a pleasing variety. Below are some of the problems that may well occur with the cakes made by this particular method.

Q. *Why is so much stress laid upon the fact that creamed fat and sugar must not curdle when the eggs are added?*
A. A curdled mixture produces a heavier cake, for it is impossible to incorporate as much air. Curdling (separating) occurs because the eggs are added too rapidly to the creamed fat and sugar and/or because the eggs were too cold. Allow the eggs to stand at room temperature for a while; beat in a basin until fluffy if they still feel cold.
Quick Remedy: If the mixture shows signs of curdling beat in 1 tablespoon of sifted flour; repeat with more flour if necessary. Stand the mixing bowl over warm, but not hot, water for a few minutes then beat hard to blend the fat, sugar and egg(s).

Q. *Why do you need plain flour and no baking powder in rich fruit cakes?*
A. If raising agent is used the mixture will rise, but it cannot carry the heavy weight of dried fruit, so this may sink.

Q. *Why does dried fruit sink in a cake?*
A. For many reasons, the most usual being that the cake mixture itself is too soft to hold the fruit in position or too much raising agent was used, see above.

Dried fruit must be allowed to dry for at least 48 hours after washing. A sudden draught in the early stages of baking could cause fruit to sink. Glacé cherries or other glacé fruit are heavy and should be floured, see page 88.

Quick Remedy: Split the cake horizontally, have the shallow fruity base as one cake and the plain top layer as a second cake.

Q. *What makes a cake sink in the centre?*
A. You must differentiate between a cake that sinks *after* it comes out of the oven and one that sinks *during* cooking.

If the cake sinks after it has come from the oven it was inadequately cooked; it is very important to test a cake carefully; see the next answer.

If the cake dropped in baking it is because the ingredients in the recipe were badly balanced, for example, too high a percentage of liquid or heavy syrup could cause a cake to sink in the middle.

If the oven temperature was incorrect the cake could sink, fail to rise properly. Too cool an oven, but more often too hot an oven which sets the outside of the cake too quickly so the heat does not penetrate through to the centre prevents the cake rising.

The reasons given for fruit sinking in a cake, see the previous answer, can also cause the cake itself to sink.
Quick Remedy: Cut the centre of the cake out and serve the remainder as a ring-shaped cake. If the centre is not heavy it could be eaten as a separate cake. If it is heavy, crumble and use the crumbs in Sherry Flan, page 208.

Q. *What are the ways of testing to see if a cake is cooked?*
A. Use these tests in the order given:
a) Press gently but firmly on top of the cake; if your finger leaves a lasting impression the cake is not cooked, a cooked cake feels firm to the touch.
b) If test a) seems to indicate the cake is cooked, remove from the oven, the cake should have shrunk from the sides of the tin, this test is less easy to see when the tin is lined.
c) If you are still uncertain whether the

cake is cooked, insert a fine metal skewer or steel knitting needle into the centre of the cake, remove carefully. If there is any uncooked mixture adhering to the skewer or needle or it seems very sticky the cake needs longer cooking. It is a good idea to warm the skewer or needle as the cold metal could make a heavy line in the cake. The reason I think this test is not completely reliable is because when you insert the skewer or needle into a rich fruit cake you might well make it sticky by inserting it into glacé cherries or the hot dried fruit; it is therefore advisable to test again by inserting the skewer or needle in an entirely different place.
d) A rich fruit cake makes a distinct humming sound if it is not cooked. The cake must be baked until silent.

Q. *Why is a Victoria Sandwich inclined to be firm like a cake rather than a sponge?*
A. Purists insist that a Victoria Sandwich *is* a cake, but frequently it is called a 'Butter Sponge'. If carefully made it should be sufficiently light to justify the term 'sponge'. It is not the easiest mixture to make well, that is why I give two methods of mixing, see pages 66 to 67.

The reasons for a less light texture are insufficient creaming of the fat and sugar; insufficient beating when the eggs are added (you may care to whisk these in a separate bowl, before beating into the creamed mixture); adding the flour too vigorously.

Q. *How can I make sure that Cup Cakes are really flat on top?*
A. By using a sufficiently moist mixture, that will not rise to a peak in the middle. If you want the mixture to rise well in the centre then use a slightly larger amount of flour, see under Butterfly Cakes, page 84. I always use a hot oven for small cakes so they do not become dry due to prolonged baking.

Q. *Why do plain cakes, such as Madeira, sometimes have an uneven texture with some rather large holes?*
A. The flour was beaten too vigorously into the mixture, add gently.

Q. *What makes a cake crack on top?*
A. Too dry a mixture; too much raising agent; too hot an oven; too small a tin, this can make the mixture over-flow, but also it can cause the cake to peak in the centre and then crack.

Q. *How does one achieve a very moist Wedding Cake?*
A. By using a rich fruit cake mixture, see page 93; by soaking the cake with alcohol, see the recipe on page 93.

Q. *Why is it advised that some cakes should be allowed to cool in the tin in which they were baked?*
A. There are two reasons, the first is that cakes that are heavy with fruit (i.e. have at least twice as much fruit as flour) or have a high percentage of treacle or syrup are inclined to break if turned out when hot.

The second reason for allowing a rich fruit cake to cool in the tin is that the condensation formed, as the cake cools, makes the outside softer.

All cakes should stand for 1–2 minutes before being turned out (except cakes like Swiss Roll) for they contract slightly and therefore are easier to remove from the tin; if they seem to be sticking a gentle tap on the tin generally loosens them.

CHAPTER 4

The Melting Method

This method of combining the ingredients produces a very moist type of cake, such as the Gingerbread, which is the Master Recipe on the next page. It is also used for some biscuits, of which Brandy Snaps or Flapjacks are the best known, see page 176. Although popular this method of mixing is used less than the rubbing-in and creaming processes, detailed in the previous chapters.

Cakes made by the melting method keep well, for they have a high proportion of syrup or treacle or honey. Often they are flavoured with ginger or other spices.

WHAT DOES MELTING MEAN?

It means that the fat and sugar are put into a saucepan and heated until melted. Often golden syrup or black treacle or honey or even marmalade are melted too. This gives a very liquid consistency. After melting, the flour, and other ingredients, are beaten into the mixture; you can do this in the saucepan or a large mixing bowl. Recipes made by this method are easily mixed, for the ingredients can be beaten briskly, either by hand or with an electric mixer or food processor, see page 112.
In most recipes you will find a high proportion of raising agent is used; this is to counteract the syrup, treacle, honey or preserve. The melting method is used for:

Small and large cakes
Biscuits and biscuit-type cakes
A few puddings
A sponge-type pastry (Genoese pastry)

Cakes made by the melting method – Chocolate Bran Brownies (top, recipe page 119), Rich Gingerbread (recipe page 115), Gilacgi (recipe page 122), Gingerbread Men (recipe page 115)

GINGERBREAD

The gingerbread, given as the Master Recipe, is an economical cake; but it keeps moist for some days, if stored in an airtight tin. There are a number of other cakes based upon the proportions given, together with richer gingerbreads, see pages 113 to 115.

Baking Utensils: A 20 × 15 cm/8 × 6 inch oblong tin or an 18 cm/7 inch square tin without a loose base. Line with greased greaseproof paper.

Oven Setting: Preheat the oven at very moderate, 160°C, 325°F, Gas Mark 3. Cook in the centre of the oven.

Cooking Time: Approximately 45–50 minutes in the oblong tin, 50–55 minutes in the square tin.

Makes a 20 × 15 cm/8 × 6 inch oblong or 18 cm/7 inch square cake

225 g/8 oz plain flour
1–2 teaspoons ground ginger
1 teaspoon bicarbonate of soda
85 g/3 oz black treacle or golden syrup
85 g/3 oz butter or cooking fat or dripping or margarine
85 g/3 oz moist brown or granulated sugar
1 egg
5 tablespoons milk

CERTAIN SUCCESS

Choice of Ingredients: Use plain flour with bicarbonate of soda, to counter-balance the heavy treacle or golden syrup.
I list the fats in the order of preference; you can use well-clarified dripping in this cake, see page 118 for details on clarifying dripping for baking.
Brown sugar adds to the flavour and good colour of a gingerbread.
Black treacle gives a much darker colour to the cake than golden syrup.
The amount of liquid given should be measured carefully; obviously the mixture will look very soft, due to the fact the fat and sugar have melted, to form a liquid, but never try and cut down on the liquid content, otherwise the cake will be over-dry.

Handling the Mixture: This type of cake is easy to mix and a pleasure for those cooks who are brisk and energetic and who find gentle folding troublesome; you can beat as hard as you like without harming the texture of the gingerbread. Do sift the bicarbonate of soda with the flour to make sure it is mixed thoroughly, and heat the milk in the pan used to melt the ingredients.

Consistency: The consistency of the Master Recipe and other cakes in this section is a pouring one; if you tip the bowl you can pour most of the mixture into the prepared tin. Obviously you will need to scrape out the mixing bowl with a knife or spoon to make sure no mixture is wasted. The consistency is shown in step 7 opposite.

Preparing Tins: Line the tin with well-greased greaseproof paper, for this gingerbread, and all recipes in this chapter with a high proportion of treacle or syrup. This keeps the cake from sticking to the tin or breaking. To remove paper, see step 9 opposite.

Baking: Preheat the oven at the temperature given in the recipe. If you have not made a gingerbread before there will be a tendency to look at the cake during baking, but cakes in this section will sink very easily if exposed to a draught or moved in any way, so it is advisable to wait until almost the end of the cooking time. Test the oblong cake after 40 minutes and the square one after 45–50 minutes cooking time.

1 Sift the flour, ginger and bicarbonate of soda into a mixing bowl. It is important to measure the bicarbonate of soda correctly and the illustration shows how you should level-off any spoon measure with a knife so you do not exceed the amount in the recipe.

2 To weigh the treacle or golden syrup, either flour the scale pan, or weigh the empty saucepan and then put an extra 85 g/3 oz weight on the scales, then add the treacle or syrup. Put the selected fat and sugar into the saucepan with the black treacle or golden syrup.

3 Stir over a low heat to melt the ingredients; remove from the heat as soon as the fat and sugar have melted then pour into the flour mixture and beat very well with a wooden spoon. Do not wash the saucepan as the milk is heated in this, see step 5.

4 Break the egg into a cup to ascertain that it is fresh, then drop it into the other ingredients. Beat the gingerbread very well at this stage, making quite certain that there is no unblended flour in the mixture.

5 Pour the milk into the saucepan, heat slowly, stirring well so the milk absorbs the residue of the black treacle or golden syrup mixture that was left-over in the saucepan after heating at step 3.

6 Allow the milk to cool slightly then pour the warm milk gradually on to the gingerbread mixture and beat very well indeed; you may see small bubbles as you do so, this is caused by the combination of mixing and the bicarbonate of soda.

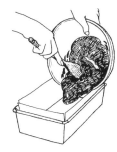

7 Pour and spoon into the lined tin, as you will see from the illustration the greased greaseproof paper is taken just above the top rim of the tin, so the gingerbread is protected as it rises slightly.

8 Bake the cakes as the timing given on page 110. Do not open the door during baking, but test at 40–50 minutes, as given under 'Baking' opposite. To test if cooked, press gently and firmly in the centre of the cake; this cake will not rise in the centre, it should be quite flat on top with no peaking.

9 Allow to cool for at least 10 minutes in the tin, then remove and carefully pull away the paper, do this while the cake is warm as the paper tends to stick when the gingerbread becomes cold.

111

Using modern equipment

MELTING METHOD BY MIXER

The details given in the Master Recipe, page 110, is typical of the way in which to use a mixer for this method of blending ingredients. All cakes can be prepared with a small or large mixer, if you follow the advice given.

Never exceed the manufacturers' recommendations as to the amount of mixture that can be dealt with in one batch, for the melted mixture is inclined to splash and too great an amount could splash over the top of the bowl and be wasted.

A MIXER FOR GINGERBREAD

Use the single or double whisks for this type of mixture; as it is light in texture.

Sift the dry ingredients into the mixer bowl, see step 1 on the previous page. Heat the treacle, syrup, fat and sugar, as steps 2 and 3 on the previous page; add to the dry ingredients, switch the mixer to the lowest speed; leave running only until all ingredients are blended. Add the egg, switch on for a few seconds, then add the warmed milk slowly, with the machine running; see steps 4–6. When adequately mixed follow steps 7–9.

Points to Watch: Do not over-whisk the mixture; add milk gradually; use low speed.

MELTING METHOD BY FOOD PROCESSOR

The detailed method to follow is given in the Master Recipe, on page 111.

All the cakes made by the 'Melting' method can be prepared in a food processor, provided the advice given on pages 110 and 111, and below, is followed.

Many cakes made by the 'Melting' method contain dried fruits; when these are added to the cake mixture you must switch on the processor for 1–2 seconds only, to blend the fruit with the other ingredients. The double-bladed cutting knife is so efficient, that it would chop the fruit finely if the processor is used for a longer period. If the recipe gives glacé cherries, or nuts, among the ingredients you can switch on for a slightly longer period. Watch carefully and switch off the moment the cherries or nuts are diced or chopped.

To remove the mixture from the processor bowl, remove the lid, the rather soft mixture may have splashed onto this, so remove with the plastic spatula and add the mixture to the processor bowl. Often you can pour a gingerbread mixture from an ordinary mixing bowl, be careful if you try to do this from the processor bowl, either remove the cutting knife or hold this by the centre disc, so it does not fall out. Scrape any surplus mixture from the processor bowl with the spatula provided.

Always consult the manufacturers' handbook as to the maximum amount of mixture that can be dealt with at one time and do not exceed this.

A FOOD PROCESSOR FOR GINGERBREAD

Fix the double-bladed cutting knife and the food processor bowl in position. Sift the dry ingredients into the bowl, as step 1, previous page.

Heat the treacle or syrup with the fat and sugar, as step 2, add to the dry ingredients and put on the processor lid. Switch on and process for 25 seconds. Add the egg and warmed milk, see steps 4–6 on the previous page, blend again for about 25 seconds. After this continue as steps 7–9.

GINGERBREADS

A family Gingerbread is Master Recipe in the melting section. It forms the basis for a good number of variations and adaptations as you will see from this and the next page. Originally a gingerbread was, as the name suggests, a well-flavoured bread to be spread with lots of butter. That is why it is usual to bake the cake in a square or oblong tin to make it easy to cut neat slices. I find the oblong tin makes a very satisfactory cooking utensil, for the baking time needed for this shape is relatively short, so you retain the sticky texture, a feature of a good gingerbread; also the mixture is less likely to sink slightly in the centre.

Black treacle is the ideal ingredient to use in a gingerbread and this is an excellent source of iron. If however you dislike the strong taste of black treacle substitute golden syrup.

You will see that under 'Baking Utensils' on page 110 I stress that the tin should not have a loose base. This is to prevent the liquid uncooked cake mixture running through any cracks at the bottom of the tin. If you have only a tin with a loose base then put a thick layer of foil over the bottom of the tin. I appreciate the fact that in many cakes in this section you are advised to line the tin with greased greaseproof paper but, if this is done a little too quickly, you could have a small gap between base and sides through which the uncooked mixture could run.

You may prefer to substitute a round tin for the square tin recommended in many recipes in this section. If so you need to use a tin of about 2.5 cm/1 inch greater diameter to accommodate the same amount of mixture and to require the same cooking time, e.g. an 18 cm/7 inch square cake tin is equivalent to a 20 cm/8 inch round tin. Cook and test in the way given in the recipe.

ECONOMICAL GINGERBREAD

Makes a 20 × 15 cm/8 × 6 inch oblong or an 18 cm/7 inch square cake

Although the Master Recipe on pages 110 and 111 is not an extravagant one, it can be made slightly more economical if you omit 25 g/1 oz treacle or syrup, 25 g/1 oz of the selected fat and 25 g/1 oz sugar. Proceed as the basic recipe but add 150 ml/¼ pint milk. Make as before but test about 5 minutes earlier.

This cake should be eaten within 1 or 2 days of making.

WHEATMEAL GINGERBREAD

Wheatmeal flour can be used in the Master Recipe on pages 110 and 111, the Economical Gingerbread above or the Rich Gingerbread on page 115. Whichever recipe you select you will need to increase the amount of liquid by about 2 tablespoons, to compensate for the fact that wheatmeal flour absorbs more liquid. This means that the baking time will be from 5 to 10 minutes longer.

Bake at the temperature given in the recipe and test carefully.

Gingerbread as Desserts

Any gingerbread is excellent served hot as a pudding. This is an advantage if you are a small family, for you can serve half the cake hot, let the remainder cool, to serve later as a cake.

If you intend having the gingerbread as a pudding it can be served with hot apple purée, see under Cider Dripping Cake on page 118 or with heated golden syrup or heat diced canned pineapple rings with a little syrup from the can and spoon over the portions of hot cake.

FLAVOURING A GINGERBREAD

The Master Recipe on page 110 and the richer recipe on page 115 are both cakes that can be adapted in various ways. In one case the more economical recipe is recommended as the richer cake is less suitable for the ingredients to be added.

Almond Gingerbread: Ingredients as the Master Recipe on page 110 or the Rich Gingerbread on page 115, but omit 25 g/1 oz flour and add 25 g/1 oz ground almonds. Put the mixture into the baking tin and top with 25 g/1 oz blanched flaked almonds. Bake as the recipe on pages 110 and 111, or on page 115.

Coconut Gingerbread: Ingredients as the Master Recipe on page 110 or the Rich Gingerbread on page 115, but omit 25 g/1 oz flour and add 50 g/2 oz desiccated coconut to the mixture. Bake as the recipe on pages 110 and 111, or on page 115. Allow the gingerbread to become cool, then top with sieved apricot jam and sprinkle with desiccated coconut. Put under a grill, set to a low heat, leave for a few minutes to allow the coconut to become a delicate golden brown.

Dried Fruit Gingerbread: Ingredients as the Master Recipe on page 110. Add up to 175 g/6 oz mixed dried fruit to the mixture and bake as pages 110 and 111. You can add the fruit to the Rich Gingerbread on page 115, but it tends to sink to the bottom of the cake. If it does then all you do is to turn the cake upside down to serve.

Lemon Gingerbread: Ingredients as the Master Recipe on page 110 or the Rich Gingerbread on page 115. Add 1–2 teaspoons finely grated lemon rind to the sifted flour in either recipe. In the Master Recipe heat only 3 tablespoons milk in the pan, add to the other ingredients together with 2 tablespoons unheated lemon juice. Do not heat the milk and lemon juice together, as the mixture would curdle.

In the Rich Gingerbread, substitute the 2 tablespoons lemon juice for the 2 tablespoons milk given in the recipe; the lemon juice can be heated in the pan.

Bake as the recipe on pages 110 and 111, or on page 115.

This cake is delicious if topped with a lemon flavoured icing made by blending 175–225 g/6–8 oz sifted icing sugar (use the larger amount for the oblong cake) with lemon juice to make a spreading consistency.

Marshmallow Gingerbread: As this is a rather luxurious topping I would suggest using the Rich Gingerbread. Make and bake this as page 115. Allow to become a little cooler in the tin, then spread with sieved apricot jam. Press white or pink marshmallows on top, covering the cake completely. Heat the grill on low, put the cake underneath, and heat for a minute or two until the marshmallows soften slightly and take on a light golden colour, watch the cake throughout this time. Cool slightly then remove from the tin.

Oatmeal Gingerbread: Ingredients as the Master Recipe on page 110 or the Rich Gingerbread on page 115. In either case, omit 50 g/2 oz flour and add 50 g/2 oz medium oatmeal instead. Bake as the recipe on pages 110 and 111, or on page 115.

Orange Gingerbread: Follow the advice given for Lemon Gingerbread and use orange juice and rind instead. In the Master Recipe, pages 110 and 111, you could use 5 tablespoons orange juice and omit the milk. In the richer recipe you can only use 2 tablespoons liquid, so increase the amount of grated rind if you want a more definite orange flavour.

Spiced Cakes: If you dislike ginger you can still use any gingerbread recipes but simply substitute mixed spice, ground cinnamon or nutmeg for the ginger.

GINGERBREAD MEN

Illustrated in colour on page 109

Makes 6–8

225 g/8 oz plain flour
1 teaspoon baking powder
1–2 teaspoons ground ginger
75 g/3 oz butter or margarine
50 g/2 oz caster sugar
1 tablespoon golden syrup
approx. 1 tablespoon milk
1 egg

to decorate
approx. 36 currants
approx. 4–5 glacé cherries

These Gingerbread Men are a combination of cake and biscuit and of the technique of rubbing-in and melting. Sift the flour, baking powder and ground ginger into a mixing bowl. Rub in the butter or margarine, add the sugar. Put the golden syrup in a basin and stand over hot water until warm and liquid, add to the ingredients in the mixing bowl (the warmed syrup blends better). Pour the milk into the basin, stir to absorb any syrup that may be left, then blend into the other ingredients with the egg.

Knead very well, if necessary add a very little more milk to give a firm rolling consistency. If the dough is a little sticky, cover and chill for a short time. Roll out on a lightly floured board until just over 5 mm/¼ inch in thickness. Either use a biscuit cutter in the shape of a man, or cut out the figure in thick paper, lay this on the dough and cut around it.

Lightly grease a baking tray or trays. Put the figures on this. Press currants into the dough for 'eyes' and 'buttons'; cut the cherries into small pieces for a 'nose' and 'mouth' on each figure.

Bake above the centre of a moderately hot oven, 200°C, 400°F, Gas Mark 6 for 12–15 minutes. The Gingerbread Men should feel firm on the edges, but they should not be as crisp as a biscuit.

RICH GINGERBREAD

Illustrated in colour on page 109

Makes a 20 × 15 cm/8 × 6 inch oblong or an 18–19 cm/7–7½ inch square cake

225 g/8 oz plain flour
1 teaspoon baking powder
½ teaspoon bicarbonate of soda
1½–2 teaspoons ground ginger
110 g/4 oz butter or margarine or
    cooking fat
110 g/4 oz moist light brown sugar
175 g/6 oz black treacle or golden syrup
1 egg
2 tablespoons milk

Line a 20 × 15 cm/8 × 6 inch oblong or 18–19 cm/7–7½ inch square tin with well greased greaseproof paper. Sift the flour, baking powder, bicarbonate of soda and ginger into a mixing bowl.

Put the butter, margarine or cooking fat, sugar and treacle or golden syrup into a saucepan, stir over a low heat until dissolved. Add to the dry ingredients and beat well. Do not wash-up the saucepan. Whisk the egg, warm the milk in the saucepan in which the ingredients were melted, stir well to make sure none of these ingredients are left in the pan, add the egg and milk to the other ingredients. Stir briskly then spoon into tin.

Bake in the centre of a very moderate oven, 160°C, 325°F, Gas Mark 3 for approximately 1 hour or until just firm to the touch, see step 8, page 111.

Allow to cool in the tin for about 15 minutes; loosen or remove the paper before the cake becomes quite cold. When cold store in an airtight tin. This cake keeps moist for up to 3 weeks.

GOLDEN ALMOND CAKE

Makes a 20 × 15 cm/8 × 6 inch oblong cake

175 g/6 oz self-raising flour or plain
    flour with 1½ teaspoons baking
    powder
50 g/2 oz ground almonds
110 g/4 oz butter or margarine
150 g/5 oz light brown or granulated
    sugar
150 g/5 oz golden syrup
few drops almond essence
2 eggs
1 tablespoon milk

for the topping
25–40 g/1–1½ oz blanched flaked
    almonds

Line a 20 × 15 cm/8 × 6 inch tin with well-greased greaseproof paper. Sift the flour, or flour and baking powder, into a mixing bowl.

In this particular recipe it is advisable to use the amount of raising agent given above rather than bicarbonate of soda with plain flour. Add the ground almonds.

Put the butter or margarine, sugar, syrup and essence into a saucepan, stir over a low heat until the ingredients have melted, spoon out carefully (but do not wash-up the pan). Add to the flour mixture; beat well. Stir in the eggs. Heat the milk in the saucepan, pour into the mixing bowl, blend all the ingredients thoroughly. Spoon into the prepared tin.

Scatter the almonds on top, do not use whole blanched almonds, they are too heavy. Bake in the centre of a slow oven, 150°C, 300°F, Gas Mark 2 for approximately 1 hour or until firm to the touch; test after about 50–55 minutes though, as this mixture should not be over-cooked, it is a pleasantly moist cake.

Note: Do not substitute black treacle in this cake, the flavour is too strong.

ICED GOLDEN ALMOND CAKE

Make and bake the Golden Almond Cake. You can still top the cake with almonds before baking, but this is not essential. If icing the cake you may like to reduce the sugar to 75–100 g/3–4 oz but do not reduce the syrup, for this gives the cake its moist texture.

When cold top with the Ground Almond Butter Icing, made as page 147, using 75 g/3 oz ground almonds, etc.

DATE AND GINGER LOAF

Makes a 675 g/1½ lb loaf-shaped cake

50 g/2 oz butter or cooking fat or
    margarine
50 g/2 oz light brown or granulated
    sugar
2 tablespoons golden syrup
75 g/3 oz dates, weight without stones
200 g/7 oz self-raising flour or plain flour
    with 2 teaspoons baking powder
1 teaspoon ground ginger
1 egg
4 tablespoons milk

Grease and flour, or line, a 675 g/1½ lb loaf tin. Put the butter or cooking fat or margarine, sugar and syrup into a saucepan, stir over a low heat until melted. Chop the dates, add to the hot melted ingredients then allow to cool.

Sift the flour, or flour and baking powder, with the ground ginger into a mixing bowl. Add the melted ingredients, egg and milk, and beat together. Spoon into the prepared tin.

Bake in the centre of a very moderate oven, 160°C, 325°F, Gas Mark 3 for 45–50 minutes or until firm to the touch. Allow to cool in the tin for 10 minutes; turn out.

Cinnamon Date Loaf: Use ground cinnamon in place of ground ginger.

SPICED TREACLE CAKES

Makes 12–18

50 g/2 oz butter or margarine
50 g/2 oz black treacle
50 g/2 oz caster sugar
175 g/6 oz plain flour
½ teaspoon bicarbonate of soda
½ teaspoon grated nutmeg
½ teaspoon ground cinnamon
1 egg
75 g/3 oz sultanas

It is important to grease the 12–18 patty tins well. The mixture rises well in cooking so use fairly deep tins and do not over-fill.

Put the butter or margarine, treacle and sugar into a saucepan, heat gently until melted. Sift the dry ingredients into a mixing bowl, add the melted treacle mixture then beat in the egg and add the sultanas. Spoon into the patty tins and bake above the centre of a moderately hot oven, 200°C, 400°F, Gas Mark 6 for 15 minutes or until firm to the touch.

Spiced Raisin Cakes: Use syrup in place of treacle and raisins instead of sultanas.

MARMALADE AND DATE CAKE

Makes an 18 cm/7 inch square cake

225 g/8 oz self-raising flour or plain flour with 2 teaspoons baking powder
1–2 teaspoons grated orange rind
100 g/4 oz orange marmalade, see method
75 g/3 oz butter or margarine or cooking fat
75 g/3 oz granulated sugar
5 tablespoons orange juice
100 g/4 oz dates, weight without stones
1 egg

Grease and flour, or line, an 18 cm/7 inch cake tin. Sift the flour, or flour and baking powder, into a bowl, add the orange rind. Put the marmalade into a pan, you can of course weigh this in the pan, as shown in step 2 on page 111. If the marmalade has large lumps of peel it is advisable to cut these into smaller pieces, add the butter or margarine or cooking fat and sugar. Stir over a low heat until melted, then add to the flour and beat well. Do not wash-up the saucepan in which the marmalade was melted, but put in the orange juice, heat gently. Chop the dates, add to the other ingredients with the egg and orange juice, stir briskly to blend. Spoon into the prepared tin.

Bake in the centre of a very moderate oven, 160°C, 325°F, Gas Mark 3 for 45–50 minutes or until firm to the touch. Do not allow this cake to over-cook, since it should be pleasantly moist, test as step 8 on page 111. Remove from the tin and allow to cool. Eat when fresh or see the adaptation below.

Note: Lemon or lime marmalade is equally good in this cake.

STICKY MARMALADE DATE CAKE

Make and bake the Marmalade and Date Cake.

Towards the end of the cooking time put 4 tablespoons orange juice into a saucepan. Remove any pieces of peel from marmalade, put back into the jar but leave 4 tablespoons of the jelly or syrup part, add to the orange juice with 25 g/1 oz sugar if you like foods rather sweet. Bring to boiling point and heat for 2–3 minutes until slightly thickened.

Take the cake out of the tin and place on a serving dish. While still hot, make a number of small holes on top with a fine skewer. Spoon the orange and marmalade syrup over the cake and allow to soak in. Either serve hot as a pudding with lots of cream or allow to cool and serve as a very moist cake.

CIDER DRIPPING CAKE

Makes an 18 cm/7 inch round cake

75 g/3 oz clarified dripping, see below
75 g/3 oz granulated sugar
1 tablespoon golden syrup
100–175 g/4–6 oz mixed dried fruit
225 g/8 oz self-raising flour or plain flour
**   with 2 teaspoons baking powder**
½ teaspoon mixed spice
1 egg
150 ml/¼ pint sweet cider

for the topping
2 tablespoons Demerara sugar

Grease and flour, or line, an 18 cm/7 inch round cake tin. Put the dripping, sugar and golden syrup in a saucepan, stir over a low heat until the dripping and sugar have dissolved. Remove the pan from the heat, add the dried fruit and allow to stand for 15 minutes.

Sift the flour, or flour and baking powder, with the spice into a mixing bowl. Add the melted ingredients with the fruit then the egg and cider. Mix well and spoon into the prepared tin. Top with the Demerara sugar. Bake in the centre of a moderate oven, 180°C, 350°F, Gas Mark 4 for 1 hour or until firm to the touch. Allow to cool for 2 minutes in the tin then turn out carefully (so the topping is not disturbed) on to a wire cooling tray.

This cake is best when eaten fresh.
Using Apple Juice: When cider is not available use apple juice.

To Clarify Dripping
Dripping has a more definite flavour than other fats and it is therefore unsuitable for cakes except when used in a few well-flavoured recipes. In order to use dripping it must be clarified; i.e. well-cleaned.

To clarify dripping put it into a saucepan and cover with cold water. Bring the water to boiling point and heat gently until the dripping has melted. Pour the water and dripping into a container. Allow to cool; you will find the dripping has set on top with the water, containing most particles of food, underneath. Lift the block of dripping from the container, turn it upside down and cut away any brown residue, so leaving the dripping clean and firm.

In addition to the recipe on this page you will find that dripping is one of the fats you could use in the Economical Gingerbread, page 113.

CIDER AND APPLE PUDDING

Serves 4–6

ingredients as Cider Dripping Cake

for the sauce
450 g/1 lb cooking apples
3 tablespoons cider or water
2–3 tablespoons sugar

The cake on this page makes an excellent pudding if served hot. This could be practical for a small family of two or three persons, for the cake could be halved immediately after baking, the one half served with apple sauce, the other allowed to cool for a cake.

To serve as a pudding, bake as the instructions on this page. Meanwhile peel and slice the apples, put into a saucepan with the cider or water and sugar and simmer until a thick purée; spoon into a sauce boat. Turn out the cake, remove the paper and cut into 4–6 neat portions. Serve with the apple sauce.

MOIST CHOCOLATE CAKE

Makes an 18–19 cm/7–7½ inch cake

110 g/4 oz golden syrup
110 g/4 oz moist light brown sugar or
  caster sugar
110 g/4 oz butter or margarine
175 g/6 oz plain flour
1¼ teaspoons bicarbonate of soda
50 g/2 oz cocoa or chocolate powder
1 egg
150 ml/¼ pint milk

Line the bottom of an 18–19 cm/7–7½ inch cake tin with greaseproof paper, grease well; grease and flour the sides of the tin. Put the syrup, sugar, butter or margarine into a saucepan, stir over a low heat until melted.

Sift the flour, bicarbonate of soda and cocoa or chocolate powder into a mixing bowl. Cocoa gives a strong chocolate flavour; chocolate powder a milder taste. Blend the melted ingredients with the flour mixture; beat in the egg and the milk. Spoon into the prepared tin.

Bake in the centre of a very moderate oven 160°C, 325°F, Gas Mark 3 for 50–55 minutes or until firm to the touch. Cool for a few minutes in the tin, then turn out.

Note: This can be served plain or topped with 150 g/5 oz melted chocolate. It can be split and filled as the Chocolate Layer Sponge page 74. It is a good basis for a Black Forest Gâteau, page 134.

JAMAICAN CHOCOLATE CAKE

Use Molasses sugar in place of other sugar in the cake above; this gives a treacle flavour, which goes well with the chocolate mixture. Split the cake, fill and top with whipped cream, or the following cream and with sliced fresh pineapple.

Economy Cream: Pour 150 ml/¼ pint milk into a saucepan, add 100 g/4 oz unsalted butter (cut into small pieces) and 1 teaspoon gelatine. Heat until dissolved; add ½ teaspoon sugar and a few drops of vanilla essence. Keep lukewarm and put through a cream maker or cream attachment of a mixer. You can blend this at top speed in a liquidizer or food processor for 30 seconds. Chill for at least 3 hours then whip. Makes 300 ml/½ pint.

CHOCOLATE BRAN BROWNIES

Illustrated in colour on page 109

Makes 16

50 g/2 oz All-bran
85 g/3 oz wheatmeal self-raising flour or
  plain flour with ¾ teaspoon baking
  powder
65 g/2½ oz butter or cooking fat or
  margarine
100 g/4 oz caster sugar
2 tablespoons water
175 g/6 oz plain chocolate
½ teaspoon vanilla essence
2 eggs
100 g/4 oz walnuts or other nuts

Line a 20 cm/8 inch square cake tin with greased greaseproof paper. Put the bran into a mixing bowl, sift the flour, or flour and baking powder, mix with the bran.

Put the butter, fat or margarine, sugar and water into a saucepan, heat gently until the fat has melted, remove from the heat. Break the chocolate into pieces, add to the hot melted ingredients, together with the essence. Leave until the chocolate has melted then blend with the bran and flour. Beat in the eggs. Chop the walnuts, or other nuts, fairly coarsely, add to the other ingredients. Pour into tin.

Bake in the centre of a moderate oven, 180–190°C, 350–375°F, Gas Mark 4–5 for 30 minutes or until firm to the touch. Allow to cool then cut into 16 squares.

BAKING WITH OIL

It is very easy to make cakes using oil, rather than butter, margarine or cooking fat. As you will find, the recipes are extremely successful and quite versatile. Measure the oil and all the other ingredients carefully. Each 30 ml/1 fl oz is equivalent to 1⅗ tablespoons oil, i.e. just over 1½ tablespoons.

I have included these recipes in the 'Melting' section for, although you do not melt any of the ingredients, the liquid consistency is similar to the other recipes in this chapter.

Use a cake tin without a loose base for cakes made with oil.

Lemon or Orange Corn Oil Sponge: The basic sponge below is delicious if lemon or orange juice is used instead of, or with, the water. In the case of lemon juice you may prefer to use just 2 tablespoons of juice and make it up with water, a little grated fruit rind can be added.

CORN OIL SPONGE

Makes an 18 cm/7 inch sponge sandwich

100 ml/3½ fl oz corn oil
100 ml/3½ fl oz water
150 g/5 oz plain flour
2 teaspoons baking powder
25 g/1 oz cornflour
150 g/5 oz caster sugar
2 egg whites
4–5 tablespoons jam

to decorate
1–2 tablespoons caster sugar

Grease and flour, or line, two 18 cm/7 inch sandwich tins. Blend the oil and cold water together. Sift the flour with the baking powder and cornflour into a mixing bowl. Gradually beat in the oil and water to make a smooth mixture then add the sugar. Whisk the egg whites in a separate bowl until they are stiff, fold gently and carefully into the batter. Divide the mixture between the prepared tins.

Bake just above the centre of a moderate oven, 180°C, 350°F, Gas Mark 4 for 15–18 minutes or until firm to the touch. Cool for 2–3 minutes in the tins then turn out on to a wire cooling tray. Cool then sandwich with the jam and top with sugar.

COFFEE CORN OIL SPONGE

Makes an 18 cm/7 inch sponge sandwich

ingredients as the Corn Oil Sponge, but use strong liquid coffee not water
Allow the coffee to become quite cold before mixing with the oil, then proceed as the basic recipe.

Sandwich the cold sponges together with apricot jam or Coffee Butter Icing, as on page 147. Top the sponge with more Coffee Butter icing or coffee-flavoured Glacé Icing, see page 146. Decorate with chopped or halved walnuts.

CHOCOLATE CORN OIL SPONGE

Makes an 18 cm/7 inch sponge sandwich

ingredients as the Corn Oil Sponge, but omit 15 g/½ oz flour and substitute 15 g/½ oz cocoa powder or omit 25 g/1 oz flour and substitute 25 g/1 oz chocolate powder
Sift the cocoa or chocolate powder with the flour, baking powder and cornflour, then proceed as the basic recipe.

Sandwich the cold sponges together with apricot jam and a little whipped cream or with Chocolate Butter Icing, as on page 147. Top the sponge with more Chocolate Butter Icing or chocolate-flavoured Glacé Icing, see page 146, or whipped cream and grated chocolate or melted plain chocolate.

FLAPJACK CRUMBLE

Serves 4–6

**550–675 g/1¼–1½ lb fruit, weight when
      peeled and cored or stoned
2–4 tablespoons liquid
sugar or honey or syrup to taste**

for the crumble
**50 g/2 oz butter or margarine
50 g/2 oz brown sugar
2 tablespoons golden syrup
175 g/6 oz rolled oats**

Prepare fruit, as Basic Fruit Crumble on
page 56, pre-cook if necessary.

Put the butter or margarine, sugar and
golden syrup into a pan, heat until the fat
and sugar have melted. Add the rolled
oats. Mix well then spoon over the partially cooked, or raw, fruit. Flatten with a
knife and bake in the centre of a very
moderate oven, 160°C, 325°F, Gas Mark 3
for 30–35 minutes. Serve hot or cold.

AUSTRIAN CHOCOLATE CAKE

Makes a 20–23 cm/8–9 inch cake

**150 g/5 oz self-raising flour with ¾
      teaspoon baking powder or
      150 g/5 oz plain flour with 2
      teaspoons baking powder
25 g/1 oz cocoa powder
150 g/5 oz light brown sugar
2 large eggs
100 ml/3½ fl oz corn oil
100 ml/3½ fl oz milk
¼ teaspoon vanilla essence**

for the syrup
**100 g/4 oz granulated sugar
150 ml/¼ pint water
2 tablespoons rum**

for the topping
25 g/1 oz icing sugar

Line the bottom of a 20–23 cm/8–9 inch
cake tin with greased greaseproof paper,
grease and flour the sides of the tin. Sift
the flour, baking powder and cocoa into a
mixing bowl, add the sugar.

Separate the eggs, whisk the egg yolks,
corn oil, milk and essence together until
well blended then add to the dry ingredients, beat until a smooth batter. Whisk
the egg whites until stiff then fold into the
soft mixture. Spoon carefully into the prepared tin.

Bake in the centre of a moderate oven,
180°C, 350°F, Gas Mark 4 for approximately 40 minutes or until firm to the
touch. Turn out carefully, remove the
paper and allow the cake to cool then
return it to the cake tin. Put the sugar and
water for the syrup into a saucepan, stir
until the sugar has dissolved then boil
briskly for 4–5 minutes. Remove from the
heat, add the rum then spoon over the
cake. Leave for at least 12 hours then lift
out of the tin.

Sift the icing sugar
over the top of the cake
to give a thick layer.
Heat part of a metal
skewer under the grill,
hold the unheated end
carefully and mark the
icing in an attractive
lattice design.

CRUNCHY OAT CRUMBLE

Serves 4–6

**follow the recipe for Flapjack Crumble,
      but use 100 g/4 oz rolled oats,
      50 g/2 oz flour, 50 g/2 oz
      desiccated coconut instead of all
      rolled oats**

For an even crisper topping use the ingredients above and 50 g/2 oz chopped walnuts or other nuts; mix these last with the
other ingredients.

GILACGI

Illustrated in colour on page 109

Serves 4–6

for the filling
225 g/8 oz dates, weight without stones
50 g/2 oz walnuts or blanched almonds
150 ml/¼ pint water
1 tablespoon honey
1 tablespoon lemon juice
½ teaspoon ground cinnamon

for the crumble
100 g/4 oz butter
100 g/4 oz flour
100 g/4 oz fine semolina
50 g/2 oz caster sugar

Chop the dates and nuts. Boil the water, pour over the dates, blend with the honey, juice and cinnamon, stand for 15 minutes.

Melt the butter; mix the flour, semolina and sugar with the butter. Spoon half the semolina mixture into a greased shallow 20 cm/8 inch tin or ovenproof dish. Add the nuts to the date mixture, spread evenly over the crumbly base, being careful not to dislodge any crumbs. Cover with the remainder of the semolina mixture, flatten with a palette knife.

Bake in the centre of a moderately hot oven, 190°C, 375°F, Gas Mark 5 for about 45 minutes; lower the heat to moderate after 20 minutes if the mixture is becoming too brown. This is delicious hot as a dessert or cold as a cake.

APRICOT ALMOND SLICES

Use 225 g/8 oz dried apricots instead of dates in the recipe above, chop and add to the boiling water, honey and lemon juice. Leave for 1 hour. Add 50 g/2 oz ground almonds, 50 g/2 oz blanched flaked almonds. Proceed as above.

Modern baking methods

In a Microwave Cooker
All the cakes in this section can be 'baked' in a microwave cooker. The moist sticky type of texture is ideally suited for this method and the syrup or black treacle used in many of the recipes adds colour. You will find that both texture and colour compare very favourably with cakes baked in a conventional oven.

Read the comments made in the previous section, page 104, about the choice of utensils. Cakes made by the melting method tend to rise a great deal in the early stages of cooking, so choose a sufficiently large baking utensil.

It is advisable to line the base of this for the cakes in this section. Use greased greaseproof paper, do not flour. As an example of the cooking time, allow approximately 10 minutes for the Moist Chocolate Cake, page 119 and about 15 minutes for the Master Recipe, i.e. the Gingerbread on pages 110 and 113. Use the SIMMER position. If your cooker has no variable control and therefore you need to cook on the HIGH setting, which is less desirable for this group of cakes, then I would only bake half quantities and allow about 5 minutes. This makes sure the cakes are not overcooked on the outside before being set in the middle. Test as information on page 104.

The recipe on this page is excellent for a microwave cooker. Allow 10 minutes on HIGH, turn frequently.

In a Crock-Pot
All the cakes in this section are highly successful in a crock-pot. Follow the information given on page 104. Allow 2½–3 hours on HIGH.

In a Pressure Cooker
Make up half quantities, for the full amount will probably take too large a container to fit into the cooker. Cook as information on page 105.

In a Table Cooker (Electric Frying Pan)
Follow advice on page 105. The cakes are not quite as sticky and moist as when baked in a conventional oven.

Storing

No cakes in this section keep for a very long time, they are nice when eaten fairly fresh. The Rich Gingerbread does keep well for up to 3 weeks, so do all recipes based on this. Although relatively economical, I find the Cider Dripping Cake stores well for some days.

There is an old belief that if you put an apple in the container in which a fruit cake or gingerbread is stored, it keeps moist for a longer time. However, you must check that the apple does not go mouldy; if it does the mould will spread and will ruin the cake.

If a gingerbread has become rather stale for a cake, slice thinly and spread with butter. As stated on page 113, a gingerbread originated as a bread.

Freezing

All the cakes in this section freeze well and freezing is a sensible way of storing the more economical mixtures.

Open-freeze or put in a container which does not touch the mixture for wrappings could adhere to the soft and slightly moist top of the cake.

The cooked cakes can be frozen for up to 3 months. I think they are nicer if defrosted slowly at room temperature then left a few hours for the flavour to mature.

The uncooked mixtures could be frozen for up to 6 weeks.

Do not freeze the Flapjacks, the crisp topping is spoilt by being left in contact with the moist fruit.

PROBLEM SOLVING

Most of the recipes in this melting method section should be pleasantly moist and light in texture.

Q. *Why did the Gingerbread bubble up over the top of the tin?*
A. If the ingredients were carefully measured it could well be that the tin was slightly shallow and the paper lining the tin was not sufficiently deep either, see step 7 page 111. These liquid mixtures tend to bubble fairly briskly in the initial stage of cooking. It could be that the amount of raising agent was too generous. Always measure these carefully.
Quick Remedy: Turn the cake, which will be rather 'untidy' looking, upside down after neatening the edges.

Q. *The Gingerbread sank very slightly but tasted delicious.*
A. If the cake sank during baking it could be too little raising agent was used and the cake never rose enough in the middle. If it sank after removing from the oven, it was insufficiently cooked.

If the cake was slightly heavy in the centre it is because too much liquid was used or because the cake was moved or subjected to a draught during cooking, see comments on page 110.
Quick Remedy: Remember it is forgivable (almost) if a gingerbread sinks slightly and certainly if it tastes delicious. You can cut out the sunken centre or turn the cake upside down or fill the little central cavity with Ginger flavoured icing and top with pieces of crystallised or preserved ginger.

Q. *Is it possible to replace the oil in the recipes in this chapter with fat of some kind?*
A. No, the recipes are created for oil and would not be the same with fat, even if melted.

123

CHAPTER 5

The Whisking Method

In this chapter you will find recipes for the very lightest kinds of cakes, together with interesting variations and recipes based upon the same method of mixing. The Master Recipe, on the next page, is the classic sponge, made by using just eggs, sugar and flour. The technique involved in producing a perfect cake by the whisking method is fully explained on the next two pages. The advice and illustrated stages should be followed very carefully, for this method of mixing is not quite as simple as the processes detailed in the previous chapters.

You will, however, feel a great sense of achievement when you have made a perfect feather-light sponge.

WHAT DOES WHISKING MEAN?

It means that the eggs and sugar are whisked together until they are thick and creamy and you see the trail of the whisk. This can be done with either a hand or electric whisk, but only a very limited number of food processors have the type of blade suitable for aerating such a light mixture, see page 128.

After whisking the eggs and sugar correctly the next stage is to add the flour; this must be done by a gentle folding action, and is fully explained under the Master Recipe.

The whisking method is used for:

Small and large sponge cakes
Some biscuits
A very few puddings

Cakes made by the whisking method – Chocolate Cream Roll (recipe page 130), Chocolate Soufflé (recipe page 141), Rum and Chocolate Gâteau (recipe page 138)

SPONGE CAKE

This is often called the 'true' sponge for its texture is so light. It is also referred to as a 'fatless' sponge, although a little fat is sometimes added, see page 129. Many small and large cakes are based on the proportions or method of the Master Recipe, see this page and page 127.

Baking Utensils: Grease and flour an 18–19 cm/7–7½ inch cake tin, or line it with greased greaseproof paper.

Oven Setting: Preheat the oven at moderate, 180°C, 350°F, Gas Mark 4. Arrange the shelf in the centre of the oven (with a fan-assisted oven any position can be used).

Cooking Time: Approximately 30 minutes.

Makes an 18–19 cm/7–7½ inch round cake

85 g/3 oz plain or self-raising flour, see under 'Choice of Ingredients'
3 large eggs
110 g/4 oz caster sugar
few drops warm water (optional), see step 7 opposite

to decorate
little caster sugar (optional)

CERTAIN SUCCESS

Choice of Ingredients: You will note that plain flour is given as first choice in the recipe above. The amount of air incorporated into the eggs and sugar by competent whisking is so great that any form of raising agent should not be necessary. If you are a little worried as to whether the sponge will rise as much as it should, then use self-raising flour, or sift ¾ teaspoon baking powder with the plain flour. Always use caster sugar in this cake except in a few recipes where icing sugar or other sugar is given. There is a recipe on page 129 for the sponge with a little melted fat added.

Handling the Mixture: Sift the flour some little time before making the sponge and leave it on a plate in a warm, but not hot, place. This lightens the flour, which is very important in this recipe.
Whisk the eggs and sugar so well that you see the trail of the whisk, shown quite clearly in step 4. I am not an advocate of whisking over hot water, but give this method on page 129. Fold the flour gently and carefully into the whisked eggs and sugar, see step 6 – *never* beat this into the whisked eggs and sugar.

Consistency: The consistency of the sponge is a soft one that is like lightly whipped cream; for a Swiss roll you need to make the mixture slightly softer, see pages 130 and 131. If the mixture is rather runny, it sadly means you have insufficiently whisked the eggs and sugar and/or over-handled the mixture when incorporating the flour. The consistency is shown in steps 7 and 8.

Preparing Tins: As this sponge is inclined to stick, grease and flour the tin well, I lightly grease even a silicone ('non-stick') tin. If you are at all worried about the sponge sticking, line the base and sides of the tin with greased greaseproof paper.

Baking: *It is essential to preheat the oven* at the temperature given for this recipe. The delicate sponge over-browns easily, so check the oven temperature at the end of 10 minutes, if the cake is getting slightly brown lower the oven temperature by 10°C, 25°F, or 1 Gas Mark. Test at the end of 25 minutes cooking time, the cake should be pale in colour but firm to a gentle touch, see step 9.

1 Sift the flour, or flour and baking powder, see the comments under 'Choice of Ingredients', on to a plate or a small shallow container. It is best to leave in the warmth of the kitchen for a short time to become **slightly** warm.

2 Break each egg separately into a cup, then transfer all the eggs to a mixing bowl; add the sugar. Stand the mixing bowl on a folded teacloth so it does not slip on the table as you whisk.

3 When whisking the eggs and sugar by hand you can use a rotary whisk but a balloon whisk, see left, or flat-type whisk tends to give a more aerated mixture and therefore produces a greater volume from the whisked eggs and sugar. Various whisks are discussed on page 29. The next page gives useful information on electric mixers for whisking.

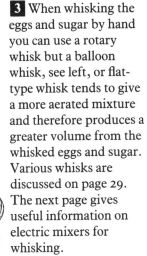

4 Steady the bowl with your left hand and whisk briskly until the mixture is thick and creamy, do this in a clockwise direction, you should be able to see the trail of the whisk, as shown in the illustration. If you cannot do this then the mixture is insufficiently whisked and you should continue the process and test again. Sift the flour, or flour and baking powder, into the whisked ingredients.

5 Change the whisk for either a metal spoon or palette knife; most cooks find it easier to use the spoon.

6 Fold the flour gently, but thoroughly, into the whisked ingredients, folding in a figure of eight movement. Every now and then part the mixture with the spoon or knife to make sure all the flour (which tends to sink to the bottom of the mixture) is incorporated.

7 When satisfied that all the ingredients are blended together, check the consistency, it should be like lightly whipped cream. If too thick then doubtless this is because the eggs were small, fold in a few drops of warm water.

8 Spoon the mixture into the prepared tin and bake in the centre of the oven for approximately 30 minutes, check baking progress, test at the end of 25 minutes as information left and step 9.

9 This sponge is very delicate, so your pressure should be firm, but light. Press with your finger in the centre of the cake. If no impression is left then the sponge is cooked.

10 Cool for 2–3 minutes in the tin then turn out on to a folded teacloth held on the palm of your hand and then invert on to a wire cooling tray as illustration page 67.

127

Using modern equipment

WHISKING METHOD BY MIXER

A small or large electric mixer is an ideal piece of equipment for whisking the eggs and sugar in the Master Recipe, page 126, and all other recipes in this section. In some recipes the eggs are separated, the egg yolks and sugar are whisked until thick and creamy; then the egg whites are whisked separately, so the mixer is used in two ways.

Where you have a choice of whisk or beater, always use the whisk, for this gives better aeration.

If using a small portable mixer make quite certain that the two whisks are used for a sufficient period of time; often the mixture looks light and fluffy, but does not hold the trail of the whisk when tested, as in step 4, on the previous page.

Make quite certain there is adequate space in the mixer bowl for the whisked mixture to increase in volume and still leave room to add the flour, or flour and other ingredients.

In certain recipes in this section there is no flour, but chopped nuts or crisp crumbs are folded into the whisked eggs and sugar.

Points to Watch: Allow the mixer to whisk the eggs and sugar thoroughly. Sift and warm the flour and do not be tempted to add this by machine; it is too vigorous and it will spoil the light texture.

A MIXER FOR A SPONGE CAKE

Use either a small or large mixer for whisking the eggs and sugar in this recipe, given on page 126. Fix the whisk(s) in position and make sure that the mixer bowl and whisk(s) are dry and scrupulously clean.

Put the eggs and sugar into the bowl, as steps 2 and 4 on the previous page. Switch on, using a low speed at first, so the liquid mixture does not splash; as the mixture begins to thicken you can increase the speed.

Continue whisking until you can see the trail of the whisk in the thick creamy mixture, see step 4 on page 127.

Sift the flour, or flour and baking powder, (warmed as in step 1 on the previous page) into the whisked egg and sugar mixture. Remove the whisk(s); then fold the flour into the eggs and sugar with a spoon or knife, as described in step 6. Complete the process by following steps 7–10 on the previous page.

WHISKING METHOD BY FOOD PROCESSOR

Food processors were not designed to whisk eggs and sugar until thick; only a few processors are now adapted so that air can be incorporated into the mixture.

A FOOD PROCESSOR FOR A SPONGE CAKE

Fix the processor bowl and the double-bladed cutting knife in position; add the eggs and sugar. Put on the lid and process until the eggs and sugar are thick and creamy.

It is difficult to fold the flour in by hand, so I would suggest removing the light mixture from the processor bowl into another container (use the spatula provided by the manufacturer), then fold in the sifted flour, or flour and baking powder, with a spoon or knife as step 4 on the previous page. After this continue as steps 7–10.

Points to Watch: Check with the manufacturers' handbook and instructions that the particular food processor is equipped to whisk eggs and sugar. Allow the motor to run only until the eggs and sugar are thick; but never permit a food processor to be switched on for too long a period.

WHISKING OVER HOT WATER

Many people recommend whisking the eggs and sugar over hot, not boiling, water. The whisking process for this can be done with a hand whisk or a portable electric whisk.

Put the eggs and sugar into the mixing bowl then whisk for a few seconds to blend. Stand the mixing bowl over a saucepan of hot, but not boiling, water, make quite sure it is balanced safely and will not tip over.

Whisk the eggs and sugar until thick and creamy as step 4 on page 127. During the whisking process make quite sure that the egg mixture does not set at the bottom of the mixing bowl, where it is nearest to the hot water. When the eggs and sugar have thickened, remove the bowl from the heat and continue whisking until cold. Fold the sifted flour, or flour and baking powder, into the whisked egg and sugar mixture as step 6 on page 127, and continue as steps 7–10.

The advantage of using this method is that the eggs and sugar thicken more rapidly than when whisked without standing over hot water. In my opinion the disadvantage is that without the utmost care the egg mixture begins to 'cook' slightly and you do not get such a light texture.

FLAVOURING A WHISKED SPONGE

The sponge on pages 126 and 127 can be flavoured in various ways; as it has a delicate flavour, as well as a light texture, additional flavours should not be too strong, nor affect the basic proportions of the mixture. The amounts given below refer to the Master Recipe on page 126 using 3 large eggs. The flavourings can be used also in the Genoese Pastry on page 132.

Almond and Vanilla Essences: Add ¼–½ teaspoon to the eggs and sugar.

Chocolate: Omit 15 g/½ oz flour and substitute 15 g/½ oz cocoa powder, or omit 25 g/1 oz flour and substitute 25 g/1 oz chocolate powder. Sift the cocoa or chocolate powder with the flour.

Coffee: Add 1–2 teaspoons coffee essence to the eggs and sugar after whisking, then whisk again until thickened. Omit the water in the sponge cake and reduce this slightly in the Swiss Roll.

Lemon or Orange: Add ½–1 teaspoon very finely grated lemon or orange rind to the eggs and sugar before whisking. Use lemon or orange juice instead of water in the recipe.

Add ½ teaspoon juice to the Genoese Pastry before folding in the final amount of sifted flour and butter.

Liqueurs: Add ½–1 tablespoon of your favourite liqueur to the mixture, after folding in the flour.

Adding Butter to Sponges
A little melted butter helps to keep a true sponge moist. Use up to 25 g/1 oz in the Master Recipe, pages 126 and 127. Read the hints about heating and incorporating butter given under Genoese Pastry, see page 132.

Flour for Sponges
A light sponge, such as the classic recipe made as pages 124 and 125, needs the light texture of white flour. Neither wholemeal nor wheatmeal flour are suitable for whisked sponges.

Easy Fillings for Sponges
Fill with whipped cream and fruit or jam or a flavoured Butter Icing, as page 147. It makes a pleasant change of texture if the whipped cream is blended with chopped nuts or diced chocolate or crushed crisp Praline, see page 137.

129

SWISS ROLL

Makes 1 large roll

**ingredients as Master Recipe for
    Sponge Cake on page 126, using
    3 eggs etc.**
1 tablespoon warm water

to fill and coat
approx. 6 tablespoons jam
2 tablespoons caster sugar

Line a Swiss roll tin measuring 30.5 ×
20–23 cm/12 × 8–9 inches with lightly
oiled or greased greaseproof paper or use
'non-stick' ungreased silicone paper.

Sift the flour as in the Master Recipe
and warm, see step 1 page 127. Whisk the
eggs and sugar until thick and creamy as
under steps 2–4 on page 127 then re-sift
the flour into the egg mixture. Fold gently
and carefully into the egg mixture with a
metal spoon then fold in the warm water.
This gives a soft pouring consistency.
Spoon or pour into the prepared tin, tilt
the tin so the mixture runs evenly all over
the paper and bake towards top of moderate to moderately hot oven, 190–200°C,
375–400°F, Gas Mark 5–6 for 8–10
minutes or until firm to a gentle touch.

Meanwhile warm, but do not overheat,
the jam. Place a sheet of greaseproof paper
on a working surface. If you have problems in rolling a sponge, it is a good idea to
damp a teacloth in hot water, wring this
out firmly and place it *under* the greaseproof paper. Sprinkle the paper with a
generous layer of caster sugar. Turn the
tin upside down to release sponge.

Pull away the greaseproof paper from
the sponge, if you hold the edges of the
paper it is easy to do this. If by chance the
paper seems to be sticking to the sponge,
damp this with a pastry brush dipped in
cold water and it will be easy to remove.
Feel the edges of the sponge, if crisp cut
off with a sharp knife.

Spread the sponge
with the warm jam,
keep this away from the
extreme side edges of
the sponge. Make a
slight cut across the
sponge about 1.5 cm/½
inch from the end
nearest you, then make
a firm fold.

Lift the sugared pap-
er and use this to help
roll the sponge. Lift on
to wire tray and cool
away from draughts.

CHOCOLATE CREAM ROLL

Illustrated in colour on page 125

Makes 1 large roll

Follow the chocolate sponge variation of
the Master Recipe on page 129 which
gives a chocolate-flavoured sponge. Make
the Swiss Roll, turn out, roll round the
sugared paper and allow to cool.

Meanwhile whip a generous 150 ml/¼
pint double cream, this can be sweetened
with a little caster sugar or sifted icing
sugar and flavoured with a few drops of
Kirsch or rum.

Unroll the sponge, spread with a little
apricot jam, then with the whipped cream
and roll again. Dust the roll with more
caster sugar or sifted icing sugar.

SMALL SWISS ROLL

Line a Swiss roll tin, measuring 25 ×
18 cm/10 × 7 inches as the Swiss Roll.

Weigh, sift and warm 50 g/2 oz plain or
self-raising flour. Whisk 2 large eggs with
85 g/3 oz caster sugar, see step 1–4 on
page 127.

Bake the sponge as described in the
recipe left, but allow 7–8 minutes only.
Turn out, spread with jam and roll.

BÛCHE DE NOEL

Makes 1 large roll

Make and bake the large Swiss Roll on page 130. Roll around the greaseproof paper if filling with a butter icing or the Chestnut Filling and allow to cool. As this is a family Christmas cake, which small children will be eating, I often fill the sponge with warmed apple or redcurrant jelly then allow to cool before coating with the Crisp Chocolate Icing as page 146.

Chestnut Filling and Coating: Cream together 50 g/2 oz butter or margarine and 75–100 g/3–4 oz sifted icing sugar. Blend in 350–450 g/12–16 oz unsweetened canned chestnut purée (amount depends upon thickness of filling required) and 1–2 tablespoons Kirsch (this is not essential).

Unroll the sponge, spread with about half the Chestnut mixture, then re-roll. Spread the remaining mixture over the roll, then drag a flat bladed knife downwards to smooth the icing and then to give the 'ridges' of a tree trunk.

Sift a little icing sugar over to look like snow and add an ornamental robin.

NUSS ROULADE

Makes 1 large roll

85 g/3 oz ground or whole hazelnuts
3 large eggs
100 g/4 oz caster sugar
15 g/½ oz sweet biscuits
little extra caster sugar

for the filling
300 ml/½ pint double cream
25 g/1 oz icing sugar
1 tablespoon Kirsch

Line a Swiss roll tin as on page 130. Ground hazelnuts are available from Health Food stores but if you can only obtain whole nuts, grind these until very fine in a blender (liquidiser) or food processor. Whisk the eggs and sugar until thick and creamy, as described on page 127. Fold the nuts into the light egg mixture; do this just as carefully as when adding flour in an ordinary whisked sponge.

Make the biscuits into fine crumbs and sprinkle evenly over the prepared tin, then add the nut mixture.

Bake above the centre of a moderate oven, 190°C, 375°F, Gas Mark 5 for approximately 10 minutes or until firm to the touch. Sprinkle a light coating of sugar over a sheet of greaseproof paper. Turn the nut sponge on to this, roll with the sugared paper inside the sponge, see Chocolate Cream Roll page 130. Cool.

Whip the cream, sift the sugar; add to the cream together with the Kirsch. Unroll the nut sponge; spread with the cream, then re-roll.

Note: Ground walnuts could be used as hazelnuts, but ground almonds should be dried for a few minutes in a moderate oven.

BREAD ROULADE

Makes 1 large roll

Follow the directions for the Nuss Roulade but substitute dried breadcrumbs (kind used for coating food) for the nuts, roll and fill as the Nuss Roulade.

INDIVIDUAL SWISS ROLLS

Makes 10–12

Prepare the sponge mixture, as for the Small Swiss Roll, pour it into the largest lined tin possible, to give a wafer thin layer. Bake as page 130 for 5–6 minutes. Cut into portions, spread with jam and roll.

GENOESE PASTRY

This is a strange name to give a cake; and it is not a pastry but an adaptation of the whisked sponge, which is the Master Recipe, see page 126. Nowadays it is often termed Genoese Sponge. The difference between Genoese Pastry, or Genoise as it is known in Italy, where it is a great favourite, and the true sponge is that an appreciable amount of butter is folded into the whisked egg mixture.

Genoese Pastry can be the basis for a plain cake, although rarely served like that, or elaborate gâteaux. It is firmer than a Victoria Sandwich mixture so is excellent for cutting into various shapes to make small decorated cakes, see page 133. It keeps moist for several days; it also freezes well.

You must melt the butter carefully, so it does not discolour by being overheated; allow to cool, but not solidify again. Unsalted butter is better than salted.

Follow all the advice given in the Master Recipe on pages 126 and 127.

50 g/2 oz unsalted butter
85 g/3 oz self-raising or plain flour with
¾ teaspoon baking powder, see
method
3 large eggs
110 g/4 oz caster sugar

Always preheat the oven well, see page 126. Grease and flour, or line, the tin(s), see below. Melt the butter in a saucepan or basin over hot water, allow it to cool. Sift the flour, or flour and baking powder, and warm, see step 1 on page 127. In this recipe I like to use a little raising agent but this could be omitted, see Choice of Ingredients on page 126.

Whisk the eggs and sugar until thick as steps 2–4 on page 127; re-sift the flour, gently and carefully fold half into the egg mixture with a metal spoon. Next fold in a little of the cool liquified butter. Finally fold in all the remaining flour and butter.

Spoon the mixture into the prepared tin(s), bake as below. Cool in the tin(s) for 1–2 minutes, turn out and allow to cool. If serving as a plain cake, top with caster sugar.

A deep cake made with Genoese Pastry should be baked in the centre of a moderate oven, 180°C, 350°F, Gas Mark 4; lower heat to 160°C, 325°F, Gas Mark 3 after 25 minutes if the cake is getting too brown.

Shallow cakes should be baked at the same temperature but just above the centre of the oven.

To make two 18–20 cm/7–8 inch sandwiches or one 18–20 cm/7–8 inch cake or a shallow oblong cake measuring 30.5 × 20 cm/12 × 8 inches:
Use ingredients as given left.

Bake the sandwiches or oblong cake for approximately 20 minutes.

Bake the deep cake for 40 minutes.

To make two 21.5–24 cm/8½–9½ inch sandwiches or one 21.5–24 cm/8½–9½ inch cake or to fill a deeper oblong tin measuring 30.5 × 20 cm/12 × 8 inches:
Use 85 g/3 oz unsalted butter, 110 g/4 oz self-raising or plain flour with 1 teaspoon baking powder, 4 large eggs, 150 g/5 oz caster sugar.

Bake the sandwiches or oblong cake for approximately 25 minutes.

Bake the deep cake for 45–50 minutes.

Wafer Thin Layers of Genoese: In some gâteaux the recipe needs 4–6 very thin layers of Genoese Pastry. Cut rounds of silicone (non-stick) paper or grease rounds of greaseproof paper 20–21.5 cm/8–8½ inches in diameter. Put on to baking sheets. Make the Genoese mixture, using 4 large eggs etc. Spread carefully over the paper rounds. Bake as many layers as possible in a moderate oven, 190°C, 375°F, Gas Mark 5 for 7–8 minutes until firm, see page 127.

SMALL SPONGE CAKES

Use the Master Recipe, pages 126 and 127.

Sponge Fingers: You need the special tins as shown right. Grease with melted butter, sprinkle lightly with caster sugar. The quantities on page 126, using  3 large eggs etc., will make 18–24 fingers. Spoon the mixture into the tins. Sprinkle caster sugar over the top of the fingers and bake towards the top of a moderate oven, 190°C, 375°F, Gas Mark 5 for about 10 minutes.

If you require crisp firm fingers, like Savoy Fingers (Boudoir) Biscuits, then bake in a very moderate oven, 160°C, 325°F, Gas Mark 3 for about 20 minutes. Allow to cool; store in an airtight tin.

Savoys: Use the Master Recipe on page 126. Spoon or pipe tiny rounds of mixture on to well-greased baking trays. Bake as for Sponge Fingers, allow about 8 minutes. Cool and sandwich together with whipped cream and jam.

DECORATED SPONGE CAKES

Use the Genoese Pastry on page 132 or the Victoria Sandwich mixture as pages 66 and 67 or the Master Recipe for this section on pages 126 and 127. Bake in an oblong tin, see pages 80 and 132.

Iced Fancies: Cut the cakes into required shapes – fingers, rounds, diamond shapes. They are nicer if the top and sides are coated with a very little sieved apricot jam before icing. Make Glacé Icing as page 146. It should be a soft consistency.
Insert a skewer into the base of the first small cake and dip into the bowl of icing, coating top and sides. Continue like this.

Place the iced cakes on to a wire cooling tray, with a plate underneath, to catch any drips of icing. Decorate with crystallised rose and violet petals, glacé cherry and angelica or nuts.

Cauliflower Cakes: Cut small rounds of cake, spread the sides and top with sieved apricot jam. Make Marzipan as page 148, colour this pale green. Roll out thinly on a sugared board, cut large leaf shapes, press against the sides of the cake to give the appearance of a green cauliflower. Top each cake with a rosette of whipped cream.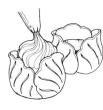

Chocolate Boxes: Melt plain chocolate in a basin over hot water then pour the melted chocolate on to a pastry slab or metal tin, to give a wafer thin layer. Cut into neat squares with a sharp knife; you can, of course, buy these chocolate squares. Cut the cake into similar sized squares as the chocolate. Brush the top and sides of the cakes with sieved apricot jam; press the chocolate squares to the sides only. Top with whipped cream and grated chocolate.

Rose Petal Cakes: Cut the cake into small shallow rounds. Coat the sides and top with sieved apricot jam and coat with chopped pistachios or green coloured chopped nuts or coconut, see page 136.
Make the Marzipan as page 148 but colour pale pink; cut into small petal shapes. Arrange these on top of the rounds of cake like a flower. Pipe a rosette of cream in the centre.

133

GORGEOUS GÂTEAUX

There are many gâteaux throughout this book, these can be served as a dessert or for tea. A sponge or Genoese Pastry will give unlimited variations, for you can combine your favourite fillings, toppings and flavourings. On this page are ideas using seasonal fruits.

In some recipes, such as the Sachertorte on page 139, two mixing processes are combined, i.e. creaming and whisking. Read the advice under the Master Recipes for both these sections, pages 67 and 127 – a successful result depends upon careful blending of the ingredients.

BLACK FOREST GÂTEAU

Serves 6–8

This delicious chocolate and cherry gâteau is easily made. You can select whichever chocolate cake is the most popular in your family, I would suggest:

The Sachertorte on page 139, which is rich and full of flavour, the moist, but more economical, Chocolate Cake made by the melting method on page 119 or the Chocolate Sponge on page 74. You could use the very light and delicate whisked sponge from this section on page 129 but then you must serve the cake very soon after it is prepared otherwise it will collapse with the weight of fruit.

Split the cake horizontally to give three layers. Spread the first layer with cherry jam and moisten either with Kirsch or a little concentrated syrup (made by boiling the syrup from canned cherries). Spread with whipped cream and stoned black cherries. Put on the second layer, repeat the filling. Add the top layer of chocolate cake.

Coat the whole cake with whipped cream, press grated chocolate against the sides. Decorate the top of the cake with black cherries and rosettes of cream.

ORANGE RUM GÂTEAU

Serves 6

ingredients as Sponge Cake on pages 126 and 127
2 teaspoons grated orange rind

for the filling and topping
3 medium oranges
300 ml/½ pint double cream
2 tablespoons rum
50 g/2 oz caster sugar

Add the orange rind when whisking the eggs and sugar then make and bake as the instructions on pages 126 and 127. Allow to cool.

Cut away the peel from two of the oranges, remove the segments of fruit. Whip the cream, add the rum and sugar, blend half the rum-flavoured cream with the orange segments.

Split the Sponge Cake horizontally and spread half with the orange mixture. Top with the second sponge and the remaining rum-flavoured cream. Cut the remaining orange into thin rings and arrange on top of the gâteau.

VIENNESE MAY GÂTEAU

Serves 6

ingredients as Sponge Cake on pages 126 and 127
1 teaspoon grated lemon rind

for the topping
675 g/1½ lb small strawberries
150 ml/¼ pint double cream
50 g/2 oz caster sugar

Add the lemon rind when whisking the eggs and sugar then make and bake as the instructions on pages 126 and 127. Allow to cool.

Make about 225 g/8 oz of the strawberries into a purée. Whip the cream until stiff then blend with the strawberry purée and sugar. Spoon on top of the Sponge Cake and leave for 1 hour to stand. Top with the remaining whole strawberries.

CHESTNUT GÂTEAU

Serves 6–8

450 g/1 lb unsweetened chestnut purée, fresh or canned, see page 20
1 tablespoon Kirsch
¼ teaspoon vanilla essence
3 large eggs
225 g/8 oz caster sugar

for the filling and topping
300 ml/½ pint double cream
75 g/3 oz plain chocolate
1 tablespoon Kirsch
50 g/2 oz icing sugar

Grease and flour, or line, an 18 cm/7 inch cake tin. Blend the chestnut purée, Kirsch and vanilla essence. Beat well until well blended. Separate the eggs, beat the yolks and sugar into the chestnut mixture. Finally whisk the egg whites until stiff, fold into the rest of the cake ingredients. Spoon into the prepared tin.

Bake in the centre of a very moderate oven, 160°C, 325°F, Gas Mark 3 for 50 minutes or firm to the touch. Allow to cool in the tin.

When cold, split the cake to make three layers. Whip the cream; grate the chocolate and fold into the cream together with the Kirsch. Sift the icing sugar, fold three-quarters into the cream mixture. Sandwich the layers together with some of the cream, then coat the sides and top of the gâteau with the remainder of the mixture.

Shake the rest of the icing sugar over the top of the cake. Keep gâteau cool in refrigerator before serving.

TUTTI-FRUITTI TORTE

Makes a 23 cm/9 inch cake

4 large eggs
150 g/5 oz caster sugar
25 g/1 oz dates, weight without stones
25 g/1 oz dried figs
25 g/1 oz unblanched almonds
15 g/½ oz mixed candied peel
50 g/2 oz plain chocolate
85 g/3 oz self-raising flour or plain flour with ¾ teaspoon baking powder
25 g/1 oz seedless raisins

If possible use a 23 cm/9 inch cake tin with a loose base or a spring form tin, see pages 25–29, line the bottom of the tin with well-greased greaseproof paper or 'non-stick' silicone parchment. Grease and flour the sides of the tin.

Separate the eggs, beat the egg yolks and 110 g/4 oz caster sugar until thick and creamy, as described on page 127. Chop the dates, figs, almonds and peel very finely; grate the chocolate. Sift the flour, or flour and baking powder. Fold all the ingredients, except the egg whites, into the thickened egg yolks and sugar. Whisk the egg whites until stiff, fold into the cake mixture. Spoon gently and carefully into the prepared tin.

Bake in the centre of a slow oven, 150°C, 300°F, Gas Mark 2 for 50 minutes to 1 hour until firm to the touch. Allow to cool in the tin for 3–4 minutes then turn out carefully and allow to cool. Top with the remaining caster sugar.

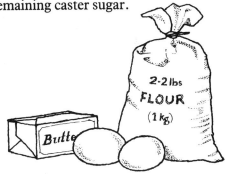

135

DOBOS TORTE

Makes a 21.5–24 cm/8½–9½ inch cake

This caramel-topped rich layer cake should be made with the whisked Sponge mixture baked in wafer-thin layers, as described under Genoese Pastry on page 132.

I rather prefer the gâteau made with Genoese Pastry because it is rather firmer yet more moist. If the thought of baking in this less usual way bothers you, make a deep cake and cut it into layers; this will give softer layers than the real recipe, but it is very pleasant.

for the cake
Sponge Cake mixture made with 4 large eggs, 150 g/5 oz caster sugar, 110 g/4 oz self-raising or plain flour with 1 teaspoon baking powder, see page 126, or Genoese Pastry on page 132 made with 4 large eggs, etc.

for the caramel topping
175 g/6 oz caster sugar

for the filling and coating
175 g/6 oz plain chocolate
2 egg yolks
175 g/6 oz icing sugar
175 g/6 oz unsalted butter
50 g/2 oz blanched almonds or pistachio nuts

Bake the wafer-thin slices of Sponge Cake or Genoese Pastry, allow to cool. Put in layers with greaseproof paper between each layer. The rounds of sponge or pastry will require neatening at the edges, so place a deep tin of the right size over the pile and cut away the edges (some people like to cut each layer after it has been baked, but the method above gives complete uniformity). If possible keep overnight with a light weight on the tin.

Place one layer of sponge on to a flat surface. Put the sugar into a strong saucepan, stir over a low heat until dissolved, then allow to heat, without stirring, until a deep golden caramel. Immediately pour over the sponge, spread evenly with an oiled knife. Dip a sharp knife in hot water, shake dry but use while hot; mark caramel into eight sections. Allow to cool.

Break the chocolate into pieces, put in a basin over hot water and allow to melt. Whisk in the egg yolks and continue whisking for 2–3 minutes, remove from the heat and whisk as the mixture cools.

Sift the icing sugar into a bowl, add the butter, beat well until soft and light; gradually beat in the chocolate mixture. Sandwich all the layers together with nearly three-quarters of the chocolate mixture; place the caramel layer carefully on top of the other layers.

Coat the sides of the gâteau with the rest of the chocolate mixture. Chop the almonds or pistachios finely and press against the chocolate coating.

To Coat with Nuts: When making a cake like the Dobos Torte, press the nuts against the sides of the cake with a palette knife. When coating firm-textured cakes, put the chopped nuts on to a sheet of paper, roll the cake like a hoop in the nuts.

Green pistachio nuts are expensive and are sometimes difficult to obtain. Blanched chopped almonds or desiccated coconut can be tinted to take the place of pistachios. Put a few drops of green food colouring on to a plate. Add the nuts or coconut, blend with the colouring; leave in the air until dry, so the colour does not run.

SPONGE SANDWICHES

The Master Recipe on pages 126 and 127 gives directions for baking the whisked sponge in one deep tin.

You can bake the mixture on page 126,

based on 3 large eggs, etc. in two 18–20 cm/7–8 inch tins, place above the centre of a moderate oven, 190°C, 375°F, Gas Mark 5 for 12–15 minutes or until firm to the touch.

A sponge made with 2 large eggs, 85 g/3 oz caster sugar and 50 g/2 oz flour should be baked in two 15–18 cm/6–7 inch tins for 10–12 minutes.

A large sponge made with 4 large eggs, 150 g/5 oz caster sugar and 110 g/4 oz flour should be baked in two 20–23 cm/8–9 inch tins for 15–18 minutes. If your oven tends to be rather hot then you may like to use a slightly cooler setting, i.e. 180°C, 350°F, Gas Mark 4 for these larger sponges, for they should not be allowed to become too brown.

Read the comments about the use of plain or self-raising flour on page 126. The sponges can be filled and decorated as an alternative to the Victoria Sandwich mixture, see pages 74–79.

SPONGE FLAN

This special tin is essential.

use 1 large egg, 40 g/1½ oz caster sugar, 25 g/1 oz flour and scant 15 g/½ oz melted butter for a 16.5–18 cm/6½–7 inch flan and double these amounts for a 20–23 cm/8–9 inch flan tin

Grease and flour the tin well. Make the sponge as the Master Recipe on page 126 and 127. Pour into the prepared tin, make sure it is evenly spread. Bake above the centre of a moderate oven, 190°C, 375°F, Gas Mark 5 for 8–12 minutes depending on size or until firm to the touch. Cool for 2–3 minutes, turn out carefully, allow to cool. Fill with fruit, as page 207.

PRALINE SPONGE

The crispness of praline makes an excellent contrast to any sponge. You can fill the sponge with cream and some of the crushed praline, and decorate it on top with more cream and crushed praline.

To Make Praline: Put 100 g/4 oz caster sugar and 100 g/4 oz blanched whole almonds into a frying pan or saucepan. Stir over a low heat until the sugar melts, then allow to cook, without stirring, until a rich golden. Pour out on to an oiled surface and leave until cold and set. Crush with a wooden rolling pin. This is enough to decorate a large sponge.

ROSY APPLE FLAN

Serves 4–6

ingredients as 20–23 cm/8–9 inch Sponge Flan, left

for the filling and topping
2 large cooking apples
2 tablespoons Calvados or apple juice
50 g/2 oz sugar
150 ml/¼ pint double cream
2 tablespoons water
4 tablespoons apple jelly
3 rosy dessert apples

Make and bake the flan as left. Peel and thinly slice the cooking apples, simmer with the Calvados and sugar until a thick purée. Allow both flan and apple purée to cool. Whip the cream, blend half with the apple purée, put into the flan.

Heat the water and jelly in a frying pan until the jelly has melted. Slice and core, but do not peel, the dessert apples. Poach for 2–3 minutes only in the jelly mixture. Lift out, drain, cool and arrange on the purée; top with remaining cream.

AUSTRIAN COFFEE GÂTEAU

Serves 6

**ingredients as Genoese Pastry on page
    132, made with 3 eggs, etc.**
150 ml/¼ pint strong coffee
**2 tablespoons Tia Maria or rum or
    brandy**
150 ml/¼ pint double cream

Bake the Genoese Pastry in a 20 cm/8 inch
tin, as described on page 132. Turn out
carefully; prick with a fine knitting needle
while still warm. The cake should be
placed on a wire cooling tray with a plate
underneath to catch all drips.

Blend the cold coffee with the Tia Maria
or rum or brandy. Pour slowly and carefully over the hot cake. Allow to cool.
Whip the cream and pipe over cake top.

RUM AND CHOCOLATE GÂTEAU

Illustrated in colour on page 125

Serves 6–8

**Ingredients as the Sponge on page 126,
    baked in 2 tins, as page 137**

to fill and decorate
300 ml/½ pint double cream
1½ tablespoons sifted icing sugar
2 teaspoons rum
6 small chocolate flake bars

Make the sponges, allow to cool. Whip the
cream, fold in the sugar and rum. Sandwich the sponges with a little cream (a
little grated chocolate or crumbled flake
bar may be added to this cream filling);
spread a thin layer over the top of the
gâteau. Use the remaining cream to pipe
over half the top of the gâteau (as shown in
the photograph). Halve the flake bars, use
these to cover the remaining half of the
gâteau.

138

YOGURT CAKES

Makes 14

100 g/4 oz butter
4 large eggs
225 g/8 oz caster sugar
**300 g/10 oz self-raising flour or plain
    flour with 2½ teaspoons baking
    powder**
¼ teaspoon bicarbonate of soda
250 ml/8 fl oz natural yogurt

for the syrup
**100 g/4 oz granulated or caster
    sugar**
150 ml/¼ pint water
strip lemon rind
5 cm/2 inch cinnamon stick

to decorate
50 g/2 oz flaked almonds

Grease and flour, or line, an oblong tin
measuring 28 × 18 cm/11 × 7 inches.
Melt the butter, allow to cool. Separate
the eggs; whisk the egg yolks and caster
sugar until thick and creamy, add the
butter gradually and blend. Sift the flour,
or flour and baking powder, with the
bicarbonate of soda, fold into the egg and
butter mixture with the yogurt. Whisk the
egg whites until stiff, fold gently and carefully into the cake mixture. Pour into the
prepared tin.

Bake in the centre of a moderate oven,
180–190°C, 350–375°F, Gas Mark 4–5 for
approximately 35 minutes or until firm to
the touch. Allow the cake to cool in the tin.
Turn out when cold and place the cake on
a dish.

To make the syrup, put all the ingredients into a saucepan; stir until the sugar
has dissolved then boil rapidly until a
slightly thickened mixture. Strain and
spoon carefully and evenly over the cake.
Toast the almonds lightly under the grill.
Sprinkle them over the cake then cut into
fingers to serve.

SACHERTORTE

Makes a 23 cm/9 inch cake

**150 g/5 oz plain chocolate
1 tablespoon water
150 g/5 oz butter or margarine
150 g/5 oz icing sugar
5 large eggs
150 g/5 oz self-raising or plain flour with
    1 scant teaspoon baking powder
1 egg white**

to fill and coat
**3–6 tablespoons apricot jam, see
    method
175 g/6 oz plain chocolate
1 tablespoon water
2 drops olive oil**

Unless the 23 cm/9 inch cake tin is the non-stick type, it is advisable to line the bottom and sides with greaseproof paper, see page 32. Lightly grease the paper. If using a 'non-stick' tin, grease this lightly but do not flour.

Break the chocolate for the cake into pieces, put into a large mixing bowl, add the water. Put over a pan of hot water or into a microwave cooker and allow to melt, do not overheat. Leave the chocolate until cool then add the butter or margarine and beat.

Sift the icing sugar, spoon all but about 25 g/1 oz into the chocolate and butter mixture, cream until soft and light. Separate the eggs, gradually beat the yolks into the creamed chocolate mixture, take care not to add too rapidly otherwise the mixture will curdle, if there are any signs of this happening beat in 1–2 tablespoons of the flour. Sift the flour or flour and baking powder; whisk the 6 egg whites until stiff, but not dry and crumbly, fold the last 25 g/1 oz icing sugar into the egg whites. Add the flour and egg whites alternately to the chocolate mixture, do this slowly and carefully, so the light texture of the egg whites is retained. Spoon into the prepared tin.

Bake in the centre of a slow oven, 150°C, 300°F, Gas Mark 2 for 50–60 minutes or until firm to the touch. Allow the light cake to cool in the tin for 2–3 minutes then turn out carefully and remove the paper. Allow to cool.

There is no need to split the cake as it is so rich and light without a jam filling, but it can be split and sandwiched with jam. Sieve the apricot jam, use 3 tablespoons to sandwich the two layers together. Spread the top of the cake with 3 tablespoons jam. Break the chocolate for the icing into pieces, put into a basin, add the water and oil and melt over a pan of hot water or in a microwave cooker. Spoon over the jam and allow to set.

CHOCOLATE FRUIT GÂTEAU

Makes a 23 cm/9 inch cake

Make and bake the Sachertorte. Prepare a generous 300 ml/½ pint very thick sweetened fruit purée – apple or apricot is particularly suitable. Whip 300 ml/½ pint double cream; grate 50 g/2 oz plain chocolate. Blend 25 g/1 oz sifted icing sugar to the cream plus 1 tablespoon apricot brandy or Calvados.

Split the chocolate cake to give three layers. Spread the first layer with apple jelly or sieved apricot jam, then a third of the fruit purée and 2–3 tablespoons whipped cream. Put on the second layer of cake, spread with jelly or jam, the second third of the fruit purée and a little whipped cream. Place on the final layer of cake, spread with jam or jelly and the remaining fruit purée. Pile or pipe the cream over the top of the cake and cover this with the grated chocolate.

It is advisable to prepare the gâteau some little time before serving, so the flavours have a chance to blend.

BATTER

I have included a Yorkshire Pudding and other recipes based upon a batter in this book, for I probably have more questions about how to make a perfect Yorkshire Pudding than anything else, except perhaps a sponge and a Christmas Cake.

YORKSHIRE PUDDING

Recipes for Yorkshire Pudding are quite standard, so I have come to the conclusion that failures lie almost entirely in the wrong baking technique.

Serves 4–6

for the batter
110 g/4 oz plain or strong flour
good pinch salt
1 egg and scant 300 ml/½ pint milk or 2
    eggs and scant 300 ml/½ pint milk
    less 2 tablespoons
25 g/1 oz fat

It is important not to use self-raising flour, or add any baking powder. If you do the pudding becomes more solid in texture. Plain flour or strong flour – the type used for making bread – are both excellent. A batter made with strong flour may rise a trifle more drastically but will be less delicate in texture than one made with plain flour.

Sift the flour and salt into a mixing bowl. Beat in the egg or eggs and the liquid. Some people like to use milk and water, rather than all milk, but that will make little, if any, difference to the way the pudding rises. Keep the batter in a cool place.

The beef will be cooking in the oven, but before cooking the batter you must raise the temperature. If worried that the meat will over-cook take it out for a time (obviously you must calculate the total cooking time accordingly). Raise the oven heat to hot to very hot, 220–230°C, 425–450°F, Gas Mark 7–8. Put the fat into the Yorkshire Pudding tin; heat for at least 5 minutes. Give the batter a final whisk, the flour tends to settle at the bottom of the liquid; pour into the very hot fat. Cook the pudding towards the top of the very hot oven for 15 minutes or until well-risen. Reduce the heat to moderately hot, 200°C, 400°F, Gas Mark 6 for a further 15–20 minutes until the pudding is firm and golden coloured. Serve at once.

Note: Individual puddings take about 15 minutes; heat a little fat in 8–9 deep patty tins, pour in the batter. Cook for 12–15 minutes, reduce the heat slightly after 10 minutes if well-risen.

RECIPES BASED ON YORKSHIRE PUDDING

The following are based upon the same method of cooking a whisked batter as in the Yorkshire Pudding.

Toad in the Hole: Heat the fat in a tin or ovenproof dish, as temperature in Yorkshire Pudding. Add 8 sausages or small cutlets of lamb; cook in the centre of the oven, for 5–10 minutes until just changing colour, then add the batter. Cook for about 10–15 minutes in the centre of the hot to very hot oven; reduce the heat to moderately hot for a further 15–20 minutes.

Norfolk Pudding: Heat 25 g/1 oz butter or margarine in an ovenproof shallow casserole, temperature as in Yorkshire Pudding. Peel and thinly slice 3 medium cooking apples, add to the hot fat with 50 g/2 oz sultanas, cover and cook for 5 minutes in the centre of the oven. Add the batter. Bake in the centre of the hot to very hot oven for 15 minutes; reduce the heat to moderately hot for a further 15–20 minutes. Top with sugar before serving.

SOUFFLÉS

I have included soufflés in the whisking section of this book for the essence of a perfect soufflé lies in its light texture.

This is produced by using a well-balanced recipe, in which the sauce or purée or basic mixture is well-flavoured and not too stiff, by whisking the egg whites until they stand in peaks in the mixing bowl and then folding them gently and carefully into the other ingredients. Never make the mistake of whisking the egg whites until they are as stiff as when making meringues, if you do you help to produce a dry soufflé.

Do not over-bake a savoury or sweet soufflé, it should be well risen, firm on the outside but pleasantly moist in the centre.

BASIC SWEET SOUFFLÉ

Serves 4

15 g/½ oz cornflour
150 ml/¼ pint milk
3 tablespoons double cream
50 g/2 oz caster sugar
15 g/½ oz butter
flavouring, see below
3 eggs
1–2 egg whites

Grease a 15–18 cm/6–7 inch soufflé dish. Blend the cornflour with the milk, pour into a large saucepan, stir over a low heat until a thickened sauce. Add the cream, sugar, butter and flavouring, see right.

Separate the eggs, beat the yolks into the hot panada (thick sauce). Whisk the whites until stiff, fold gently into the other ingredients. Spoon into the prepared soufflé dish.

Bake in the centre of a moderate to moderately hot oven, 190–200°C, 375–400°F Gas Mark 5–6 for about 30 minutes; a sweet soufflé should always be slightly soft in the centre. Serve at once. The soufflé can be topped with sifted icing sugar or served with a hot fruit purée or hot jam.

Flavourings: Almond, vanilla or other essences can be added, use up to 1 teaspoon. Liqueurs give a delicious flavour. Use a fruit purée instead of the milk.

Chocolate Soufflé: Add 25 g/1 oz cocoa or 50 g/2 oz chocolate powder to the cornflour (*illustrated in colour on page 125*).

CHEESE SOUFFLÉ

Serves 2–4

25 g/1 oz butter or margarine
25 g/1 oz flour
150 ml/¼ pint milk
2–3 tablespoons double cream
100 g/4 oz Gruyère or other cooking
    cheese
3 eggs
salt and pepper
1–2 egg whites

Grease the soufflé dish, see left. Heat the butter or margarine in a large saucepan, stir in the flour and cook gently for 2–3 minutes; gradually blend in the milk and cream. Stir as the sauce comes to the boil and thickens. If you like a firm texture to a soufflé, omit the cream. Grate the cheese. Separate the eggs, beat the yolks, then the cheese into the sauce, do not cook again. Add salt and pepper to taste.

Whisk all the egg whites until just stiff, fold into the other ingredients. Spoon into the prepared soufflé dish and bake as the recipe left.

Flavourings

Use flaked cooked fish or chopped shellfish instead of cheese; flavour the sauce with chopped herbs; add chopped chicken or ham or breast of game.

Vegetable Soufflé: Use a spinach or other vegetable purée instead of the milk.

141

SAVOY FINGER SOUFFLÉ

Serves 4

100 g/4 oz Savoy sponge finger biscuits
2 tablespoons sweet sherry
50 g/2 oz sultanas
25 g/1 oz glacé cherries
25 g/1 oz angelica or glacé pineapple
**   (optional)**
300 ml/½ pint milk
4 eggs
75 g/3 oz caster sugar

Lightly grease an 18 cm/7 inch soufflé dish. Crush the biscuits, put into a basin, add the sherry and sultanas. Chop the cherries and the angelica or pineapple, stir into the biscuit mixture. Warm the milk; separate the eggs. Whisk the yolks with the sugar, add the warm, but not too hot, milk. Pour over the biscuit mixture, mix well and allow to stand for 30 minutes. Whisk the egg whites until stiff, fold into the other ingredients then spoon into the soufflé dish.

Bake in the centre of a moderate oven, 180°C, 350°F, Gas Mark 4 for 35–40 minutes or until well-risen and firm to the touch. Serve at once.

LUXURY BREAD PUDDING

This is quite unlike an ordinary bread pudding for it has a soufflé texture.

Serves 4

ingredients as Savoy Finger Soufflé, but use 175 g/6 oz soft fine bread, brioche or plain cake crumbs, instead of Savoy Fingers

Grease the soufflé dish with 15 g/½ oz butter, sprinkle 25 g/1 oz of the crumbs over this.

Follow directions for the recipe above, using the remaining 150 g/5 oz crumbs.

Serve hot with heated lemon curd or jam.

Modern baking methods

In a Microwave Cooker

I would not choose to cook any of the whisked recipes in this section in any other way than by the conventional method of baking in an oven, but if you are in a hurry you can 'bake' either the Master Recipe on pages 126 and 127 or the Genoese Pastry on page 132 in a microwave cooker.

The mixtures rise very well, in fact the advice given on page 104 to use a container larger in diameter than if baking in the oven is particularly important for these very light textured mixtures. During the early stages of cooking the mixture rises so dramatically that it will certainly spill over the container if insufficient depth is allowed. After this stage it does 'settle down', but still rises well.

The reason I am not enthusiastic about microwave cooking of these mixtures is that some of the delicate texture is lost; also, of course, the sponge lacks the attractive appearance of oven baking. This can be camouflaged by decorating the top of the sponge. It also is so very easy to overcook by ½ to 1 minute and in so doing to loose the moist texture and toughen the sponge.

If you do decide to 'bake' in the microwave cooker, the Master Recipe on pages 126 and 127 takes 8–10 minutes at full heat or the stage just below this if possible. As the cooking time is not a great deal less than when cooking the mixture in a conventional oven, I do not choose a microwave for this purpose.

Line the container with clingfilm to avoid sticking, this is better for these sponges than greased greaseproof paper.

Do not use the crock-pot, pressure cooker or table cooker for the cakes in this section, the results will be very disappointing.

Storing

A whisked Sponge Cake keeps well for only a day unless it has a very moist filling and is put in a covered container in the refrigerator. Genoese Pastry keeps for a slightly longer period but even so it is not the kind of cake that is meant to be kept for prolonged periods.

The very thin layers as used in the Dobos Torte do keep well because they have become almost biscuit-like in texture.

Basically cakes in this section should be frozen for long term storage.

If a sponge cake has become dry it could be used as a Tipsy Cake or filled with fruit, plus a little syrup or alcohol; allow to stand so the sponge is softened.

Freezing

It may seem strange to say that the texture of a whisked Sponge Cake and Genoese Pastry are improved by freezing but the cakes seem to have a rather more moist texture and increased flavour. Even when making a plain sponge, it is advisable to open-freeze this since the delicate top of the cake can be spoilt if it comes in contact with a lid or covering. It is no longer delicate when frozen and can be wrapped easily.

Sponges filled with fruit and cream become very moist in freezing which most people like. If you want the texture to be drier, then freeze the sponge only and fill after defrosted. Separate the layers with sheets of greaseproof paper or wax or silicone (non-stick) paper.

A Swiss Roll freezes well, but the sugary outside does become slightly damp. Allow to defrost then coat with more sugar.

PROBLEM SOLVING

Whisked mixture should be light and delicate in texture.

Q. *What causes a sponge or Genoese Pastry to be close and slightly tough?*
A. Insufficient whisking of the eggs and sugar; adding the flour or flour and butter too roughly; baking too slowly; see pages 126, 127 and 132.
Quick Remedy: Serve the sponge as a Fruit Gâteau, see page 134, or in one of the other ways suggested on that page. The moist fillings and toppings counteract the less than perfect texture.

Q. *Why does a whisked sponge fail to rise well?*
A. For the reasons given above. Beginners are advised to use some raising agent in the mixture, see page 13.
Quick Remedy: Follow the suggestions given above, or continue baking slowly to make an unusual biscuit.

Q. *What causes a Swiss Roll to crack?*
A. Overbaking, test the sponge in plenty of time, see page 130; too dry a mixture, it should flow from the spoon like a thick cream.
To save the day, if you feel you may have overbaked the sponge, place a damp warm teacloth under the sugared paper. The warmth and moisture comes through the sugared paper and softens the sponge. It is advisable to cut off the crisp edges before trying to roll it.
Quick Remedy: Top the rolled cracked sponge with lots of icing sugar or with whipped cream and decorate with fruit.

Q. *Is it an advantage to add a little melted butter to the sponge mixture?*
A. Yes, this helps to keep it moist. Make quite sure the melted butter is not too hot and fold it into the sponge very gently and carefully, see page 129.

143

CHAPTER 6

Fillings, Frostings & Decorations

The term 'filling' covers a wide variety of recipes, from simple and adaptable butter icings to unusual blendings of fruits, nuts and mixtures based upon cream and preserves. Choose the filling carefully, wisely; delicate-textured sponges need a light filling whereas less fragile cakes or pastries blend with richer mixtures.

Interesting frostings, also called icings, can turn a cake into an artistic, as well as a delicious, creation.

There are many ways in which cakes can be decorated, some of the most delightful being moulded from icing, as shown on page 151.

THE SECRETS OF SUCCESSFUL ICING

Icing a cake takes both time and practice, but with reasonable practice you will achieve a high standard.
The first step towards a professional looking cake is to select the right icing; each icing recipe includes information as to the kind of cake it is suitable for.
Check that the cake is well-shaped, and prepared carefully for icing and decorating; there is advice about this under the first basic recipes.
Follow the advice about preparing the various types of frosting; be particularly careful to see any mixture is smooth and the correct consistency or texture. If using a cooked frosting, check the ingredients are heated to the correct temperature.
Always allow time for basic coatings to set before adding the final decorations or piping on the cake.

Simple Celebration Cakes – showing how Glacé and Butter Icing (recipe pages 146 and 147) can turn large and small plain cakes into special delicacies (see page 162)

GLACÉ ICING

This icing is often called 'Water Icing' for the basic icing is made with water. Although it is recommended that the icing sugar is sifted, tiny soft lumps do come out if the moist icing is left to stand for a short time.

The amount given would make a fairly thin covering over an 18–19 cm/7–7½ inch cake or about 18 small cakes.

150 g/5 oz icing sugar
approx. 1¼ tablespoons warm water
flavouring, see below

Sift the icing sugar into a basin. Gradually beat in the water. In some cases you need a stiff consistency but the above produces an icing that is easily spread over the cake(s).

For a very glossy icing, heat the sifted sugar and water in a saucepan gently for 1 minute beating well.

FLAVOURINGS
The quantities are for the icing given above.

Almond Glacé Icing: Add a few drops of almond essence to the icing.
Chocolate Glacé Icing: Sift 2 teaspoons cocoa or 1 tablespoon chocolate powder with the icing sugar or melt 50 g/2 oz plain chocolate in a basin over hot water. Sift in the icing sugar and beat well then add 1–2 teaspoons warm water.
Coffee Glacé Icing: Use very strong coffee instead of water.
Lemon or Orange or other Fruit (raspberry etc): Use strained fresh fruit juice instead of water.
Liqueur: Use liqueur instead of water.

TO COAT A CAKE WITH GLACÉ ICING

Follow the stages 3–5 under Royal Icing, page 149. The icing will be softer and

146

easier to spread. Do however make sure the icing is not too soft in texture, otherwise it will run off the top and sides of the cake.

To coat small cakes, see page 133.

FEATHERING

This is the one icing where the piping is done immediately after the ground work is put on so you have the right effect.

Coat the cake with one colour, then pipe lines in a different one.

Using a fine skewer, draw across lines towards you while they are still wet. Then draw the skewer across again, working in the opposite direction and in between the first lines.

Melted chocolate could be used instead of icing for the lines.

CRISP CHOCOLATE ICING

This is enough to coat the outside of a large Swiss Roll or give a good layer on the top of a 23–25 cm/9–10 inch cake. It is less rich than a true butter icing and is an icing that children enjoy. It sets into a pleasantly crisp icing and should be spread over the cake.

225 g/8 oz icing sugar
1 egg white
50 g/2 oz sweetened chocolate powder
50 g/2 oz butter or margarine

Sift the icing sugar. Beat the egg white until frothy and add the icing sugar. Beat until smooth then add the chocolate powder, mix well. Cream the butter or margarine until very soft then blend with the chocolate icing.

BUTTER ICING

Soft butter icing uses equal quantities of butter and icing sugar. If you would like a slightly more crisp icing use 50% more icing sugar than butter.

Butter icing can be used as a coating or a filling. It is excellent as an icing for piping.

The amount given would make a fairly thin layer of filling or topping for an 18 cm/ 7 inch cake.

50 g/2 oz butter
75 g/3 oz icing sugar
flavouring, see below

Cream the butter until soft. Sift the sugar into the butter and beat until soft and light. Add desired flavouring.

To coat top and sides and have one layer of filling you need 175 g/6 oz butter etc. or slightly more if coating a deep cake. Piping needs extra Butter Icing. A piped border of Butter Icing would use the amount given above.

FLAVOURINGS

Caramel Butter Icing: Make a caramel as under Dobos Torte, page 136. When golden caramel, blend in 4 tablespoons water, heat until blended. Make the butter icing as above then gradually blend in 2 tablespoons caramel.

Chocolate Butter Icing: Sift in ½–1 tablespoon cocoa or 1–2 tablespoons chocolate powder after creaming the butter and sugar. If preferred melt 50 g/2 oz plain chocolate, cool and blend with the icing.

Coconut Butter Icing: Blend 25 g/1 oz desiccated coconut with the butter icing plus a few drops of water or milk.

Coffee Butter Icing: Beat in 1–2 teaspoons coffee essence or blend 1 teaspoon instant coffee powder with 2 teaspoons hot milk or water, cool and add gradually to the butter icing.

Lemon or Orange Butter Icing: Add 1–2 teaspoons very finely grated fruit rind when creaming the butter and sugar. Add 2 teaspoons juice or increase icing sugar to 100 g/4 oz and use more juice.

Rum or other alcohol: Use a few drops of rum or other essence or a little real alcohol. If necessary increase the amount of icing sugar to compensate for the extra liquid.

Vanilla Butter Icing: Add a few drops essence or use vanilla flavoured icing sugar, see page 18.

GROUND ALMOND BUTTER ICING

75 g/3 oz ground almonds
100 g/4 oz icing sugar
50 g/2 oz butter
few drops almond essence

Spread the ground almonds on to a baking tray and brown in a moderate oven 180°C, 350°F, Gas Mark 4 for about 5 minutes, do not allow to become too dark. Allow to cool.

Sift the icing sugar into a mixing bowl; add the butter and essence and cream well. Stir the browned ground almonds into the creamed mixture.

CHOCOLATE FUDGE ICING

ingredients as Butter Icing
75 g/3 oz plain chocolate

Make the Butter Icing as above. Break the chocolate into pieces. Put into a basin, place over a pan of hot water and allow to melt; cool and blend with the Butter Icing. This rich icing is ideal for firm sponges.

MARZIPAN OR ALMOND PASTE

This uncooked icing makes a good coating for a rich fruit cake. It adds flavour and an excellent foundation for the top icing.

The proportions below are the usual ones for this uncooked icing, which is also known as Almond Paste. As you see you use exactly the same amount of sugar as ground almonds.

110 g/4 oz icing sugar
110 g/4 oz caster sugar
225 g/8 oz ground almonds
few drops almond essence
2 egg yolks

Sift the icing sugar into a mixing bowl, add the other ingredients. Mix well with a knife and then gather the icing together with your finger-tips. It should be a firm rolling consistency. If too dry add a little more egg yolk to bind or use a squeeze of lemon juice or a few drops of sherry.

You can make a whiter marzipan with egg whites only and a sweeter icing by increasing the amount of icing sugar by 50 g/2 oz, naturally this means you need extra liquid.

Take time and trouble to coat a cake with marzipan for if this is put on well, you will have a better foundation for the icing.

TO COAT A CAKE WITH MARZIPAN

1 Make sure the cake is quite level on top, if not either turn it upside down or cut away a thin layer. Brush away any loose crumbs from the cake.

2 Measure the diameter of the top of the cake then measure around the cake to ascertain the length of the band, use a tape measure or string. Measure cake depth.

3 Use about two thirds of the marzipan to coat the sides of the cake. Dust the working surface with caster or sifted icing sugar, roll out the marzipan to give a band of the desired measurements, you may prefer to make two shorter bands rather than one long one.

4 Coat the sides of the cake only with a little sieved apricot jam or unbeaten egg white, this makes certain the marzipan will adhere to the cake.

5 Hold a round cake like a hoop and roll along the band of marzipan; with a square or oblong shape you press the band against the sides of the cake.

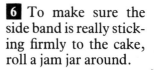

6 To make sure the side band is really sticking firmly to the cake, roll a jam jar around.

7 Coat the top of the cake with sieved apricot jam. Roll out the remaining marzipan to a round or square to fit the top of the cake. Support this over the sugared rolling pin and lay it on top of the cake.

8 Seal the join between the sides and top coating then roll the top smooth.

Most people find it better to leave the marzipan layer to dry out in the air for 48 hours before coating the cake with icing: oil from the ground almonds could soak into the icing and spoil its colour.

The disadvantage about this is that the marzipan tends to become hard. If you like soft marzipan then learn to handle the marzipan icing quickly and deftly, this decreases the possibility of oil seeping out. Lightly paint the marzipan with egg white, to form a seal, before icing.

ROYAL ICING

Royal Icing is a firm icing and is suitable for rich fruit cakes, but not for light sponges. It is the ideal icing for wedding cakes for it is sufficiently firm to support the pillars of the various tiers. See also Australian Icing, page 151.

450 g/1 lb icing sugar
2 egg whites
½–1 tablespoons lemon juice
1 teaspoon glycerine (optional)

Sift the icing sugar very thoroughly. Beat the egg whites until just frothy, do not overbeat. Add a little icing sugar, mix well then add the remaining sugar and juice.

Beat with a wooden spoon steadily for about 10 minutes or until the icing is just glossy and very white.

If using an electric mixer, beat steadily for a few minutes; overbeating creates air bubbles in the icing which makes it difficult to obtain a perfect coating and would also prove troublesome when the icing is used for piping. Finally add the glycerine.
Note: The glycerine helps to prevent the icing becoming over-hard.

Always keep the bowl of Royal Icing covered with a damp cloth or damp kitchen paper until ready to use.

Details about coating cakes, piping and the amount of Royal Icing to use for the various sized cakes are on pages 97 and 150, and below.

TO COAT A CAKE WITH ROYAL ICING

1 Make the icing as the recipe, put a little dab in the centre of the cake board 'to anchor' the cake. Place the cake on the cake board then onto an icing turntable. If this is not available use an upturned mixing bowl. The advantage of a turntable or mixing bowl is that you can turn this round and coat the cake easily and evenly.

2 Put all the icing for coating on the top of the cake, spread with a palette knife to completely coat the cake. At this stage do not try and neaten any part of the icing, concentrate on coating the cake with an even amount of the icing. Work the icing in a 'paddling' movement to avoid or remove any small bubbles of air.

3 Take the palette knife or, better still, an icing ruler.
Neaten the top of the cake by drawing the knife or ruler across the icing at an angle of about 30°.

4 Neaten the sides of the icing with the knife or ruler held upright. Never pat the icing if you want a completely smooth coat.

If putting on two coats of icing allow the first coat to dry completely, i.e. for 24–36 hours, before putting on the second coat.

5 Before putting on a second coat – check that the first coat of icing is absolutely smooth. If there are any tiny 'bumps' of uneven icing, rub these down with the finest sandpaper available.

Repeat stages 1–5 again; the second coat can be a little thinner. So if you make up the same amount of Royal Icing, you will have a little left over for a limited amount of piping.

EQUIPMENT FOR PIPING

You need a piping bag in which to put the icing pipe. Nowadays there are excellent cotton or man-made bags which wash well, or you can make a bag with greaseproof paper. To make this bag, see below: Cut a square of greaseproof paper, folded to give a triangle – you could cut this to work with a single layer.

1 Take hold of the top right hand corner and roll the points until they all meet.
2 Secure firmly by folding points inwards.
3 Cut a tiny piece from the base of the triangular bag; drop in the pipe.

If using a fabric bag for a small pipe you can obtain a screw band upon which the selected pipe can be secured.

You also need selected pipes such as:
Writing pipe: Hold the bag with the pipe like a pen so you get an even flow of icing. You can then pipe greetings or 'feathering' (page 146).

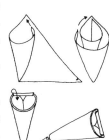

Rose or star pipe: Gives pattern as shown. To make an upright rosette or star hold the bag upright, press down gently and firmly on to the surface of the cake – until shape is formed, then sharply lift up bag, giving a perfect shape.
To make a border design, hold the bag at the angle given when using a writing pipe.

You also need an icing ruler or long palette knife, see page 149. If making Australian Icing you need a long rolling pin.
A turntable is an excellent investment.

Good Icing and Piping

Good piping depends upon practise and the willingness to take sufficient time on this rewarding skill.

Firstly coat the cake carefully, see page 149. Allow the icing to become dry and firm before piping.

Have the icing bag only half-filled; gently press the icing down to the base of the bag. If using a paper bag, fold the top paper over the icing.

Always use the pipe slowly and steadily, so ensuring an even flow of icing.

CRÈME PÂTISSIÈRE

If well made this mixture can be used for piping as well as for a filling.

This is sufficient to fill a large flan or cake or use as a filling and topping on an 18–19 cm/7–7½ inch sponge.

1 *level* tablespoon cornflour
150 ml/¼ pint milk
1–2 teaspoons sugar
few drops vanilla essence
2 egg yolks
up to 150 ml/¼ pint double cream

Blend the cornflour with the milk. Pour into a saucepan, add the sugar and essence and stir over a low heat until thickened and smooth. Remove from the heat. Whisk the egg yolks, blend with the cornflour mixture then return to the heat and cook very slowly. Allow the mixture to cool, but stir frequently to prevent a skin forming.

Whip the cream, the amount used depends upon personal taste. Fold into the cold cornflour mixture.
Note: This icing can be delicately flavoured with almond essence or a very little liqueur. Add this carefully after the cornflour mixture has thickened and cooled.

AUSTRALIAN ICING

This icing is sufficient to coat a 23 cm/9 inch round or 20 cm/8 inch square cake. It can be put over marzipan instead of Royal Icing.

2 tablespoons water
4 level teaspoons gelatine
3½ teaspoons glycerine
100 g/4 oz glucose
900 g/2 lb icing sugar

Put the water into a good-sized basin or mixing bowl, stand over a saucepan of hot water. Sprinkle the gelatine on top of the water, leave until softened, blend with the water then allow to dissolve. Add the glycerine and glucose. Heat together until blended then gradually sift in the icing sugar and blend with the other ingredients. Knead and use as below.
Note: Instead of water use all lemon juice. The icing can be tinted as required.

TO COAT A CAKE WITH AUSTRALIAN ICING

1 Make the icing as the recipe and knead well until very smooth. Form into the required shape, i.e. a ball for a round cake, a square for a square cake.

2 Sift icing sugar over the rolling pin and working surface. Roll out the icing to a size sufficiently large to cover top and sides of the cake. Put a little dab of Royal Icing or Glacé Icing in the centre of the cake board.

3 Lift the cake on to the cake board and place this on to the turntable or upturned mixing bowl. Support the icing over the rolling pin and lower this over the cake. Gently pull the icing to give a completely smooth coating.

4 Press against the cake with your hands, then pass the rolling pin firmly over the top of the cake.
Roll around the sides of the cake carefully with a jam jar.

5 Carefully cut away the surplus icing from the base of the cake with a sharp knife. Place the extra icing in a polythene bag, so that it keeps sufficiently moist to use for moulding, see below.

The cake is now ready to decorate.

MOULDING AUSTRALIAN ICING

Take tiny pieces of the icing, dust your fingers with sifted icing sugar and press out the icing until paper thin; as an example of moulding this is how you make a rose, but every kind of flower or figure can be moulded.

1 Form the centre of the rose with folded icing then make petal shapes and wrap around the centre part. Continue like this until the complete rose is formed. Allow to harden.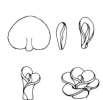

2 To make a flat petalled flower, lay the petals over one another, they can be stuck together at the centre with a little Royal or Glacé Icing. To finish pipe the centre or make a small ball of a different coloured icing.

AMERICAN FROSTING

This is a soft coating icing; it can be swept up in peaks for Christmas Cake or used on sponges.

This amount is sufficient for a thin coating over a 13–15 cm/5–6 inch cake or the top of an 18 cm/7 inch cake.

175 g/6 oz granulated or caster sugar
4 tablespoons water
1 egg white
pinch cream of tartar

Put the sugar and water into a strong saucepan, stir over a low heat until the sugar has dissolved then allow to boil without stirring until the mixture forms a soft ball when tested in cold water, i.e. 114.5°C/238°F.

While the sugar is heating, whisk the egg white until very stiff. Beat the syrup until slightly cloudy, add the cream of tartar and pour on to the egg white in a steady stream, beating all the time.

Cool slightly then spread on top or over the top and sides of the cake.

Note: For a slightly crisper icing use 225 g/8 oz sugar and boil to 115.5°C/240°F.

The icing can be flavoured by using a little orange or lemon juice or coffee instead of all water. Vanilla or almond essence can be added to the syrup.

COOKED FONDANT

This icing can take the place of Marzipan or Royal Icing or it can be used to coat delicate cakes. It keeps well, and has a pleasant shine.

This is sufficient to coat a 15–18 cm/6–7 inch cake.

225 g/8 oz granulated or caster sugar
4½ tablespoons water
pinch cream of tartar

It also can be used for moulding, but it is not as good for this purpose as Australian Icing.

Put the sugar and 4 tablespoons water into a strong saucepan, stir until the sugar has dissolved, add cream of tartar then boil until mixture reaches 115.5°C, 240°F, i.e. it forms a soft ball when tested in cold water. Beat until slightly cloudy then turn on to a board, work with a knife and then knead until smooth. If you need a softer fondant for coating little cakes, add the extra ½ tablespoon water and blend with the fondant.

To make a soft flowing consistency again place the fondant in a basin, heat gently over hot water then pour over cake.

COOKED MARZIPAN

ingredients as Cooked Fondant
1 egg white
100–175 g/4–6 oz ground almonds
few drops almond essence

Make the Cooked Fondant, allow to become cloudy. Whisk the egg white until frothy; add the ground almonds and almond essence. Blend with the fondant. Knead with a little sifted icing sugar.

Use as Marzipan.

FUDGE ICING

This is enough to make a filling and topping for an 18–19 cm/7–7½ inch sponge.

Put 225 g/8 oz granulated sugar, 3 tablespoons milk, 25 g/1 oz butter, little vanilla essence and 150 ml/¼ pint full cream sweetened condensed milk into a strong saucepan, stir until the sugar has dissolved. Boil to 114.5°C/238°F, stirring frequently, then beat until cloudy. Spread over the cake while still warm.

INTERESTING FILLINGS

In addition to the particular fillings given in recipes, you will find the fillings on this page add interest to cakes. The kind of cake or pastry for which the filling is suitable is given in each recipe.

CRÈME CHANTILLY

This is the name given to whipped and flavoured cream. Whipping cream makes a good topping and filling for cakes, but double cream a firmer one. This flavoured cream is excellent for piping.

Whip the cream until it just stands in peaks, do not over-whip; it is very easy to do this if using an electric mixer. Gradually fold in the sugar and vanilla.

Allow up to 2 teaspoons sugar and ¼ teaspoon vanilla essence to each 150 ml/¼ pint cream or use vanilla flavoured sugar. **Note:** If cream is over-whipped it curdles (separates). If this appears to be happening gently fold in a very little milk, this may restore the cream to a smooth texture.

CRISP JAM FILLING

This filling can be used in any sponge. It is sufficient for an 18–20 cm/7–8 inch cake. It is also a good filling for baked jam tartlets.

75 g/3 oz sweet biscuits
3 tablespoons jam
25 g/1 oz butter

Crush the biscuits in a blender or with a rolling pin, blend with the jam and butter.

HONEY FILLING

This butter and honey filling is excellent in plain or lemon flavoured sponges. It is sufficient for a 16–18 cm/6–7 inch cake.

2 tablespoons thick honey
50 g/2 oz butter
½ teaspoon grated lemon rind
2 teaspoons lemon juice

In a bowl, cream the thick honey, softened butter, grated lemon rind and juice together.

LEMON FILLING

This filling is excellent in a Swiss Roll or sponge. It is sufficient to fill the Swiss Roll on page 130 or a 20–23 cm/8–9 inch sponge cake.

75 g/3 oz sweet biscuits
2 lemons
50 g/2 oz butter or margarine
50 g/2 oz caster sugar
1 egg yolk

Crush the biscuits, grate the top rind from the lemons, be careful to take only the top yellow 'zest'. Halve the fruit and squeeze out 2 tablespoons juice. Put the butter or margarine, lemon juice and rind, and sugar into a saucepan. Stir over a gentle heat until the butter or margarine has dissolved, then add the biscuit crumbs. Continue heating until the mixture is thick and smooth. Take the pan off the heat, add the egg yolk, mix well then return the pan to the heat and cook very slowly for several minutes. Allow to cool before using.

Peanut Butter Fillings

Peanut butter can be used in the Honey Filling or in the Butter Icings on page 147. It does not melt in the same way as ordinary butter, so is not suitable for cooked icings but is excellent in uncooked fillings; although it does have a very distinctive taste.

JELLY GLAZE

This is not only excellent as a glaze over fruit in a flan, but to use instead of icing on top of a sponge. It is sufficient for the top of an 18 cm/7 inch sponge.

1 teaspoon arrowroot
3 tablespoons water
4 tablespoons apple or redcurrant jelly

Blend the arrowroot with the water. Put into the saucepan with the jelly. Stir over a very low heat until the jelly has dissolved and the mixture is thick and clear. Allow to cool slightly before using.

JAM GLAZE

Follow the recipe for Jelly Glaze, above, but use jam instead. Measure the jam after sieving this. The most suitable jams are apricot, raspberry or strawberry.

REDCURRANT FROSTING

This icing is excellent on delicate sponges; enough to top a 16–18 cm/6–7 inch sponge.

1 egg white
3 tablespoons redcurrant jelly
1 tablespoon water

Whisk the egg white until stiff. Heat the jelly with the water until the jelly has dissolved and the mixture is boiling. Pour steadily on to the egg white, beating well as you do so. Allow to cool slightly. Spread on top of the sponge, sweep up in peaks.

JAM FROSTING

Follow the recipe for Redcurrant Frosting, above, but use jam instead. Measure the jam after sieving this. The most suit-

able jams are apricot, damson, raspberry or strawberry.

Cashew and Brazil Nuts in Fillings
Although almonds are the general favourite for fillings followed by walnuts, do not disregard the delicious flavour of cashews or Brazils. Chop and add these to Butter Icing, page 147, to the Crème Pâtissière on page 150 or to whipped cream.

Modern Methods of Icing
A modern mixer or food processor is useful when making Royal Icing but, as instructed on page 149, over-beating can spoil the icing by creating too many air bubbles, so time carefully.

Cooked icings can be heated in a microwave cooker, but in view of the fact there is such a brief period when they are at the right temperature, I feel it is easier to do this on top of a cooker.

Storing

Icings are generally stored as part of the cake or gâteaux. Glacé Icing does not store well, that is why it is better to put this on cakes that will be eaten quickly. It cracks after about 2 days.

Royal Icing stores well but tends to harden with keeping. If you have made a large quantity of Royal Icing, to coat the cake and then for piping, you must cover the bowl with damp kitchen paper or a cloth, see page 149. Australian Icing does not harden a great deal with storage; it always remains sufficiently soft to cut easily.

Butter Icing stores well but does become crisp and harder.

Cream-filled cakes must be eaten when freshly prepared.

Freezing

Soft type icings freeze better than crisp hard ones, that is why Butter Icing is a good choice. You will find a selection of variations on this basic Icing, page 147. Make the icing a little softer than usual for a filling, if the cake is to be frozen.

Whipped cream freezes better than cartons of cream, so cakes filled and decorated with whipped cream freeze well. Soft fillings in this section freeze well.

It is unlikely you will want to freeze rich cakes topped with Royal or Australian Icing.

Open-freeze decorated cakes, so the topping is not spoiled, then pack. Remove from the packing to defrost so the decoration is not spoiled.

PROBLEM SOLVING

Icings are only really successful if the right consistency is achieved and the mixture handled correctly. If the icing does not seem quite right, read below before putting it on a cake.

Q. *I am never sure which icings can be used for piping on a cake?*
A. You can only use Glacé Icing, recipe on page 146, for piping lines, so it can be used for writing a name or a greeting, or feathering, see page 146, or a simple trellis or line design, little dots or similar purposes. Royal and Butter Icings are the icings to select for piping other shapes. You also can use whipped cream on light sponges and desserts and savoury butters on cocktail savouries.

Q. *How can I stop Royal Icing becoming too hard?*
A. By adding glycerine, see recipe on page 149, and by using a little water.

Q. *Unlike most people I love a very hard Royal Icing, any tips please?*
A. Omit any glycerine; be generous with the lemon juice and add a pinch of cream of tartar.

Q. *I hate the hardness of Royal Icing even when glycerine is used, but I need to coat a three tier rich Wedding Cake, what could I use instead. Could I coat it with Glacé Icing?*
A. No. Glacé Icing is not sufficiently firm to hold the pillars on a Wedding Cake, use the Australian Icing on page 151. American Frosting could be used, but this does not give a beautifully flat surface, so although it is ideal for the snow effect on a Christmas Cake, it is not suitable for the elegance of a Wedding Cake.

Q. *My family hates Marzipan; can I successfully omit this when coating a Christmas Cake?*
A. Yes, if you use two thick layers of Royal Icing or a thick layer of Australian Icing, recipes on pages 149 and 151, or coat the cake with Glacé Icing, allow this to dry then coat with the beautifully light American Frosting, page 152 – an excellent alternative.

Q. *I like to fill sponges with whipped cream, rather than icing; why does this curdle when whisked in my electric mixer?*
A. For the same reason it will curdle if over-whipped by hand; it has been over-beaten. Watch carefully as the cream begins to thicken and use the slowest speed possible.
Quick Remedy: If you catch the cream as it just starts to curdle, you often can rectify this by gently folding in a little milk.

Q. *Why does my white Royal Icing on our Christmas Cake become a horrid yellow colour after a time?*
A. Because the oil from the ground almonds used in Marzipan has seeped through the icing: read the advice on page 148 about handling this icing and the delay necessary before coating the cake with Royal Icing.

155

CHAPTER 7

Celebration Cakes

Birthdays, Christmas, Weddings and many other occasions mean a celebration cake. There is a particular pleasure and sense of achievement in cooking for any special festival.

In other chapters there are a wide variety of cake recipes ranging from the simple to the more elaborate. In the pages that follow are ideas to make the cakes interesting and suitable for *your* special occasion.

I have not specified which cake to select for all the easy suggestions can be carried out with a variety of recipes.

HAPPY CELEBRATIONS

A festive occasion needs an appreciable amount of preparation; so try and make the celebration cake ahead, so you have time for other tasks.

You will find advice on freezing various kinds of cake in each section of this book, for example if you are making a whisked sponge cake for a young child's celebration there is no need to make it at the eleventh hour, it freezes perfectly, see page 143. On the other hand rich fruit cakes need baking well ahead to mature in flavour.

Celebration cakes are not necessarily elaborately decorated; it is more important to create an appropriate and interesting looking cake that reflects the occasion, or special interest of the child or adult(s) for whom the occasion is planned.

A modern three-tier wedding cake – combining piping, lacework and beautiful delicate moulded flowers (see page 162)

NOVELTY CAKES FOR BIRTHDAYS

It is possible to buy a variety of small figures to put on cakes. These range from skaters and skiers, ideal for a Christmas, as well as a birthday cake, to dancers, footballers, etc.

Children love a cake that reflects their hobby or personal interest.

The cake mixture can be the type you know is popular, ranging from a rich fruit cake to a light sponge. Not all children like fruit cakes, the Victoria Sandwich is a safe choice. A range of icings are given in the previous chapter.

TAKE A ROUND CAKE

A round cake can be decorated in the usual manner, or as:

A Maypole

Stand a stick of barley sugar or a knitting needle in the centre of the cake, attach narrow pretty ribbons to this, then wind the ends around tiny dolls or characters – each little child can have one.

A Roundabout

Cut a circle of stiff coloured paper or cardboard, a little larger than the cake, make a slit in this as shown; fold to make a conical shape. Support this on a long knitting needle, push the pointed end into the cake. Arrange tiny cars or motor bikes around the edge.

A circus ring can be made in the same way with a 'parade' of clowns, dancers and animals.

TAKE A SQUARE CAKE

A square cake can make a charming Christmas cake or several unusual birthday cakes.

A Ski Jump

Cut the square cake in half as shown to make two triangles. Place these side by side to give a thicker cake, they can be joined by jam or icing. Coat the cake with marzipan and Royal Icing or American Frosting to give a snow effect. Arrange small skiers down the slope.

The Grand Old Duke of York

Make the slope as above, cover with green or chocolate icing. Arrange tiny trees up the 'hill' and lots of soldiers. This becomes the Duke who had 'ten thousand men'.

A Corral

Coat the square cake with chocolate or green coloured icing, arrange chocolate finger biscuits all around the edge when the icing is nearly set, do not add too early otherwise they become sticky. Put cattle inside, horses and small figures outside.

A Military Fort

A military fort should be made in much the same way.

A Chess Board

Coat the cake in white icing; allow to dry, then make squares of chocolate icing or melted chocolate, as page 133, and place on top of the cake. The sides can be coated with chocolate vermicelli over the icing. Mould little figures from Australian icing or buy miniature chess pieces.

TAKE AN OBLONG CAKE

There are directions for baking sponge cakes in shallow oblong tins on pages 80 and 132. If baking another mixture in this way you will need to allow only about half the cooking time as when baked in a deep tin.

Our Street

Cover the cake in green coloured or chocolate icing. Make a second oblong, cut into rectangles and shape these to be tiny houses. Coat these with different coloured icings, make windows and a door with piping. Arrange the houses on both sides of the street. Add tiny trees, figures and one or two cars.

A Farmyard

Coat the cake with chocolate icing. Arrange tiny farm animals, one or two figures, on top of the cake. Add a lorry or tractor.

A Theatre

For this you need an oblong cake and a square cake.

Cut a slice from the oblong cake. Place this on one end of the oblong – that is the raised 'platform'. Coat this and the entire oblong with icing. Place on the cake board. Ice the square separately. Use a different colour from that used for the 'auditorium'. Place on its end on the board. Allow all icing to dry. You then are ready to use a different coloured icing for drawn-back 'curtains'; to place trees or other 'scenery' against the backing and figures on the stage.

The 'audience' can be made with moulded icing or tiny biscuits or you can buy more little dolls or other figures. Make seats from squares of chocolate.

A Football Pitch or Rugby Field or Tennis Court or Cricket Pitch

Ice the cake and coat the top with green coloured coconut, as page 136.

Pipe any special lines needed to make the top like a real pitch or court on top. Buy the relevant figures. You may be able to buy the goal posts or tennis net, but these are not difficult to make with fine net and cocktail sticks, fine knitting needles or chocolate stick sweets.

159

CHRISTMAS CAKE

There is no need to use elaborate piping on a Christmas Cake, page 93. The swept-up snow effect, with colourful ornaments, is ideal.  American Frosting, page 152, can be used for a soft icing, or Royal Icing, page 149, is generally chosen. Cover the cake fairly thickly with icing; take the blade of a knife and sweep up the icing as shown.

TAKE A LOAF CAKE

A cake baked in a loaf tin can be transformed into a variety of interesting cakes for parties.

A Country Cottage

It can be a little house, complete with a garden, made on the cake board with green icing and little moulded plants. You will need to emphasise the sloping roof, either by shaping the top of the loaf or building up to a slope with marzipan. Coat the 'roof' in one colour and the rest of the 'house' in a second colour. Pipe in the windows, doors and any climbing 'flowers' up the sides of the cottage. You could have a moulded roof and windows in marzipan or icing if preferred.

A Camping Tent

Shape the loaf cake, as before, coat in icing. Make the 'canvas' of the 'tent' with very thin pieces of Australian Icing or Marzipan, pages 151 and 148, which can be tinted any colour you like. The front 'tent' pole can be a knitting needle.

Coat the cake board with coloured chopped almonds or coconut, as page 136, to look like grass.

VALENTINE CAKE

Obviously the cake must be heart-shaped; you can obtain heart-shaped tins quite easily, but you could bake an oblong sponge and cut the heart out of this.

A light sponge is ideal, for it enables you to use Glacé Icing, page 146, with Butter Icing, page 147, for the piping. You will find the Master Recipe for the Victoria Sandwich on pages 66 and 67 gives just the right amount for the average heart-shaped tin. As the mixture is spread over a slightly larger area, giving a more shallow cake, shorten the baking time given on page 67 slightly.

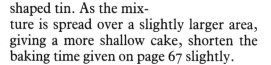

A Simnel Cake

For details and recipe see page 92.

WEDDING CAKES

The traditional British Wedding Cake is generally made from two or three tiers of rich fruit cake, as pages 92–97, coated with Marzipan and Royal Icing or the more modern Australian Icing and decorated with piping, then topped with figures or real or artificial flowers in a small holder.

The second and third tiers are mounted on pillars, easily obtainable from shops selling wedding cake decorations.

If having a small party, one large cake will be sufficient. You will find more about wedding cakes on pages 96–97.

If you do not like a rich fruit cake then you can use an idea from France or America.

Most American wedding cakes are based upon a sponge or other light mixture, there are plenty of recipes in this book. The cakes should have a difference of about 5 cm/2 inches in diameter if you are having several tiers.

Ice the cakes, but use a soft icing, like American Frosting, page 152, or you could coat them in the Australian Icing, page 151. They are then put one on the other, without pillars, and decorated with piping, crystallised violet or rose petals, silver balls. The French cake invariably has the figures of a bride and groom on top.

An American wedding cake (Bride's Cake) sometimes has a rich fruit top tier and light second and third tiers – an excellent idea to cater for all tastes.

CHRISTENING CAKES

A Christening Cake can be made from a rich fruit mixture coated with marzipan and Royal Icing, but if small children will be among the family party it is a good idea to plan to have a light sponge as well as the richer cake, or instead of this. The traditional cake is topped with a stork figure.

The appealing little crib cake shown is easily made. Use a Victoria Sandwich mixture, the Master Recipe on pages 66 and 67 would be ideal for a small party, but use a bigger quantity if desired, see page 73. Bake in an oval pie dish or casserole, depending on the size required. As the mixture

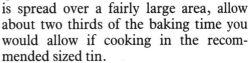

is spread over a fairly large area, allow about two thirds of the baking time you would allow if cooking in the recommended sized tin.

When cooked coat in white icing, or use pale pink for a girl and pale blue for a boy. The frilled surround is easily made. Use a single or double layer of patterned doilies, attach the edging around the sides of the 'crib', then place some over the top. Decorate with piping and ribbon.

161

SIMPLE CELEBRATION CAKES

The picture on page 145 shows how icing can turn plain cakes into special delicacies. The icing used is Butter Icing, page 147, plus a little Glacé Icing, page 146.

The plate of small cakes shows:
a) Round cakes – the sides coated with sieved jam and desiccated coconut. A halved canned peach on top of each cake with a border of Butter Icing.
b) Small cup cakes – a circle cut from each and Butter Icing spread over the cake, the circle replaced and the cakes given a border of Coffee Butter Icing.
c) Butterfly cakes – made as page 84.
d) Small cakes – with Glacé Icing.
e) Cup cakes – topped with jam and a lattice design in Glacé Icing.

The Round Cake
The cake on the right was coated on the sides with Chocolate Butter Icing. You can either pipe the lines around, using a large writing pipe, or completely coat the cake and make the lines with a fine skewer.

The top was decorated in alternate sections of piped Coffee and Chocolate Butter Icing. Complete the cake with a border around the top and base of the Chocolate Butter Icing.

The Oblong Cake
Pipe Coffee Butter Icing around the sides of the cake; spread the top with a thin layer of the icing; complete with piped borders as shown. Make Brandy Snaps as page 176. Pipe Coffee Butter Icing into each end of the Brandy Snaps. Place on top of the cake just before serving.

Cherry Topped Round Cake
Coat the sides of the cake with Butter Icing and browned flaked almonds. Make a little Glacé Icing, spread over the top of the cake. Put a glacé cherry and angelica in the centre of the cake. Finally pipe a border of Butter Icing around the edge.

A MODERN WEDDING CAKE

Illustrated in colour on page 157

While traditional methods of icing are excellent, there has been a change in the way special occasion cakes are decorated. The modern trend is away from elaborate piping and towards the use of delicate moulded flower decoration.

The three tier wedding cake, illustrated on page 157, shows how beautiful this can be.

The cake mixture was baked in three flower-shaped tins. The slight deviation from round tins does not change the baking time. Follow the advice given on pages 96 and 97 for baking round rich cakes.

Coat the cakes with marzipan and then with Australian Icing, page 151. In Britain it is possible to buy this type of icing ready prepared so all you have to do is to handle the icing as described on page 151.

The tiny flowers were moulded from the same icing, which was tinted to give variety of colour and then put on to the cake. Use a very little Royal Icing on the back of each flower to make it adhere to the cake.

The piping round the edges of the cakes was done in Royal Icing, see page 150. The illustration below shows the particular pattern used in the lacework.

The technique of this is to pipe each tiny individual piece of lacework on to a flat surface, allow it to set and then very carefully lift it off and attach it to the cake with more Royal Icing.

To make the lacework, use a oo and/or a o writing pipe.

The delicate piping was also done with a very fine writing pipe with tinted Royal Icing.

SCOTS BUN

Makes an 18 cm/7 inch cake

for the pastry
225 g/8 oz plain flour
½ teaspoon baking powder
pinch salt
120 g/4½ oz butter or margarine
25 g/1 oz caster sugar
water to bind

for the filling
450 g/1 lb currants
225 g/8 oz seedless raisins
225 g/8 oz sultanas
100 g/4 oz mixed candied peel
100 g/4 oz blanched almonds
100 g/4 oz moist brown sugar
175 g/6 oz plain flour
½ teaspoon ground ginger
1 teaspoon mixed spice
½ teaspoon ground cinnamon
½ teaspoon bicarbonate of soda
½ teaspoon cream of tartar
1 egg
4 tablespoons milk

to glaze
1 egg yolk
½ teaspoon water

Grease an 18 cm/7 inch round cake tin. Sift the flour, baking powder and salt into a mixing bowl. Rub in the butter or margarine, add the sugar and sufficient water to make a firm rolling consistency. Roll out very thinly, cut the dough into two 18 cm/7 inch rounds and a band the depth of the tin.

Put the first round into the tin, damp the edges, then put in the band of pastry and turn in a little to make a good join at the base. Seal the pastry joins very firmly.

Blend the dried fruits together, chop the peel and almonds, add to fruit together with the sugar. Sift the flour with the three spices, bicarbonate of soda and cream of tartar into the fruit mixture, then add the egg and milk and mix thoroughly. Spoon into the pastry lined tin; spread quite flat.

Damp the edges of the final pastry round, turn in a little of the band of pastry, place the round in position and seal the edges.

Beat the egg yolk and water, brush over the pastry; then prick the pastry in a neat design with a fine skewer.

Place in the centre of a very moderate oven, 160°C, 325°F, Gas Mark 3 for 1 hour, then reduce the heat to slow, 150°C, 300°F, Gas Mark 2 for a further 1½ hours. Allow to cool in the tin then turn out carefully. Store in an airtight tin.

This cake is traditionally served at Hogmanay (New Year).

GARLAND CAKE

A Garland Cake is a Norwegian speciality.

Grind 300 g/10 oz unblanched almonds, blend with 300 g/10 oz sifted icing sugar, grind again, add 2 tablespoons plain flour and bind with 2 egg whites. Rest for 24 hours.

Roll into finger-thick sausages on a surface dusted with icing sugar, the longest 14 cm/5½ inches diminishing gradually to 2 cm/¾ inch. Form into rings and place on baking trays; bake in a hot oven, 220°C, 425°F, Gas Mark 7 for 7 minutes. Cool and assemble as the illustration. Decorate with lines of Glacé Icing, see page 146. Top with suitable ornaments for the occasion, such as flags or sweets.

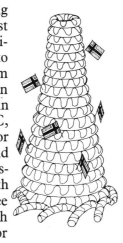

CHAPTER 8

Meringues, Biscuits & Cookies

Crisp light meringues are both versatile and practical. You can vary the flavour of meringue in many ways, the basic recipe can be adapted and used as a topping on a variety of desserts and even on savoury dishes too, as the recipes on page 168 demonstrate.

Meringues, and most biscuits, can be stored for a considerable time so that they make a good stand-by, see page 179.

Over the years I have had almost more questions about making meringues than about any other individual recipe. I hope you will find the answers to any problems in the pages that follow.

Home-made biscuits and cookies, which are very similar to biscuits, are made in a variety of ways, so that the information given under the Master Recipes in Chapters 2–5 will be helpful.

SUCCESSFUL MERINGUES, BISCUITS AND COOKIES

The term 'meringue' refers to a mixture of egg whites and sugar; although you can prepare a savoury egg white mixture as page 168. The most familiar method of making meringues is in the Master Recipe that follows.

There are however, less usual ways of blending egg whites and sugar, known as Meringue Cuite and Italian Meringue, page 168. There is no Master Recipe for a biscuit dough, since so many different principles are involved, but good biscuits and cookies (similar to biscuits) depend upon the following points:

Keep the dough as dry as possible, do not add more liquid than stated in the recipe; if the dough seems too dry and crumbly, knead it well. Most biscuits should be baked fairly slowly. Cool on the baking tray as instructed because biscuits are fragile when warm.

Biscuits made by the creaming method – Lemon Shortbread Fans (recipe page 173), Golden Peanut Biscuits (recipe page 172)

MERINGUES

As explained on page 164, a meringue can be the basis of many delicious recipes.

Baking Utensils: A lightly oiled baking tray or a tray lined with oiled paper or with silicone ('non-stick') paper.

Oven Setting: Generally as low as possible, see under 'Baking'.

Oven Position: Centre or below centre of the oven unless using a fan-assisted electric oven when any position can be used.

Cooking Time: See under 'Baking' or as recipe.

For quantity see below

2 egg whites
either 110 g/4 oz caster sugar or 50 g/2 oz
icing sugar and 60 g/2 oz caster sugar
flavouring, see page 167

These amounts will make 12 medium meringue shells or 24 small or finger meringues or about 60 tiny meringues (ideal for small children) or two 15 cm/6 inch rounds.

CERTAIN SUCCESS

Choice of Ingredients: Do not use very fresh egg whites; it is better to choose eggs that are at least 24 hours old. Left-over egg whites, that have been kept in a covered container in the refrigerator, are good. You can use a mixture of sugars or all caster sugar for the standard meringues. The inclusion of icing sugar gives a firmer mixture. Lovers of natural (unrefined) sugar will be pleased to know you can make meringues using natural light brown sugar. Variations of flavourings etc. are given on page 167.

Handling the Mixture: If whisking the egg whites by hand, stand near a draught. Make quite sure the mixing bowl is dry, clean and free from grease; ensure that no specks of egg yolk are with the whites; if they are, remove with the corner of a damp teacloth or a little egg shell. Whisk egg whites until stiff, see under 'Consistency'.

Three ways of incorporating the sugar:
a) As step 2, i.e. whisk in half the sugar; fold in the remainder – this is the usual and highly recommended method.
b) Gradually fold in all the sugar, this gives a more delicate meringue.
c) Whisk all the time, as the sugar is added gradually, this is successful with an electric mixer and gives a very firm type of meringue.

Consistency: The egg whites should be stiff when completely whisked, but not dry and crumbly – a sign of over-whisking. You should be able to turn the mixing bowl upside down, without the whisked whites falling out.

When the sugar has been added the mixture should still be stiff and firm, if 'watery' it is a sign that you have over-handled the mixture.

Preparing Tins: This is very important. If using a silicone ('non-stick') baking tray or paper on the baking tray do not use oil. If using an ordinary baking tray, brush with just a few drops of oil or place greaseproof paper on the tray and brush this with oil.

Baking: Although the temperature is so low you must allow adequate time to preheat the oven at the correct setting. Use the very coolest setting for crisp meringues, i.e. 90–110°C, 200–225°F, Gas Mark O–¼ whichever is possible on your cooker or slightly hotter 110–120°C, 225–250°F, Gas Mark ¼–½ for meringues that are slightly sticky inside. Allow 1–1¼ hours for baby meringues, 2–3 hours for larger ones. If using the slightly hotter oven, the shorter cooking time should be sufficient.

1 Prepare the baking tray as page 166. Separate the eggs, put the whites into the bowl. Use either a rotary whisk or an electric whisk and beat until stiff. See under 'Consistency' page 166.

2 Gradually whisk in half the sugar, then fold in the remainder, see under 'Handling the Mixture' page 166.

3 Fill a tablespoon with the mixture. Now take a second spoon, scoop the mixture out of the first spoon on to the baking tray in a rolling movement, this produces a good shape. The spoon used for shaping the meringues depends upon the size required.

4 It is easier to pipe the meringue mixture into the required shapes. Fit a 5 mm/¼ inch plain or rose pipe into a large piping bag, spoon in the mixture.

5 To make meringue shells, pipe into rounds. To make fingers, pipe even-sized lengths. To make Meringue Nests, pipe à small round base of mixture, then pipe a circle of the mixture around the base giving small flan shapes. Meringue Cuite, page 168, can be used for this.

6 Bake the meringues as directed on page 166 until quite firm. You can tell if small meringues are cooked: they should lift from the baking tray or paper quite easily. Allow to cool and store in an airtight tin. If the meringues seem cooked but appear to be 'sticking', dip a palette knife in very hot water, pat dry, but use while warm; slip under each meringue.

For Meringue Gâteaux, cut rounds of silicone ('non-stick') paper or oiled greaseproof paper. Spread or pipe the meringue over the paper and bake as the Master Recipe.

FLAVOURING MERINGUES

The quantities are based upon the Master Recipe on page 166, using 2 egg whites. Dry ingredients should be blended with the sugar before this is added to the egg whites.

Chocolate Meringues: Use 2–3 teaspoons sifted cocoa or 4–6 teaspoons chocolate powder.

Coconut Meringues: Prepare meringue mixture, then add 50 g/2 oz desiccated coconut, bake as usual.

Coffee Meringues: Use 1½ teaspoons instant coffee powder.

Vanilla Meringues: Blend a few drops of vanilla essence with the whisked egg whites or use all vanilla flavoured caster sugar, see page 18, instead of ordinary sugar.

NUT MERINGUES

50 g/2 oz blanched almonds, Brazils, hazelnuts or walnuts
ingredients as Master Recipe on page 166

Chop the nuts very finely; moist Brazils should be left in the air for several hours to dry out. Prepare the meringue mixture, add the nuts then bake as small meringues or as a Meringue Gâteau.

Using modern equipment

A MIXER FOR MERINGUES

An electric mixer is excellent for whisking egg whites. Use a high speed for this. Change to slow speed and gradually whisk in half the sugar, then fold in the remainder by hand. If preferred use method c), as detailed on page 166 under 'Handling the Mixture' and add all the sugar with the mixer on slow speed.

A FOOD PROCESSOR FOR MERINGUES

The comments made on page 128 about using a food processor for whisking apply when making meringues. Check that the food processor manufacturer has designed the machine to whisk egg whites. You will, I am afraid, find it quite difficult to incorporate the sugar with the cutting knife in position, this should be removed and the sugar blended in by hand.

NEW WAYS OF MAKING MERINGUE

Both the following methods of preparing a meringue mean that the mixture is partially cooked, so it is ideal for a topping where the baking time is short, such as in a Lemon Meringue Pie or Alaska.

Use caster sugar in either recipe.

Meringue Cuite: Use the ingredients as in the Master Recipe on page 166. Put the unwhisked egg whites and sugar into an ovenproof glass or a copper basin. Stand over hot, but not boiling, water; whisk until thick and fluffy. This is excellent piped as tiny meringues, Meringue Nests; bake as usual.

Do not use as a Pavlova or Vacherin.

Italian Meringue: Use the proportions as the Master Recipe on page 166, but allow 1 tablespoon water to each 25 g/1 oz sugar.

Put the sugar and water into a strong pan, stir until the sugar has dissolved, then allow to boil, without stirring, until it reaches 127°C/260°F, or it forms a hard ball when tested in cold water. Meanwhile whisk the egg whites until very stiff, pour the hot sugar mixture on to the egg whites, whisking all the time. Whisk until cold. Bake as a topping or use uncooked as a filling.

Filling Meringues

Fill meringues just before serving. Small meringues or rounds of meringue can be sandwiched together with whipped cream, Crème Chantilly, Crème Pâtissière or Butter Icing, see pages 153, 150 and 147.

Meringues Glacés means that the small shells are sandwiched together with ice cream. You can top them with whipped cream if desired.

Meringue Nests, page 167, can be filled as above and topped with fruit or grated chocolate.

CHEESE MERINGUE

Whisk the egg white(s) as said on page 167, add a little salt and pepper, then fold in 25 g/1 oz finely grated cheese to each egg white. Parmesan cheese is best since it is dry in texture. This mixture is not suitable for baking as ordinary meringues, but it makes a delicious topping on a savoury base, such as a fish or Shepherd's pie, instead of pastry or mashed potato. Make sure the base is very hot, cover with the meringue and just brown in a moderate oven, 180–190°C, 350–375°F, Gas Mark 4–5 for 10–15 minutes.

The nicest way to cook the mixture is to fry it as a hot savoury. Heat a pan of oil until very hot, 190°C/375°F. Drop in 12–15 small spoonfuls of the mixture and fry for 1–2 minutes, drain on absorbent paper and serve while hot.

MERINGUE GÂTEAUX

Follow the Master Recipe, pages 166–167.

Chamonix: These are small individual gâteaux. Flavour the Master Recipe with vanilla, pipe into 10–12 rounds and bake as meringue shells. When cold top with sweetened chestnut purée, see page 20, whipped cream and grated chocolate.

Nut Gâteau: This is nicer if baked for a short time in a very moderate oven. Make two 20–23 cm/8–9 inch rounds of silicone ('non-stick') or oiled greaseproof paper on baking trays or in large sandwich tins. Prepare the nut meringue using 4 egg whites etc. Bake at 160°C, 325°F, Gas Mark 3 for about 45 minutes. Remove paper while still slightly warm. When cold fill with whipped cream and soft fruit, such as raspberries. Top with more whipped cream and fruit.

Vacherin: This is similar to Pavlova, but omit the cornflour and vinegar. Bake slowly as meringues, then fill.

BAKED ALASKA

This is an impressive, yet easy dessert. Use double the quantities in the Master Recipe, or the variations or other recipes on pages 166–168. To serve 6 people you will need 4 egg whites etc.

Preheat the oven at very hot, 230–240°C, 450–475°F, Gas Mark 8–9.

Put an 18–20 cm/7–8 inch sponge round or square on an ovenproof serving dish. Moisten with a little liqueur or fruit juice then top with a block of ice cream and fruit, such as strawberries. Coat completely with meringue. Bake for 3–5 minutes only until the meringue is golden brown. Decorate with more fruit if wished and serve at once.

PAVLOVA

Serves 6

3 egg whites
¼ teaspoon vanilla essence
1 level teaspoon cornflour
175 g/6 oz caster sugar
¾ teaspoon white or brown vinegar

The inclusion of vinegar and cornflour in this recipe gives a slightly marshmallow texture to the meringue. To accentuate this, preheat the oven at 150°C, 300°F, Gas Mark 2, put in the meringue then reduce the heat to 140°C, 275°F, Gas Mark 1 after 5 minutes; bake for about 1–1¼ hours. You can bake the meringue at the usual low setting, see 'Baking' page 166 for 2–3 hours for a crisper result.

Either make two 18 cm/7 inch rounds of silicone ('non-stick') paper or lightly oiled greaseproof paper or make a single round about 20–21.5 cm/8–8½ inches in diameter, put on to the baking tray(s).

Whisk the egg whites until stiff, fold in the vanilla essence; whisk again for a few seconds. Sift the cornflour into the sugar, add to the egg whites, as given in the Master Recipe page 166. Lastly fold in the vinegar. Spoon the mixture over the two rounds or use about two-thirds to cover the one round and pipe remainder in a narrow band around base. Bake as above.

Cool on the baking tray, then remove paper. Serve freshly cooked unless making it crisp, by longer baking.

Fillings
The fillings can be varied; these should be put in just before serving. If using two rounds, sandwich together and top with whipped cream or ice cream and fruit.

If using the flan shape, fill with the cream or ice cream and fruit.

Another delicious mixture is to blend 225 g/8 oz lemon curd or thick fruit purée with 300 ml/½ pint whipped cream.

BISCUITS MADE BY RUBBING-IN METHOD

Although the advice given in Chapter 2 is helpful, you can handle the biscuit dough much more firmly than any cake mixture.

SCOTCH SHORTBREAD

Makes 8

100 g/4 oz plain flour
50 g/2 oz rice flour or ground rice or
    cornflour
100 g/4 oz butter
50 g/2 oz caster sugar

to decorate
little caster sugar

Preheat the oven well ahead so the shortbread keeps a good shape, see method.

Sift the dry ingredients into a mixing bowl. Cut the butter into pieces then rub into the flour, add the sugar. Turn out of the bowl and knead until smooth. To make the real shortbread shape, dust a wooden shortbread mould with rice flour or cornflour; press in the mixture; leave for an hour, so the shape will set. Turn carefully out on to an ungreased baking tray.

If you have no wooden mould, form the dough into a neat round about 1.5 cm/½ inch thick, flute the edges. Prick the biscuit with a fine skewer. Bake in the centre of a slow to very moderate oven, 150–160°C, 300–325°F, Gas Mark 2–3 for 35–40 minutes until firm, but still pale. Mark into 8 triangles, cool on the baking tray. Top with a little sugar.

The mixture can be made into small biscuits, roll out the dough until barely 5 mm/¼ inch thick, cut into desired shapes. Bake for 15 minutes at the higher temperature given.

PETTICOAT TAILS

This is the name given to very thin 'fan-shaped' pieces of shortbread. Make the Scotch Shortbread, but roll out until not much more than 3 mm/⅛ inch in thickness. Form into two large rounds, put on to ungreased baking trays, prick with a fine skewer, dust with a layer of caster sugar. Mark into triangles and bake for 15 minutes in a very moderate oven, as Shortbread. Carefully separate the triangles (the 'tails'), before storing.

FLAVOURING SHORTBREAD

The traditional Scotch Shortbread on this page can be flavoured in many ways, follow the recipe and bake for the same time.

Almond Shortbread: Prepare the mixture, work in 25–50 g/1–2 oz blanched chopped almonds. Top with blanched flaked almonds and a dusting of sugar.
Other nuts could be used.

Chocolate Shortbread: Omit 15 g/½ oz rice flour and add 15 g/½ oz sifted cocoa or omit 25 g/1 oz rice flour and add 25 g/1 oz chocolate powder. Add a few drops vanilla essence too.

Coconut Shortbread: Omit 25 g/1 oz rice flour, add 50 g/2 oz desiccated coconut instead and an extra 25 g/1 oz sugar.

Ginger Shortbread: Sift 1–2 teaspoons ground ginger with the flour, add 25–50 g/1–2 oz chopped crystallised ginger. Bake as Shortbread.

Pitcaithley Bannock: Prepare the mixture then work in 25 g/1 oz finely chopped candied peel and 25 g/1 oz finely chopped blanched almonds. Bake as Shortbread.

RICH CHEESE BISCUITS

Makes 24–36

110 g/4 oz plain flour
pinch salt, shake pepper, pinch dry
  mustard powder
85 g/3 oz butter
85 g/3 oz Parmesan cheese
1 egg yolk

to glaze
1 egg white

Sift the flour and seasonings into a mixing bowl. Rub in the butter. Grate the cheese very finely. Blend with the rubbed-in mixture; add the egg yolk to bind. The mixture may be too soft to handle, in which case cover and chill for a time. Use as below. Always grease the baking trays well and preheat the oven at hot 220°C, (use 210°C if your oven is fierce), 425°F, Gas Mark 7. The biscuits should be cooled on the baking trays, as brittle when hot.

Brush with egg white before baking.

Cheese Straws: Roll out the dough on a lightly floured board until 5 mm/¼ inch thick. Cut into fingers 5 mm/¼ inch wide and 6.5–8 cm/2½–3 inches long. Bake for 7–10 minutes towards the top of the oven.

Cheese Butterflies: Roll out the dough as above, cut into rounds about 3.5 cm/1½ inches in diameter, cut half the rounds down the centre. Bake as Cheese Straws. When cold spread or pipe centre of rounds with Savoury Butter, below, press the halved biscuits in position.

SAVOURY BUTTER

To make sufficient butter for the biscuits above, cream 50 g/2 oz butter with seasonings to taste. Flavour with a little anchovy essence or lemon juice and grated rind or tomato paste.

BISCUITS MADE BY CREAMING METHOD

The following recipes for biscuits are made by first creaming the fat and sugar together. However, there is no need to cream until the mixture is as light as for the cakes in Chapter 3.

SHREWSBURY BISCUITS

Makes 20–30

110 g/4 oz butter or margarine
75–110 g/3–4 oz caster or light brown
  sugar
225 g/8 oz plain flour
flavourings, see method
1 egg
little milk, if necessary

Cream together the butter or margarine and sugar, sift in the flour and mix well. Add the egg and mix again, you may find the dough binds together without any extra liquid, but if adding milk then put it in drop by drop, so you achieve a rolling consistency. Cut into the desired shapes. This is an excellent biscuit dough to cut into animal or other shapes for children. Put on to ungreased baking trays.

Bake in the centre of a very moderate oven, 160°C, 325°F, Gas Mark 3 for 15 minutes or until firm. Cool on trays.

FLAVOURINGS

Add a few drops of essence to the fat and sugar. Or add 1 teaspoon finely grated lemon or orange rind to the fat and sugar. Or omit 15–25 g/½–1 oz flour; substitute the same amount of sifted cocoa or chocolate powder.

Gingerbread Cookies: Sift 1 teaspoon ground ginger with the flour. Use dark brown sugar. Cut the dough into Gingerbread Men or other shapes. Bake as above.

171

ANZACS

Makes 18–20

110 g/4 oz butter or margarine
1 tablespoon golden syrup
110 g/4 oz caster sugar
110 g/4 oz self-raising flour or plain flour
    and 1 teaspoon baking powder
110 g/4 oz rolled oats
110 g/4 oz desiccated coconut

Cream together the butter or margarine, syrup and sugar until soft. Add the other ingredients, knead well. If necessary add a little milk to bind. Roll into 18–20 balls, put on to well greased baking trays, allowing space for the mixture to spread.

Bake in the centre of a very moderate oven, 160°C, 325°F, Gas Mark 3 for 15 minutes or until firm and golden. Allow to cool for about 10 minutes on the baking trays, then lift on to a wire cooling tray.

BUTTERSCOTCH WALNUT CRISPS

Makes 18–24

50 g/2 oz walnuts
100 g/4 oz butter or margarine
50 g/2 oz Demerara sugar
25 g/1 oz caster sugar
1 egg yolk
175 g/6 oz plain flour

Chop the walnuts very finely. Cream together the butter or margarine and sugars until soft and light. Add the egg yolk, flour and chopped walnuts. Knead the dough until no cracks remain. Roll out the dough until 5 mm/¼ inch in thickness and cut into 5 cm/2 inch rounds. Put on two lightly greased baking trays.

Bake in the centre of a very moderate oven, 160°C, 325°F, Gas Mark 3 for 10 minutes. Cool on the baking trays.

LANGUES DE CHAT

Makes 24

85 g/3 oz butter
85 g/3 oz caster sugar
3 egg whites
85 g/3 oz plain flour

The shape of these biscuits has given them their name, i.e. cats' tongues.

Cream together the butter and sugar until very soft and light. Whisk the egg whites until just frothy; do not overbeat these. Blend the egg whites into the creamed mixture. Sift the flour and fold into the other ingredients. Grease one or two baking trays. Put a 5 mm/¼ inch plain pipe into a large piping bag; spoon in the mixture. Pipe very thin 'tongues' on to the baking tray(s).

Bake towards the top of a hot oven, 220°C, 425°F, Gas Mark 7 for 5 minutes only. Allow the biscuits to cool for several minutes, then lift off the baking tray(s) with a warm palette knife. When cold, store in an airtight tin.

GOLDEN PEANUT BISCUITS

Illustrated in colour on page 165

Makes 48

150 g/5 oz smooth peanut butter
75 g/3 oz butter or margarine
200 g/7 oz natural granulated sugar, see
    Note
½ teaspoon vanilla essence
1 egg
150 g/5 oz plain flour
½ level teaspoon bicarbonate of soda

Cream together the peanut butter, butter or margarine, sugar and vanilla. Gradually beat in the egg. Sift the flour and bicarbonate of soda, add gradually to the other ingredients. Beat the mixture well; it may seem a little soft at this stage, in which case chill for a short time before handling.

Roll the mixture lightly with your finger tips to form 48 small balls. Place on two or three ungreased baking trays; allow a 5 cm/2 inch space between the balls.

Dip the prongs of a fork in flour then press the back of the fork against the biscuit dough to form parallel lines in one direction; turn the fork at right angles to make lines in the opposite direction.

Bake the biscuits in the centre of a moderate oven, 190°C, 375°F, Gas Mark 5 for 10 minutes. Remove from the oven, but allow to cool completely on the trays before removing. Store in an airtight tin.
Note: The golden colour and extra flavour of unrefined (natural) granulated sugar is a great asset in this and the next recipe. Various sugars are described on page 15.

LEMON SHORTBREAD FANS

Illustrated in colour on page 165

Makes 8

100 g/4 oz butter
65 g/2½ oz natural granulated sugar
150 g/5 oz plain flour
½ teaspoon baking powder
40 g/1½ oz rice flour or cornflour

for the topping
½–1 lemon
25 g/1 oz natural granulated sugar

Lightly grease the inside of an 18–19 cm/ 7–7½ inch fluted flan ring, place this on a greased baking tray and dust the ring and tray with a very little rice flour or corn-flour.

Cream together the butter and sugar until soft and light. Sift the flour, baking powder and rice flour or cornflour; add to the creamed ingredients. Knead the mixture well and press into the flan ring.

Rub the lemon against the coarse side of a grater, use only the top yellow 'zest'. Blend this very thoroughly with the 25 g/ 1 oz sugar then sprinkle over the top of the shortbread and press firmly into the biscuit mixture with a knife.

Bake in the centre of a very moderate oven, 160°C, 325°F, Gas Mark 3 for 45 minutes. Cool slightly then mark into eight portions. Allow to become quite cold before separating the portions. Store in an airtight tin.

VANILLA SHORTBREADS

Makes 10–18

75 g/3 oz butter
50 g/2 oz caster sugar
few drops vanilla essence
100 g/4 oz self-raising flour or plain flour with 1 teaspoon baking powder

Cream together the butter and sugar with the essence until soft. Sift in the flour or flour and baking powder. Knead lightly, roll into 10–12 medium or 16–18 small balls. Put on to two ungreased baking trays, allow room to spread in cooking.

Bake in the centre of a very moderate oven, 160°C, 325°F, Gas Mark 3 for 12–15 minutes. Cool on the baking trays.

COCONUT KISSES

Makes 10–12

ingredients as Vanilla Shortbread
approx. 5 tablespoons raspberry jam
approx. 25 g/1 oz desiccated coconut

Make the biscuit dough as above, roll the mixture into 20–24 small balls. Bake as above. Allow to cool on the baking tray. Sandwich the biscuits together with a little jam to make 10–12; coat the outsides with jam then roll in coconut.

173

OATIES

Makes 15–18

75 g/3 oz butter or margarine
25 g/1 oz caster sugar
175 g/6 oz plain wheatmeal flour
¼ teaspoon salt
50 g/2 oz rolled oats
milk to bind

Cream together the butter or margarine and sugar until soft. Sift the flour and salt into the creamed mixture, add the rolled oats then knead well. Gradually blend in enough milk to make a firm rolling consistency.

Place on a lightly floured board and roll out until 5 mm/¼ inch in thickness. Cut into 15–18 rounds. Place on lightly greased baking trays. Prick with a fork or fine skewer or knitting needle.

Bake in the centre of a very moderate oven, 160°C, 325°F, Gas Mark 3 for 15 minutes or until firm. Allow to cool for 10 minutes on the baking trays then remove on to a wire cooling tray. These biscuits are excellent with cheese.

SWEET OATCAKES

Makes 18–24

75 g/3 oz butter or margarine
50 g/2 oz caster sugar
50 g/2 oz self-raising flour or plain flour
     with ½ teaspoon baking powder
pinch salt
225 g/8 oz fine oatmeal
milk to mix

Cream together the butter or margarine and sugar. Sift the flour or, flour and baking powder, with the salt, add the oatmeal and blend with the creamed fat and sugar. Knead well and add milk to make a firm rolling consistency.

Roll out firmly on a pastry board, sprinkle with a little oatmeal until 5 mm/ ¼ inch in thickness. Cut into rounds and put on to lightly greased baking trays. Prick the biscuits with a fine skewer.

Bake in the centre of a very moderate oven, 160°C, 325°F, Gas Mark 3 for 15 minutes. Cool on the baking trays.

SHORTBREAD CRISPS

Makes 12–16

for the biscuit base
50 g/2 oz butter or margarine
25 g/1 oz caster sugar
100 g/4 oz plain flour
very little milk

for the topping
50 g/2 oz cornflakes
40 g/1½ oz butter or margarine
25 g/1 oz caster sugar
1 tablespoon golden syrup
50 g/2 oz rolled oats

Cream together the butter or margarine and sugar for the biscuit base; add the flour. Knead the mixture well, then add just enough milk to make a firm rolling consistency. Knead well, then roll out until just 5 mm/¼ inch in thickness and a neat oblong shape. Put on to an ungreased baking tray.

Crush the cornflakes until slightly smaller, this enables you to mix them more easily with the other ingredients.

Put the butter or margarine, sugar and golden syrup for the topping into a saucepan, heat gently until the butter and sugar have melted. Remove from the heat, cool for a few minutes, add the rolled oats and then the cornflakes. Spoon over the biscuit base.

Bake in the centre of a very moderate oven 160°C, 325°F, Gas Mark 3 for 20–25 minutes. Mark in fingers while still warm. Remove from the baking tray when cold.

174

AMERICAN BUTTER COOKIES

Makes 50–60

175 g/6 oz butter
175 g/6 oz caster sugar
¼ teaspoon vanilla essence
2 medium eggs
175 g/6 oz plain flour

Cream together the butter, sugar and essence until soft and light. Gradually beat in the eggs. Sift the flour into the creamed mixture. Put teaspoons of the mixture on to ungreased baking trays, flatten the small heaps of mixture with a fork.

Bake in the centre of a very moderate oven, 160°C, 325°F, Gas Mark 3 for 8–10 minutes. Cool on the baking trays.

BOURBON BISCUITS

Makes 10–12

110 g/4 oz butter or margarine
110 g/4 oz caster sugar
few drops vanilla essence
85 g/3 oz plain flour
25 g/1 oz rice flour or cornflour
50 g/2 oz chocolate powder
1 tablespoon granulated sugar

for the chocolate filling
40 g/1½ oz butter or margarine
50 g/2 oz icing sugar
2 teaspoons cocoa powder

Cream together the butter or margarine, sugar and vanilla essence. Sift together the flour, rice flour or cornflour and chocolate powder; add to the creamed mixture. Knead, add milk to bind.

Roll out the dough until 5 mm/¼ inch in thickness. Cut into 20–24 equal sized fingers, put on to ungreased baking trays. Sprinkle lightly with the granulated sugar and make several holes on top of the biscuits with a thick needle. Bake in the centre of a very moderate oven, 160°C, 325°F, Gas Mark 3 for 12 minutes or until firm. Cool on the baking tray.

Meanwhile make the butter icing by creaming the ingredients together. Sandwich the biscuits with icing.

TIGER CAKES

Makes 10

85 g/3 oz butter or margarine
25 g/1 oz caster sugar
85 g/3 oz plain flour
25 g/1 oz cornflour

to fill and decorate
150 g/5 oz icing sugar
85 g/3 oz butter or margarine
½–¾ tablespoon coffee essence
50 g/2 oz walnuts
50 g/2 oz caster sugar
2 tablespoons water

Cream together the butter or margarine and sugar; add the flour and cornflour; knead firmly. If necessary add a little milk to make a firm consistency. Roll out until a generous 5 mm/¼ inch in thickness; cut into 20 small rounds. Put on ungreased baking trays.

Bake in the centre of a moderate oven, 180°C, 350°F, Gas Mark 4 for 12–15 minutes until firm, but not too brown. Cool on the baking trays.

Sift the icing sugar, cream with the butter or margarine; add the essence. Finely chop the walnuts, put on a flat plate. Sandwich the biscuits with a little icing to give ten complete cakes. Coat the sides and top of the cakes with the remaining butter icing then with chopped nuts.

Put the sugar and water into a small strong saucepan, stir until the sugar has dissolved; boil steadily until a golden brown caramel. Spoon teaspoons of the caramel on top of each cake; allow to set.

BISCUITS MADE BY MELTING METHOD

Two of the most famous types of biscuits, given below, are made by this method. The ingredients must be weighed or measured carefully to ensure a successful result, see the suggestions for weighing syrup or treacle on page 111.

BRANDY SNAPS

Makes 12–14

50 g/2 oz plain flour less 1 teaspoon, see method
½–1 teaspoon ground ginger (optional)
50 g/2 oz butter or margarine
50 g/2 oz golden syrup
50 g/2 oz caster sugar

Grease two or three flat baking trays very well and grease the handles of two or three wooden spoons. Sift the flour and ground ginger. The mixture is a better consistency if 1 teaspoon flour is taken away from the 2 oz, there is no need to do this when using the metric measure. Put the butter or margarine, syrup and sugar into a saucepan, heat only until the ingredients have melted. Add the flour and ginger, mix well.

Put teaspoons of the mixture on the baking trays, allow about 8 cm/3 inches around each small amount of mixture. It is easier if only one tray of biscuits is put into the oven, so giving time to roll these biscuits before the next batch are cooked.

Bake in the centre of a moderate oven, 180°C, 350°F, Gas Mark 4 for 8–10 minutes or until the biscuits are uniformly golden brown. Bring the first tray out of the oven, allow the biscuits to stand for 1–2 minutes only, until the first biscuits can be lifted with a palette knife.

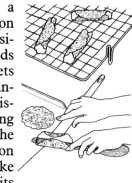

Roll around a greased wooden spoon handle. Hold in position for some seconds until the biscuit sets round the spoon handle. Place the rolled biscuit on to a wire cooling tray. Repeat with the rest of the biscuits on the first tray and bake the remaining biscuits then roll these.

If you find any biscuits have hardened on the baking tray and cannot be removed with the palette knife, simply return them to the oven for 1–2 minutes.

BRANDY CORNETS

Roll the biscuits round lightly greased cream horn tins instead of spoon handles. Fill with whipped cream, or ice cream, and fruit just before serving.

FLAPJACKS

Makes 12–16

75 g/3 oz butter or margarine
50–75 g/2–3 oz light brown or caster sugar
1 tablespoon golden syrup
175 g/6 oz rolled oats

Grease an 18 cm/7 inch square sandwich tin well. Put the butter or margarine, sugar and syrup into a large saucepan. Stir over a low heat until the fat and sugar has melted. Add the rolled oats, stir well to blend. Put into the prepared tin.

Bake in the centre of a moderate oven, 180°C, 350°F, Gas Mark 4 for 25 minutes or until evenly golden brown. Mark into fingers while warm; allow to become almost cold in the tin before removing. Store away from other biscuits.

BISCUITS MADE BY WHISKING METHOD

The egg whites should only be lightly whisked for Macaroons; if stiffly whisked the biscuits become over-dry. You can however whisk the egg whites more stiffly for Coconut Pyramids.

ALMOND MACAROONS

Makes 12–18

2 egg whites
few drops almond or ratafia essence
150 g/5 oz ground almonds
150–175 g/5–6 oz caster sugar
rice paper

to decorate
few glacé cherries or blanched almonds

Whisk the egg whites until just frothy, add the essence, ground almonds and sugar. If slightly soft, add more almonds.

Put sheets of rice paper on baking trays, form the mixture into 12–18 soft balls, put on the rice paper. Allow room to spread as the mixture flattens. Top each with a piece of cherry or a blanched almond.

Bake in the centre of a moderate oven, 180°C, 350°F, Gas Mark 4 for approximately 20 minutes. Cool enough to handle, then cut round the rice paper.

Note: To produce sticky macaroons either put a bowl of water in the oven under the biscuits as they bake or use 75–100 g/3–4 oz ground almonds and pipe the soft mixture on to the rice paper.

BISCUITS BASED ON ALMOND MACAROONS

In each case the biscuits are baked as the Almond Macaroon recipe.

Chocolate Macaroons: Use 75 g/3 oz ground almonds, 25 g/1 oz rice flour and 50 g/2 oz chocolate powder.

Coconut Macaroons: Use half ground almonds and half desiccated coconut.

Cornflake Macaroons: Use 75 g/3 oz ground almonds and 50 g/2 oz lightly crushed cornflakes.

Ratafias: Use the macaroon biscuit recipe but form into about 60–70 tiny balls. Bake for 10 minutes only.

These keep for weeks in a container and can be used on trifles and desserts.

Rout Biscuits: Blend 110 g/4 oz ground almonds, 110 g/4 oz caster sugar, a few drops almond or ratafia essence; bind with an egg yolk. Roll into 48–60 tiny balls, top with whole or flaked almonds and brush with lightly whisked egg white. Bake in the centre of a moderately hot oven 200°C, 400°F, Gas Mark 6 for 6 minutes.

Chocolate Petits Fours: Omit the almonds, recipe above, coat in melted chocolate and chocolate vermicelli.

COCONUT PYRAMIDS

Makes about 18

2 egg whites
175 g/6 oz desiccated coconut
½ level tablespoon cornflour
75–100 g/3–4 oz caster sugar
rice paper, optional

Whisk the egg whites until stiff, add the rest of the ingredients. Form into pyramid shapes. Put on to rice paper or on lightly greased baking trays.

Bake in the centre of a very moderate oven, 160°C, 325°F, Gas Mark 3 for about 10 minutes. Cool slightly, lift from the tray. Tear or cut away the surplus rice paper.

Note: These can be coated with a little melted chocolate.

177

BISCUITS MADE WITHOUT COOKING

The three recipes on this page are excellent as petits fours. If you make a selection of tiny biscuits, you could add these to give a pleasing variety.

ALMOND TRUFFLES

Makes 12–36

75 g/3 oz icing sugar
175 g/6 oz sponge cake
50 g/2 oz ground almonds
4 tablespoons apricot jam
1 tablespoon sweet sherry
few drops almond essence

for coating
225 g/8 oz plain chocolate
50 g/2 oz chocolate vermicelli

Sift the icing sugar with the sponge cake, blend with the rest of the ingredients, except coating ingredients.

If making cakes, form the mixture into 12 balls.

If making petits fours, form the mixture into about 36 balls.

Should the mixture be a little soft to handle chill for a short time in the refrigerator, then chill again before coating.

Break the chocolate into pieces and melt in a basin over hot water, remove from the heat when melted. Put one truffle into the chocolate, turn round with two forks until thinly coated. Place the chocolate vermicelli on to a flat dish or sheet of greaseproof paper, put the chocolate coated truffle on this and turn until covered with the vermicelli. Continue like this until all the truffles are coated.

Allow to set on a wire cooling tray. Put the larger truffles into cake sized paper cases and the petits fours into sweetmeat cases.

RUM AND ORANGE TRUFFLES

Makes 12–36

ingredients as Almond Truffles, but add 1–2 teaspoons finely grated fresh orange rind
use orange jelly marmalade instead of apricot jam
use rum instead of sherry

Proceed as the Almond Truffles, mixing the orange rind with the other ingredients.

GUM NUT CHEWS

Makes 18–36

Chop 25 g/1 oz Maraschino cherries, lightly crush 225 g/8 oz cornflakes, blend with 100 g/4 oz mixed dried fruit, 100 g/4 oz desiccated coconut, 1 × 175 g/6 oz can full cream sweetened condensed milk and ½ teaspoon vanilla essence.

Roll into 18–36 balls, leave for 12 hours to set. Serve as cakes or petits fours.

Modern baking methods

Although you can just set the outside of a meringue, such as the topping on a Lemon Meringue Pie, see page 201, in a microwave cooker, this appliance is not suitable for cooking meringues in the same way as an oven. Indeed none of the appliances described in previous chapters can be used for this purpose.

In a microwave cooker
You can cook some biscuits, e.g. shortbread, in a microwave cooker. Use a HIGH setting. Line a dish with clingfilm, put in the biscuit and cook for 3–3½ minutes. Flapjacks are also quite satisfactory in a microwave cooker, allow 3 minutes, or as advised by the manufacturer.

Storing

Unfilled meringues should be stored in an airtight container away from biscuits. Biscuits must be stored in completely airtight containers in order to remain crisp. If they do become slightly soft, put them on a baking tray and crisp for a few minutes at the temperature given in the initial recipe.

Do not store chocolate biscuits or Brandy Snaps or Flapjacks with ordinary plain biscuits.

Store cheese-flavoured biscuits apart from other biscuits.

Freezing

If you have sufficient airtight containers there is no need to freeze either meringues or biscuits. If, however, you are short of storage space, pack meringues or biscuits into tightly-sealed containers and freeze. The high percentage of sugar in meringues means they never freeze completely. Use within 3 months, eating cream filled meringues as soon as they defrost.

Brandy Snaps do not freeze, they soften and collapse.

Macaroons become very crumbly, but do not harden as they would with storage in a tin.

PROBLEM SOLVING

Meringues cause many problems to cooks, here are some of the usual ones.

Q. *Why do meringues 'weep' on the baking tray and so become horribly sticky?*
A. Because the sugar was insufficient or overbeaten into the egg whites. Because the egg whites were insufficiently whisked. Because the oven was not adequately preheated before putting the meringues into the oven.

Q. *Many biscuit doughs are difficult to handle, why?*
A. It is because recipes contain little, if any, liquid.
Remedy: If the dough seems slightly sticky, wrap and chill for a time or handle with slightly dampened (not wet) finger-tips. If too dry handle very roughly, kneading it hard, you will not spoil the dough. When the dough has to be rolled out, do this far more roughly than when rolling pastry.

Q. *Why are biscuits so difficult to remove from the baking tray, they seem either to break or stick?*
A. Very crisp shortbread-type biscuits, Rich Cheese Biscuits and others are very fragile when hot, that is why it is advisable to allow them to cool completely on the baking tray. Some biscuits, like Flapjacks, will stick in the tin if they are left until absolutely cold. Lift out when just warm.

The instructions in the various recipes about removal from the trays or tins are important and so is the information about greasing or not greasing trays.

Q. *What can one do with broken meringues?*
A. Crush finely and use as a topping over cream or icing on a cake.

Break into fairly large pieces, add to slightly softened ice cream and refreeze.

Q. *Why do meringues break when I try to take them off the baking tray?*
A. It could be because the tray was inadequately greased, see page 166 for advice. Modern silicone ('non-stick') paper is a great help and so is a warm knife, see page 167. Often it is because you are trying to remove them before they are 100% cooked.

Check on the baking temperature, the oven may be a little too hot and therefore the meringues appear cooked on the outside before they are quite ready, see page 166 for temperature.

CHAPTER 9

Scones, Teacakes & Yeast Baking

I find people appreciate these plainer foods very much indeed when they are made at home, for their taste and texture are so excellent.

Scones are both quick and economical to prepare. Most of these are made by rubbing the fat into the flour so the information given in Chapter 2 will be helpful.

Many teacakes, something between a scone and a cake, are also made by this quick rubbing-in process; although some famous teacakes need a yeast dough.

One has only to visit Ireland and taste their wonderful Soda Breads to appreciate the fact that good bread can be made without yeast. What a delight to be able to make this and other breads at home.

Yeast gives a unique texture to a mixture. It is important to appreciate the fact that fresh yeast is a living organism and as such it needs careful storage and handling.

WHAT DOES A YEAST DOUGH MEAN?

It means that the dough is lightened by the use of yeast rather than an ordinary raising agent, such as baking powder. A yeast dough must be given time to rise after mixing and before baking.
The mixed dough is left in a warm place for some time until it is virtually double in size, it is then kneaded, formed into the desired shapes and left to prove again. The various stages are fully explained under the Master Recipe, for home-made White Bread, which is covered on the pages that follow.
An electric mixer or food processor can be used to knead the dough; it is important to follow the advice given on page 182.
A yeast dough is used in this book for:

Many kinds of plain and fancy breads
Teacakes and buns
Some interesting cakes

A selection of baked goods – Cottage Loaf (recipe page 187), Babas au Rhum (recipe page 193), Apricot and Walnut Bread (recipe page 185)

GOOD SCONES

Really good scones should be very light in texture, a good shape, golden in colour on the outside and with absolutely no taste of raising agent. I make this last point because all too often one tastes scones with a clearly defined flavour of baking powder or bicarbonate of soda. Measure carefully if adding raising agent(s) to plain flour. I find modern self-raising flour makes excellent scones, without the addition of any raising agent, which once was used.

Scones are made by the rubbing-in technique covered in Chapter 2, see page 39. Never make the dough too dry, it should be a soft rolling consistency.

Preheat the oven very thoroughly; cook scones in a hot oven, see recipe. Too slow cooking hardens and dries the mixture. To test if cooked, press gently but firmly at the sides of the scones, they should feel firm to the touch.

If you like a very soft scone, use plenty of milk to brush the top before cooking and cover with a teacloth when on the wire cooling tray.

PLAIN SWEET SCONES

Illustrated in colour on the jacket

Makes 12–18

225 g/8 oz self-raising flour or plain flour with 2½ level teaspoons baking powder or with ½ level teaspoon bicarbonate of soda and 1 level teaspoon cream of tartar
pinch salt
25–50 g/1–2 oz butter or margarine
25–50 g/1–2 oz caster sugar
approx. 150 ml/¼ pint milk to mix

Sift the flour or flour and baking powder or flour and bicarbonate of soda and cream of tartar with the salt. Rub in the butter

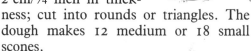

or margarine, add the sugar and enough milk to make a soft rolling consistency. Knead lightly until a smooth round, put on to a lightly floured surface. Roll out until approximately 2 cm/¾ inch in thickness; cut into rounds or triangles. The dough makes 12 medium or 18 small scones.

Brush each scone with a little milk to give a shiny topping. Put on to an ungreased baking tray; this can be dusted with a little flour if desired, preventing the bottom of the scones becoming too brown. Bake towards the top of a hot oven 220°C, 425°F, Gas Mark 7 for 10 minutes. Remove from the baking tray on to a wire cooling tray. Serve with butter and/or whipped cream and jam.

A MIXER FOR SCONES AND YEAST DOUGHS

The remarks on pages 40 and 68 apply when making scones, teabreads and other mixtures without yeast.

A mixer is excellent for kneading a yeast dough; use the special dough hook at a low speed. Never over-mix the dough, stop and test as step 4 on page 187.

A FOOD PROCESSOR FOR SCONES AND YEAST DOUGHS

The remarks on pages 40 and 69 apply when making scones, teabreads and other mixtures without yeast.

A food processor can be used for kneading the yeast dough, but you must switch off after 10 seconds and test the dough as step 4 on page 187.

RECIPES BASED ON PLAIN SWEET SCONES

All these scones are baked as Plain Sweet Scones; add dry ingredients before adding the milk.

Almond Scones: Add 25–50 g/1–2 oz blanched chopped almonds to the dough. Top each scone with a little sugar and chopped almonds before baking.

Cheese Scones: Omit the sugar in the basic recipe. Sift a pinch of pepper and dry mustard with the flour and salt. Rub in the fat, add 50–75 g/2–3 oz grated cheese. Mix with 1–2 eggs and milk.

Coconut Scones: Increase the sugar to 75 g/3 oz, add 50 g/2 oz desiccated coconut to the dough, mix with 1 egg and milk.

Cream Scones: Mix the dough with single cream instead of milk; or use sour cream and only ½ level teaspoon of cream of tartar with plain flour.

Date Scones: Add 50–75 g/2–3 oz chopped stoned dates before adding the milk. About 25 g/1 oz chopped walnuts can be added.

Fruit Scones: Add 50–75 g/2–3 oz dried fruit to the dough.

Orange Scones: Add 1–2 teaspoons grated orange rind and 25–50 g/1–2 oz finely chopped candied orange peel to the dough. Bind with orange juice and milk.

Rich Scones: Blend the scones with 1–2 eggs and use less milk.

Savoury Scones: Omit sugar and add seasoning to the flour; or blend with yeast extract dissolved in the milk or with tomato juice. Add up to 1 tablespoon chopped fresh mixed herbs (chives, parsley, etc.).

Treacle Scones: Sift ½ teaspoon ground cinnamon and ½ teaspoon mixed spice with the flour. Use 25 g/1 oz sugar (this can be soft moist brown sugar). Add 1–2 tablespoons black treacle before mixing with milk.

WHOLEMEAL SCONES

Wholemeal flour makes delicious scones. Use it in the basic recipe or any of the variations. You will need more milk to bind the mixture and the scones will take a little longer to cook.

Scones made with wheatmeal flour are excellent and very light in texture.

Brown Scones can be made by using half white and half wholemeal or wheatmeal flour.

FAT RASCALS

Makes 10–12

These teacakes are very like the Plain Sweet Scones on page 182, use the same amount of flour and raising agent, but rub 100 g/4 oz butter or margarine into the flour, add 25–50 g/1–2 oz moist brown sugar, 50 g/2 oz currants. Mix with milk, then roll out and cut into rounds as described on page 182. Sprinkle with a little caster sugar before baking. Bake as Plain Sweet Scones, serve with butter.

GRIDDLE SCONES

Any of the recipes given on this page and page 182 can be baked on a griddle (often called a girdle or bakestone). Rub the griddle with a little melted fat and preheat. To test if the right heat, shake on a little flour; if the right heat it should turn golden in 1 minute.

Roll out the dough until just under 1.5 cm/½ inch in thickness, cut into rounds. Put on to the griddle, cook steadily for 8–10 minutes, turn once or twice.

HONEY BRAN MUFFINS

Makes 12–15

50 g/2 oz **All-Bran**
150 ml/¼ pint milk
50 g/2 oz **butter or margarine**
50 g/2 oz **caster sugar**
3 tablespoons **thin honey**
1 egg
100 g/4 oz **self-raising flour with 1
    teaspoon baking powder or plain
    flour with 2 teaspoons baking
    powder**

Grease and flour 12–15 deep patty tins.
Put the bran into a basin and add the milk,
allow to stand for 30 minutes. Cream
together the butter or margarine, sugar
and honey. Add the bran with any liquid
left and the egg. Beat well to blend. Finally sift the flour and baking powder into the
mixture and blend with the other ingredients. Spoon into the prepared tins.

Bake just above the centre of a moderately hot oven, 200°C, 400°F, Gas Mark
6 for 15–20 minutes (the time depends
upon the depth of the mixture) or until
firm to the touch. Serve buttered.

CRANBERRY NUT LOAF

Makes 1 loaf

50 g/2 oz **cooking fat or margarine**
6 tablespoons **orange juice**
225 g/8 oz **self-raising flour or plain flour
    with 2 teaspoons baking powder**
pinch salt
1 tablespoon **grated orange rind**
225 g/8 oz **caster sugar**
1 egg
75 g/3 oz **walnuts**
100 g/4 oz **cranberries**

Grease and flour a 900 g/2 lb loaf tin. Heat
the fat or margarine with the orange juice
until melted, then allow to cool. Sift the
flour, or flour and baking powder, and
salt. Add the orange rind and sugar. Gradually blend in the orange juice and fat.
Add the egg and mix thoroughly. Chop
the nuts, then stir into the teabread mixture together with the cranberries. Spoon
into the prepared tin.

Bake in the centre of a moderate oven,
180°C, 350°F, Gas Mark 4 for approximately 55 minutes or until firm to the
touch. Allow to cool in the tin for 3–4
minutes then turn out on to a wire tray.

GOLDEN SYRUP LOAF

Makes 1 loaf

4 tablespoons **golden syrup**
150 ml/¼ pint milk
225 g/8 oz **self-raising flour or plain flour
    with 2 teaspoons baking powder**
½ teaspoon **bicarbonate of soda**
¼ teaspoon **salt**

Grease and flour, or line, a 675 g/1½ lb loaf
tin. Put the syrup and milk into a saucepan, warm gently; do not overheat. Sift
the flour, or flour and baking powder,
bicarbonate of soda and salt into a mixing
bowl. Add the syrup and milk, beat well.
Spoon into the prepared tin.

Bake in the centre of a moderate to
moderately hot oven, 190–200°C, 375–
400°F, Gas Mark 5–6 for 35–40 minutes or
until firm to the touch; check the baking
after 25 minutes and slightly lower the
heat if necessary. The flavour improves if
the loaf is kept for 24 hours before cutting.

TREACLE OR HONEY LOAF

Use black treacle or honey instead of
syrup in the loaf above.

ORANGE APRICOT BREAD

Makes 1 loaf

175 g/6 oz dried apricots
225 ml/7½ fl oz orange juice
2 teaspoons grated orange rind
50 g/2 oz candied orange peel
50 g/2 oz walnuts
85 g/3 oz butter or margarine
350 g/12 oz self-raising flour or plain
    flour with 3 teaspoons baking
    powder
100 g/4 oz caster sugar
2 eggs
1 tablespoon lemon juice

Grease and flour a 900 g/2 lb loaf tin. Cut the apricots into small pieces, put into a mixing bowl, add the orange juice and orange rind. Leave soaking for 12 hours.

Chop the peel and nuts, mix with the apricots (by this time most of the liquid will have been absorbed). Melt the butter or margarine, sift in the flour, or flour and baking powder, add the apricot mixture with the sugar, eggs and lemon juice. Spoon into the prepared tin.

Bake in the centre of a moderate oven, 180°C, 350°F, Gas Mark 4 for 30 minutes then reduce the heat to very moderate, 160°C, 325°F, Gas Mark 3 for a further 1 hour or until firm to the touch. Turn out and keep for 24 hours before cutting.

APRICOT AND WALNUT BREAD

Illustrated in colour on page 181

Prepare the apricots, as in Orange Apricot Bread, but soak in water instead of orange juice. Omit the grated orange rind and candied peel; add 50 g/2 oz chopped glacé cherries and 75 g/3 oz chopped walnuts instead. Bake as the Orange Apricot Bread.

WALNUT BANANA BREAD

Makes 1 loaf

100 g/4 oz butter or margarine
100 g/4 oz caster sugar
½ teaspoon vanilla essence
1 egg
225 g/8 oz self-raising flour or plain flour
    with 2 teaspoons baking powder
¼ teaspoon salt
450 g/1 lb ripe bananas with skins
75 g/3 oz walnuts
50 g/2 oz seedless raisins

Grease and flour a 900 g/2 lb loaf tin. Cream together the butter or margarine, sugar and essence. Beat in the egg. Sift the flour with the salt. Skin and mash the bananas and chop the walnuts.

Beat the flour and banana purée gradually into the creamed mixture. Add 50 g/2 oz of the nuts and the raisins. Spoon into the prepared tin. Top with the remaining walnuts; press these gently into the teabread mixture.

Bake in the centre of a moderate oven, 180°C, 350°F, Gas Mark 4 for 45–50 minutes or until firm to the touch. Cool in tin for 2–3 minutes then turn on to tray.

DATE LOAF

Makes 1 loaf

Grease and flour a 900–1.2 kg/2–2½ lb loaf tin. Put 350 g/12 oz chopped stoned dates into a basin, add 150 ml/¼ pint boiling water, stand for 10 minutes.

Sift 350 g/12 oz self-raising flour, or plain flour with 3 teaspoons baking powder, and a pinch salt. Rub in 50 g/2 oz margarine, add 50 g/2 oz sugar, 2 eggs, 3 tablespoons milk and the dates. Beat well. Put into the prepared tin and bake in the centre of a moderate oven, 180°C, 350°F, Gas Mark 4 for 50–60 minutes.

WHITE BREAD

I have given the recipe based upon a small amount of flour only, for beginners may feel happier if handling this, rather than a larger amount, but see page 188.

Baking Utensils: Lightly greased 900 g/2 lb loaf tin or flat baking tray or sheet.

Oven Setting: A hot oven 220°C, 425°F, Gas Mark 7, see under 'Baking' on this page.

Oven Position: Centre of the oven, unless using a fan-assisted electric oven, when any position can be used; see batch baking on page 188.

Cooking Time: Approximately 45 minutes.

Makes 1 loaf
300 ml/½ pint water
15 g/½ oz fresh yeast or 7 g/¼ oz dried yeast
    with 1 teaspoon caster sugar or honey
★500 g/1 lb strong or plain white flour
1 teaspoon salt
25 g/1 oz lard or butter or margarine

★This is the amount in a small bag of flour, but you can weigh out the usual 450 g.

CERTAIN SUCCESS

Choice of Ingredients: Check that fresh yeast really is fresh, it should smell pleasant, be an even putty colour and crumble easily. Dried yeast has had the moisture removed, that is why half the amount only is needed.

Strong flour is better for bread, see page 12, it gives the best result.

Measure the salt carefully, too much not only spoils the flavour of the bread but has a harmful effect upon the yeast.

Fat is not essential, but makes a more moist bread. Water is used in the Master Recipe, but milk is excellent, see page 188. The liquid must not be over-heated, if too hot it will harm the yeast.

Some kind of sugar is not necessary when using fresh yeast, but must be used with dried yeast, see step 1 opposite.

Handling the Mixture: Handling, or kneading, is an essential part of bread making. It distributes the yeast and incorporates air into the mixture. It must be done thoroughly, but not overdone, see steps 3 and 7. Over-kneading spoils bread texture.

'Proving', i.e. rising is another essential stage, see steps 6 and 8, right.

Consistency: It is important that a bread dough is not too stiff, if it is it cannot be beautifully light. The average amount of liquid is given in the Master Recipe above, but you may have to adjust this for metric amounts and with various kinds of white flour. As explained on page 189, wholemeal or wheatmeal flours absorb much more liquid.

Preparing Tins: Not only the tins but all the equipment used in yeast cookery should be pleasantly warm. The tins or baking trays for bread and other yeast dishes should be lightly greased, unless silicone ('non-stick') when this is unnecessary.

Baking: It is essential that dishes made with yeast should be put into a hot oven, this destroys the action of the yeast at the right time. The average baking time is given but to test the bread, remove from the tin or baking tray, knock at the bottom. Cooked bread sounds hollow.

If the sides of a tin loaf are not sufficiently brown for your taste then put on to a flat baking tray and cook for a further 5 minutes.

1 Warm the water to 43°C/110°F, i.e. just tepid, blend with the fresh yeast. If using dried yeast, dissolve the sugar or honey in the tepid liquid. Sprinkle the dried yeast on top, leave for 10 minutes; after this use as fresh yeast.

2 Sift the flour and salt into a mixing bowl, rub in the fat. Pour the yeast liquid into the centre of the rubbed-in mixture and blend thoroughly. Different makes of flour vary so you may need to add more liquid if necessary.

3 Turn the dough on to a lightly floured working surface, knead thoroughly to stretch and develop the dough. To do this, fold the dough towards you then push

down and away from you with the base of the palm of the hand (called the 'heel'). Continue until the dough feels firm, elastic and no longer sticky.

4 To test if sufficiently kneaded, press firmly with a floured finger. If the impression comes out, the dough is ready for the next stage.

5 Either return the dough to the bowl and cover with a teacloth or put into a very large saucepan and cover with the lid or place inside a large lightly oiled polythene bag. Tie loosely to allow room for expansion. The dough should then be left to rise. The word used is 'prove'. There are various ways in which this can be done.

6 *Quick Rise:* 45–60 minutes in a warm place. *Slower Rise:* 2 hours at average room temperature. *Overnight Rise:* up to 12 hours in a cold larder or room or up to 24 hours in a refrigerator – in the normal storage part of the cabinet, NOT freezing compartment. Return to room temperature – leave for 20 minutes before baking.

7 Turn the risen dough on to a lightly floured surface. Flatten with the knuckles to knock out air bubbles, then knead to make the dough firm and ready for shaping, this is known as 'knocking back'.

8 To shape the dough:
Tin Loaf: Press out to a neat oblong the length of the tin but three times the width. Fold neatly in three and fit into the tin – with the fold underneath.
Cottage Loaf: Divide the dough into two portions, the base to be twice as large as the top. Place the small ball of dough on top of the large one, press firmly with the handle of a wooden spoon through the centre to join the two balls (as shown below). Snip the sides with scissors. *Illustrated in colour on page 181.*
Bloomer Loaf: Shape the dough into a fat sausage, make cuts along the top (as shown below right).
Cob Loaf: Shape the dough into a ball and place on the greased baking tray. Mark the top with a well-floured knife.

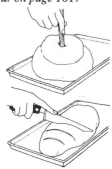

9 Cover the dough lightly and allow to prove once more for 30–40 minutes in a warm place, for 1–1½ hours in a cooler place or up to 16 hours in a refrigerator. The bread is then ready to bake, see page 186 and the next page.

SPEEDY BREAD MAKING

It has been discovered that if you use a small amount of ascorbic acid (vitamin C) you can hasten the first process of 'proving' i.e. stage 5 on page 187.

If making the Master Recipe, pages 186 and 187, crush and then dissolve 1 × 25 mg ascorbic acid tablet in the warm liquid. Proceed as stages 1–4. At stage 5 you will then only require 10 minutes 'proving'. Continue as stages 6–8. Allow slightly longer 'proving' i.e. 45 instead of 30–40 minutes in a warm place at stage 9 then continue as the recipe.

RECIPES BASED ON WHITE BREAD

The following recipes are based upon the proportions used in the Master Recipe on page 186.

Batch Baking
It is possible to make a large batch of dough as the Master Recipe; allow it to 'prove' as stage 5, divide it into portions, knock back and add various flavourings to each batch, so giving an interesting selection of breads.

Obviously some of the ingredients suggested need to be blended with the yeast and flour from the initial stage; these are given in the various recipes in the next column.

Amount of Yeast to Use
When making larger amounts of bread dough you do not use the amount of yeast in proportion to the quantity of flour, e.g. in the Master Recipe you use 15 g/½ oz fresh yeast or 7 g/¼ oz (1½ level teaspoons) dried yeast.

If you use 1.5 kg/3 lb flour, you only need 30 g/1 oz fresh yeast or 15 g/½ oz (3 level teaspoons) dried yeast i.e. twice not three times as much.

Use the proportions as the Master Recipe on page 186 with the following alterations. Remember when you change the flour you may need to adapt the amount of liquid.

Apple Bread: Use approximately 300 ml/ ½ pint apple purée instead of water in the Master Recipe; heat to the temperature described in Step 1 on page 187. The purée can be unsweetened or sweetened with honey or sugar. You can add about 50 g/2 oz sultanas to the dough.

Brown Bread: Use half strong white and half strong wheatmeal flour.

Cheese Bread: Allow the dough to prove as step 5, page 187; add up to 175 g/6 oz cheese; this can be grated Cheddar, or other hard cheese, or crumbled feta or curd or cottage cheese. Blend thoroughly then proceed as the recipe on pages 186 and 187. About 1 tablespoon mixed finely chopped fresh herbs (chives, crushed garlic, parsley) also can be added.

Fruit Bread: Knead up to 100 g/4 oz mixed dried fruit into the dough.

Granary Bread: This is a proprietary make of flour which contains some malt flakes, some bran, some cracked wheat. Use instead of white flour in the Master Recipe. The bread has a slightly sweet flavour. It rises well. You can use two-thirds Granary and one-third wholemeal flour for a very delicious loaf.

Milk Bread: Use butter as the fat in the recipe and mix the dough with warm milk instead of water.

Oatmeal Bread: Substitute 40–50 g/1½–2 oz medium oatmeal or rolled oats for the same amount of flour in the Master Recipe.

Rye Bread: If you use all rye flour you produce a somewhat heavy loaf. A better result is obtained by using half rye and half strong white flour or you can use two thirds white flour and one third rye flour.

CROISSANTS

Makes 12–18

basic yeast dough made with 450 g/1 lb
flour etc, see page 186 and below
175–225 g/6–8 oz butter or margarine

to glaze
1 egg yolk
2 tablespoons water

Prepare the dough as steps 1 to 6 see pages 186 and 187. If taking the dough from a large batch, knead on a generously floured board until a soft rolling consistency.

If preparing the dough especially use 1 tablespoon less water than usual to give a slightly firmer mixture. Knead the dough thoroughly as step 3 and allow to 'prove' as step 6. 'Knock back' the dough, then roll out to a neat oblong shape.

Leave the butter or margarine in a warm room to soften slightly. Put one third of the butter or margarine over two thirds of the dough, in exactly the same way as shown in Flaky Pastry on page 211.

Fold the dough in three, turn at right angles then roll out again. Repeat this stage twice until all the fat is used.

After all the fat has been used roll out the dough again, fold as before. Allow to stand for 10–15 minutes, then roll, fold and re-roll once more.

Roll out the dough very thinly. Cut first into 6–9 squares, then divide into triangles, twist the dough from the long side to the point, as shown, then turn into a horseshoe shape. Put on to baking tray(s).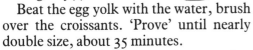

Beat the egg yolk with the water, brush over the croissants. 'Prove' until nearly double size, about 35 minutes.

Bake above the centre of a very hot oven, 230°C, 450°F, Gas Mark 8 for 15 minutes. Reduce heat slightly after 10 minutes if becoming brown.

TOPPINGS FOR YEAST BREAD

A loaf of bread looks more interesting with a shiny or decorated crust. To give a very good shine, blend the yolk of an egg and a tablespoon water or milk over the dough before the final 'proving'.

To give a pleasantly moist shiny top, brush the dough with a little oil before the final 'proving'.

Sprinkle rolled oats, wheat flakes, poppy, caraway, celery or sesame seeds over the dough before the final 'proving'.

To give a sticky shine to sweet breads, brush with the glaze used for buns on page 191 after cooking.

WHOLEMEAL BREAD

Use wholemeal flour in the Master Recipe. You will require more moisture to bind the dough, for wholemeal bread must be a really soft texture. Proceed as for White Bread on pages 186 and 187.

Wholemeal loaves look attractive if topped with a little oatmeal, or rolled oats or sesame or poppy seeds before baking.

Another incredibly easy way of making wholemeal bread is as follows:

Use the same amount of ingredients except for the water. You need 390 ml/13 fl oz water.

Follow steps 1 and 2 on page 187. The dough will be very soft. Mix well with a wooden spoon or your hand or an electric dough hook until the dough feels springy and leaves the sides of the mixing bowl clean. Put into a greased and warmed 900 g/2 lb loaf tin without 'proving' first, then allow to 'prove' in the tin for 20–25 minutes. Bake in the centre of a moderately hot oven, 200°C, 400°F, Gas Mark 6 for approximately 40–45 minutes.

PIZZA ALLA NAPOLETANA

Serves up to 8

**basic yeast dough made with 450 g/1 lb
    flour etc, as pages 186 and 187**
1½ tablespoons olive oil
900 g/2 lb tomatoes
1–2 garlic cloves
2 medium onions
salt and pepper
225 g/8 oz Bel Paese or Mozzarella
1 small can anchovy fillets
few black olives

Prepare the dough as page 187, allow it to 'prove', then 'knock back'.

A Pizza is so adaptable that the dough can be rolled out to fit a large oblong tin or made into two 20–23 cm/8–9 inch rounds, these can be put on flat baking trays or into large sandwich tins. Grease the tins well before adding the dough. Brush with a few drops of the oil.

The filling should be prepared while the bread dough is originally rising. Skin the tomatoes and garlic, peel the onions, chop all these ingredients. Heat the remaining oil and simmer the vegetables until a thick purée, season well; cool slightly. Spread over the top of the bread dough and allow to 'prove' again for 25–30 minutes. Grate or slice the cheese, spread over the tomato mixture.

Bake in the centre of a hot oven, 220°C, 425°F, Gas Mark 7 for about 20–25 minutes; reduce the heat slightly after 10 minutes and add the anchovy fillets and olives. This prevents these becoming rather dried; they can of course be put on to the tomato mixture at the same time as the cheese if preferred.

Note: The topping can be varied in many ways, use chopped cooked bacon, sardines and other savoury ingredients. You can sprinkle grated Parmesan over the mixture before baking; or use other good cooking cheese.

RECIPES BASED ON BREAD DOUGHS

The following can be made with the basic yeast dough on pages 186 and 187 or the variations page 188, or the enriched dough on page 191.

Devonshire Splits: Prepare the selected dough, allow to 'prove', then 'knock back'. Divide into small balls, put on to warm and lightly greased baking tray(s). Allow to 'prove' for 15–20 minutes or until nearly double the original size. Bake near the top of a hot oven, 220°C, 425°F, Gas Mark 7 for 12–15 minutes. When cold, top with sifted icing sugar. Serve with Devonshire cream and jam. In Cornwall these are known as Cornish Splits.

Doughnuts: Prepare the dough as for Devonshire Splits. If making round doughnuts, roll into balls then make an indentation in each ball, put in 1 teaspoon of jam or thick apple or other fruit purée. Re-roll the dough, so the jam or purée is completely covered. This is very important for it would burn in frying. Place the doughnuts on to a warmed and lightly greased baking tray and allow to 'prove' as above.

Meanwhile heat a deep pan of oil or fat to 170–175°C/340–350°F (use the higher setting for small or ring doughnuts). Fry the doughnuts steadily for 5–7 minutes until golden in colour. Drain on absorbent paper, then roll in caster sugar. Cream doughnuts must be filled after baking.
Illustrated in colour on the jacket

Small Doughnuts: Roll into small balls and proceed as above. The dough can be made in rings too.

Fruit Doughnuts: Roll the dough around stoned, ripe apricots, plums or well-drained cooked prunes. The stoned fruit can be filled with cream cheese. Proceed as Doughnuts, but allow longer cooking time; if necessary lower the heat after 5 minutes so the outside is not over-cooked.

ENRICHED YEAST DOUGH

Although fruit and other buns can be made from the basic bread dough, this richer dough is worth making.

15 g/½ oz fresh yeast or 7 g/¼ oz dried yeast
25–50 g/1–2 oz caster sugar
approx. 150 ml/¼ pint milk or milk and water or water for firmer dough, see method
350 g/12 oz strong white flour
pinch salt
50 g/2 oz butter or margarine
1 egg

Cream the fresh yeast with 1 teaspoon sugar, warm the liquid, add to the yeast. Or dissolve 1 teaspoon sugar in the warm liquid, add the dried yeast, leave for 10 minutes, see page 187, then continue as though using fresh yeast. Add a sprinkling of flour to the yeast liquid, leave in a warm place for about 15 minutes or until the surface is covered with bubbles i.e. 'the sponge breaks through'.

Sift the flour and salt into a mixing bowl. Rub in the butter or margarine, add the yeast liquid then the egg and knead lightly. The dough is ideal for a rolling consistency, as needed for Chelsea Buns, but add 1–2 tablespoons extra liquid for soft doughs required for Fruit Buns, Devonshire Splits etc.

Knead the dough as step 3, page 187, and allow to 'prove' as step 6. The dough is then ready to use in individual recipes.

RECIPES BASED ON ENRICHED DOUGH

You can make up the one batch of Enriched Yeast Dough but it is very easy to make up three or four times the amount, divide this into sections and add the various extra ingredients. Quantities below are based on the 350 g/12 oz flour etc.

Fruit Buns: Blend 75 g/3 oz dried fruit and 25 g/1 oz chopped candied peel into the dough, allow to 'prove' as described in the Master Recipe on page 187. Knead again and divide into 12 portions. Form into neat balls, put on to a warm lightly greased baking tray and allow to 'prove' for 20–25 minutes or until nearly double in size.

Bake near the top of a hot oven, 220°C, 425°F, Gas Mark 7 for 12–15 minutes.

Blend 2 tablespoons caster sugar with 2 tablespoons boiling water; brush over the hot buns to glaze.

Hot Cross Buns: Sift 1 teaspoon ground cinnamon and ½ teaspoon grated nutmeg with the flour. Proceed as Fruit Buns above but mark the buns with a cross before 'proving'. Bake and glaze as Fruit Buns.

Rich Fruit Loaf: Proceed as for Fruit Buns above, put the dough into a 675–900 g/1½–2 lb loaf tin. Glaze as on page 189. Allow to 'prove' for 25–30 minutes. Bake in the centre of a hot oven, as above, for 40–45 minutes, reduce heat slightly after 20 minutes if necessary.

SWISS BUNS

Makes 15–18

ingredients as Enriched Yeast Dough

for the topping
Glacé Icing made with 225 g/8 oz icing sugar etc., as page 146
food colouring

Prepare the dough, allow to 'prove'. Divide into 15–18 small portions and roll each portion to a finger shape. Put on to warm greased baking trays, allow to 'prove' and bake as Devonshire Splits, on page 190. Cool before icing.

Make the icing, as page 146, add a few drops of colouring. Top the buns with the icing, allow to set.

MAKING ROLLS

The dough in the Master Recipe or any of the variations on pages 186 and 188 will make about 12 rolls. Continue to stage 9 page 187, divide the dough into equal sized pieces, form into interesting shapes. Put on to warmed and lightly greased baking trays. Glaze and top as the suggestions above. Allow to 'prove', this takes about 15 minutes in a warm place or 30 minutes in a cooler position or 6–8 hours or overnight in a refrigerator.

Bake for 12–15 minutes towards the top of the hot oven.

SALLY LUNNS

These teacakes are made with the Enriched Yeast Dough on page 191 but without sugar or with only 1 teaspoon sugar (if using dried yeast). Knead the dough after it has 'proved' (stage 5 on page 187), divide into two portions. Press into two warmed and greased 12.5–15 cm/5–6 inch sandwich tins. Allow to 'prove' as stage 9 page 187, then bake for 25 minutes in a hot oven, as the rolls above. Brush with the sugar and water glaze as under Chelsea Buns.

TRADITIONAL BUNS

Chelsea Buns: Make the Enriched Yeast Dough as page 191, allow to 'prove' as described on page 187. Roll out to an oblong, 1.5–2 cm/½–¾ inch in thickness. Warm 50 g/2 oz butter or margarine to a spreading consistency. Spread over the dough, add 50 g/2 oz caster or light brown sugar, 100 g/4 oz mixed dried fruit, a pinch of ground cinnamon and a pinch of grated nutmeg.

Roll up like a Swiss Roll do this quite lightly, for the dough will rise again. Cut into 9–12 portions.

Place in a warmed 23–25 cm/9–10 inch square tin, they should fit the tin fairly tightly to keep a good shape as they rise.

Allow to 'prove' again in warm place for approximately 25–30 minutes or until nearly double the original size. Bake just above the centre of a hot oven, 220°C, 425°F, Gas Mark 7 for about 15–20 minutes; you can reduce the heat slightly after 12 minutes if the buns are becoming sufficiently brown.

Blend 2 tablespoons sugar and 2 tablespoons boiling water together. Brush the buns with this as soon as they come from the oven.

Bath Buns: Take the ingredients for the Enriched Yeast Dough on page 191, but increase the butter or margarine to 100 g/4 oz and the eggs to 2 (this means you will have a softer dough). Add 100 g/4 oz mixed dried fruit and 50 g/2 oz chopped candied peel to the other ingredients. Proceed as for the Enriched Yeast Dough and allow to 'prove' as the instructions on page 187. Form into 12 rounds. Put on to greased warmed baking trays; allow room for the buns to spread in baking. Lightly crush 5–6 sugar lumps, press the pieces of sugar on to the buns. 'Prove' again and bake as Chelsea Buns above.

BABAS AU RHUM

Illustrated in colour on page 181

Makes 8–10

15 g/½ oz fresh yeast or 7 g/¼ oz dried
    yeast
150 ml/¼ pint milk or milk and water
50 g/2 oz caster sugar
225 g/8 oz plain flour
pinch salt
2 eggs
¼ teaspoon vanilla essence
50 g/2 oz butter or margarine
25 g/1 oz currants, optional

for the syrup
4 tablespoons water
4 tablespoons caster sugar or honey
squeeze lemon juice
3–6 tablespoons rum

You need 8–10 individual flan rings or small ring tins; if not available use 12–14 castle pudding tins or dariole moulds. Grease and warm the tins before filling.

Cream the fresh yeast, warm the milk or milk and water and blend with the yeast. Or dissolve 1 teaspoon of the sugar in the warm liquid, sprinkle the dried yeast on top and leave 10 minutes: use as fresh.

Sift the flour and salt into a mixing bowl. Beat the eggs and vanilla essence together. Add the yeast liquid and the eggs to the flour and blend very thoroughly with your finger-tips. Place the butter or margarine in small pieces on the dough. Cover and allow to 'prove' for 45 minutes.

Blend in the butter or margarine, the remaining sugar and the currants, if including these. Divide the mixture into portions and half fill the prepared tins. Place a cloth or polythene over the tins.

Allow the dough to 'prove' again for 20 minutes then bake just above the centre of a hot oven, 220°C, 425°F, Gas Mark 7 for 10–15 minutes or until firm. Turn out on to a dish. Heat the water with the sugar or honey and lemon juice until the sugar has dissolved. Add the rum.

Prick the Babas gently with a fork and spoon the syrup over the cakes. **Note:** Decorate with whipped cream and glacé cherries.

SAVARIN

Serves 6–8

**ingredients as Babas au Rhum, but omit
    currants**

Prepare the dough as for the Babas au Rhum but put into a 20 cm/8 inch greased ring mould. Allow to 'prove' for 25–30 minutes then bake for 10 minutes in a hot oven as for Babas, reduce the heat to 190°C, 375°F, Gas Mark 5 and cook for a further 15–20 minutes or until firm. Turn out, prick and coat with the syrup.
Note: Can be filled with fresh fruit salad.

BRIOCHES

Makes 10–12

15 g/½ oz fresh yeast or 7 g/¼ oz dried
    yeast
3 tablespoons warm milk
25 g/1 oz caster sugar
350 g/12 oz plain flour
pinch salt
150 g/5 oz butter
2 eggs

Dissolve fresh yeast in the milk, or milk and 1 teaspoon of the sugar with dried yeast (see Babas au Rhum). Sift the flour and salt into a bowl, rub in the butter, add the yeast liquid, eggs and knead until smooth. Allow to 'prove' until double in size. Knead again and put into greased and warmed brioche tins. 'Prove' for 10–15 minutes then bake as Babas au Rhum.

IRISH SODA BREAD

Makes 1 loaf

450 g/1 lb plain white or wheatmeal flour
½–1 level teaspoon salt
½ level teaspoon bicarbonate of soda
½ level teaspoon cream of tartar
approx. 300 ml/½ pint buttermilk or
    sour or fresh milk

Sift together the dry ingredients, bind to a soft, but not over-sticky, dough with the buttermilk or milk. Turn the dough on to a floured board, form into a round about 2.5 cm/1 inch in thickness, put on to an ungreased baking tray. Lightly mark into 4–6 sections, known as 'farls'. Do not mark right through the loaf.

Bake in the centre of a hot oven, 220°C, 425°F, Gas Mark 7 for approximately 30 minutes.

BATTER RECIPES

Crumpets: Heat 150 ml/¼ pint milk with 15 g/½ oz butter; cool until just warm, blend with 7 g/¼ oz fresh yeast. Mix 100 g/4 oz plain flour, pinch salt and the yeast liquid. Beat hard then 'prove' until double in bulk, beat again. Grease and thoroughly heat a griddle, test as page 183 under Griddle Scones. Put about 8 crumpet rings or large metal cutters on the griddle, spoon some of the mixture into the rings. Cook for 2–3 minutes, then turn and cook on the second side.

Scotch Pancakes (Drop Scones): Blend 100 g/4 oz self-raising flour, pinch salt, 1 egg, 150 ml/¼ pint milk and 25 g/1 oz melted butter. Grease and heat a griddle. Drop on about 12–18 spoonfuls of the mixture. Cook for 2 minutes or until the top surface is covered with bubbles, turn and cook on the second side.

Modern baking methods

In a Microwave Cooker

You can bake scones in this cooker, although scones made with white flour look pale in colour. Allow about 2 minutes on the HIGH or FULL position. The scones should be arranged in a ring with one in the centre. Use a flat ceramic plate, turn once or twice.

If you have a microwave browning dish treat this like a griddle. Preheat as instructed by the manufacturer. Cook the scones for about 2 minutes, turn over half-way through cooking.

The particular teabreads in this book should be baked in a conventional oven.

I find different microwave cookers vary appreciably in their results when cooking bread or yeast mixtures. It is possible to 'prove' the dough in a microwave cooker, but I much prefer the usual methods, see page 187. If using the microwave put the dough in a large bowl, cover with clingfilm (allow plenty of space in the bowl for the dough to rise). Give 15 seconds on HIGH setting; allow the dough to stand for 10 minutes. Repeat this process until the dough has risen to twice its original size, test as step 5, page 187. To make a tin loaf as the Master Recipe, place the dough in a lightly oiled or greased 900 g/2 lb ceramic loaf tin. Cover and 'prove' as the method above; bake for approximately 5 minutes at the FULL setting. In my opinion the result is acceptable, but is not to be compared with oven baking. Softer mixtures, such as the Savarin, usually give better results.

In a Table Cooker (Electric Frying Pan)

Scones and small yeast rolls can be cooked on the base of the cooker, just as Rock Cakes. Preheat the cooker, see page 62, and cook as the advice on that page. Allow about the same cooking time as when baking in the oven.

Storing

Scones and yeast buns keep for about 24 hours in a covered container. Bread made without yeast keeps for several days. Bread must be quite cold before it is stored. Put white bread into a bread crock, tin or other container or wrap and put it into the refrigerator.

Wholemeal and wheatmeal bread keeps more moist if wrapped in a cloth.

You can freshen day-old scones or stale bread by warming in a moderate oven. Cover with foil to prevent the outside drying before the centre becomes warm and fresh. When warm, remove the foil and leave for a few minutes.

Do not store scones or bread with pastry or cakes; these must be kept separate.

Freezing

Scones and baking powder breads freeze perfectly for up to 3 months. Defrost at room temperature or in the oven or microwave cooker.

Yeast breads also freeze perfectly for up to 6 weeks. It is a good idea to slice a loaf before wrapping and freezing and just to remove the number of slices required for that particular meal. Bread slices can be toasted without defrosting.

You can freeze bread or other yeast doughs before or after 'proving'; knead into a neat shape or put into a tin. To compensate for freezing, use 50% more yeast than in the recipe. Wrap in a well-oiled freezer quality polythene bag. Loosen the bag and allow the dough to defrost and rise slowly; this will take some hours; then proceed as usual. Use within 3–4 months.

PROBLEM SOLVING

Although the dough is easy to handle some people are nervous about yeast cooking.

Q. *What gives a close texture to bread and makes it rise less than it should?*
A. The wrong kind of flour, it is worthwhile using strong flour; too much salt, measure this carefully. Allow adequate time for 'proving'.

Q. *Why can't I make the bread I enjoy in France?*
A. Because the French use a special flour. Try a mixture of 425 g/15 oz flour and 25 g/1 oz cornflour in the Master Recipe, pages 186 and 187. It will not produce bread exactly like French bread, but it is very good. Form the dough into long batons; allow to 'prove' and bake as page 186 for 30–35 minutes.

Q. *What makes bread and yeast buns have very large uneven holes?*
A. Insufficient kneading, see Steps 3 and 7 on page 187. Do not use an excessive amount of yeast or allow the bread to 'prove' until it is over-risen. If that happens 'knock back' and 'prove' again.

Q. *Why can I taste yeast in my home-made bread?*
A. Because you are using too much yeast or not blending this with the liquid carefully. Insufficient kneading is another cause of a yeast taste and baking in too cool an oven, see temperature on page 186.

Q. *Why do the tin loaves I make have a poor shape?*
A. The dough may be put unevenly into the tin; see page 187. The tin may be too small, the Master Recipe on page 186 using 450 or 500 g/1 lb flour, must be put into a 900 g/2 lb loaf tin, so it is supported as it rises and fills the tin.

CHAPTER 10

Pastry and Pastries

There is a belief that good pastry cooks are born and not made. There may be some fortunate people who ARE born with a gift for handling mixtures, so instinctively that they produce good pastry. However, this ability can be learned following recipes carefully and by practice.

There are many kinds of pastry, all of which are covered in this section. Having mastered the art of making good pastry you can then produce wonderful pies, exotic French pastries, crisp professional looking flans, filled with seasonal fruit, together with many other sweet and savoury delicacies, see below.

Cooked and uncooked pastry freezes well, so you can batch-bake and store the extra food for another occasion.

WHAT DOES GOOD PASTRY MEAN?

It means that the pastry is light and crisp in texture and is baked to just the right colour.

The very full instructions given enables you to make every kind of pastry well, from the family shortcrust to the ultra-light choux pastry.

It is possible to use an electric mixer or food processor for blending the ingredients in some kinds of pastry.

The secrets of good pastry lie in using correct proportions of ingredients, blending and handling these correctly; knowing about rolling and folding and lastly choosing the right baking temperature.

Pastry is used for:

Small and large tarts and flans
Sweet and savoury pies
Pastries, such as Cream Horns, Palmiers, Eclairs,
Gâteau St. Honoré and many others
Cocktail nibbles and vol-au-vents

Savoury baked dishes using different pastries – Prawn-filled Choux (recipe page 209), Cheese and Onion Quiche (recipe page 205), Bacon and Apple Roll (recipe page 205)

GOLDEN RULES IN PASTRY MAKING

Since the various methods of making pastry differ in many ways it is not possible to have just one Master Recipe, but rather to follow the advice given in previous chapters 1 to 5. In addition:

Choose the right ingredients, i.e. the kind of flour and fat recommended in the recipe.

Keep all the ingredients and utensils used as cool as possible, except when dealing with the melting method of preparing pastry on pages 208 and 210.

Handle the dough lightly and deftly; it is important to incorporate as much air as possible into the mixture when rubbing fat into the flour, or creaming the fat and sugar or folding the flour and fat mixture. Roll out the pastry dough as lightly as possible; use short sharp movements and not a continual hard 'pressing-down' movement. Do not turn the rolling pin in all directions for that stretches the pastry. Bake at the recommended temperature, most pastries require a hot oven, but this varies somewhat with the type of filling. Pastry containing a relatively high percentage of sugar must not be baked at too great a heat.

Wholemeal Flour in Pastry

Wholemeal or wheatmeal flours can be used in shortcrust or similar pastries. As pointed out throughout this book these flours absorb more liquid than white flour, but do add the liquid gradually, so you use the minimum amount for a satisfactory result.

QUANTITY OF PASTRY

In this particular book the quantity of flour, etc. required is clearly stated in the various recipes. In some publications you may find recipes that give the weight of pastry, e.g. '225 g/8 oz shortcrust pastry'. This means, or should mean, pastry made with that amount of flour and not the total weight of the completed pastry.

Frozen Pastry: You need 375 g/13 oz shortcrust instead of 225 g/8 oz flour, 110 g/4 oz fat, water to bind. Or 375 g/13 oz puff pastry instead of 175 g/6 oz flour, 175 g/6 oz fat, water to bind.

ONE-STAGE PASTRY

Shortcrust and similar types of pastry can be made in one stage, just as when making a cake; if you use the soft type of margarine or soft cooking fat.

Put all the ingredients, including the liquid, into a bowl or large basin and blend with a fork. Do not continue mixing after the dough forms a soft ball.

VARIATIONS ON SHORTCRUST PASTRY

Cheese Pastry: Use only 85 g/3 oz fat; add 50 g/2 oz finely grated Cheddar or other good cooking cheese to the rubbed-in mixture, also see page 205.

Flan or Biscuit Crust Pastry: Add 40 g/1½ oz caster sugar to the rubbed-in mixture; bind with 1 or 2 egg yolks and very little water, also see page 206.

Nutty Pastry: Add 25 g/1 oz finely chopped walnuts, or other nuts, to the basic rubbed-in mixture or the variations above and below and pages 205 and 206.

Sweet Shortcrust Pastry: Add 1 tablespoon caster sugar, see also page 206.

PASTRY MADE BY RUBBING-IN METHOD

The favourite pastry for most people, i.e. Shortcrust, is made by the rubbing-in method.

The information at the beginning of Chapter 2 is therefore very important, see pages 38 to 40.

You can use either a mixer or food processor for making this rubbed-in pastry, providing it is not over-handled.

The information is on page 40; Shortcrust pastry is crumbly and difficult to roll out if over-handled.

SHORTCRUST PASTRY

225 g/8 oz plain flour
pinch salt
**110 g/4 oz fat – this can be all butter or
all margarine or half butter or
margarine and half cooking fat or
lard**
cold water to mix

Important Points: Using proportions above. Rubbing the fat into the flour lightly and carefully, see page 39; adding the liquid slowly and carefully.

Sift the flour and salt into a mixing bowl. Cut the fat into pieces, drop into the flour, as steps 1 to 3 on page 39. Gradually add the liquid and blend the dough with a palette knife. Flours vary in the amount of liquid they absorb but you will need just over 2 tablespoons; the mixture should form a ball and leave the mixing bowl clean.

Dust the pastry board and rolling pin with a little flour, roll out the dough to the required shape. Shortcrust pastry is generally baked in a moderately hot to hot oven, 200–220°C, 400–425°F, Gas Mark 6–7.

TO MAKE A FRUIT PIE

A pie made in a 1.2 litre/2 pint pie dish serves 4–6 people. For this use Shortcrust or Sweet Shortcrust Pastry made with 175 g/6 oz flour, etc. if you like a very thin crust, or 225 g/8 oz flour, etc. for a thicker topping. Have sufficient fruit to support the pastry as it cooks. You need about 750 g/1½ lb prepared fruit. If insufficient use a pie support or upturned ovenproof egg cup.

1 Prepare the fruit, put into the pie dish, add a little water and sugar to taste. Do not put sugar on the very top of the fruit, it makes the pastry soggy. To thicken the juice as the fruit cooks blend 1–2 teaspoons arrowroot, cornflour or fine semolina with the sugar.

2 Roll out the pastry, as described left, to the size of the pie dish, plus an extra 5 cm/2 inches all around. Cut a narrow strip or strips the width of the rim of the pie dish.

3 Moisten the rim of the pie dish with water, press the strip(s) on this. Support the large pastry shape over the rolling pin as shown; lower over the fruit. This stage is easier than it sounds and it prevents the pastry breaking.

4 Cut away any surplus pastry and 'flute' the edges of the pastry. This means pressing between your forefinger and thumb to give a scalloped effect. Bake in the centre of a moderately hot to hot oven, 200–220°C, 400–425°F, Gas Mark 6–7 for 10–15 minutes to set the pastry; reduce the heat to moderate, 190°C, 375°F, Gas Mark 5 for a further 20–25 minutes or a little longer with hard fruit. Dust the pie with caster sugar and serve hot or cold.

SYRUP TART

Serves 4–6

ingredients as Shortcrust Pastry on page 199, made with 175 g/6 oz flour, etc.

for the filling
1 lemon
6 tablespoons golden syrup
75 g/3 oz soft fine breadcrumbs

Make, roll out the pastry and line either a 23 cm/9 inch pie plate or tin or an 18–20 cm/7–8 inch deeper flan dish or tin. Bake 'blind' as described on page 206–207 in the centre of a moderately hot to hot oven, 200–220°C, 400–425°F, Gas Mark 6–7 for 10–15 minutes only until just firm; do not allow the pastry to brown.

Meanwhile finely grate the rind from the lemon, halve and squeeze out 1 tablespoon juice, blend with the syrup and breadcrumbs. Remove the pastry case from the oven, remove the paper or foil from the pastry. Reduce the oven heat to moderate, 180°C, 350°F, Gas Mark 4. Spoon the syrup mixture into the pastry case, do not spread too near the edges of the pastry or the pie plate. Bake for 20 minutes. Serve hot or cold.

CUSTARD TART

Serves 4

ingredients as Shortcrust or Sweet Shortcrust Pastry on pages 199 and 198, made with 175 g/6 oz flour, etc.

for the filling
1 large egg
2 egg yolks
1–2 teaspoons sugar
300 ml/½ pint milk
nutmeg

Make and partially bake the pastry as described in the Syrup Tart left. Meanwhile beat the egg and egg yolks with the sugar. Warm the milk and pour over the egg mixture. Strain the warm custard into the warm pastry case. Grate a little nutmeg over the top. Return the tart to the oven, reducing the heat to slow to very moderate, 150–160°C, 300–325°F, Gas Mark 2–3 for a further 40 minutes until the filling is set.

BAKEWELL TART

Serves 4–6

ingredients as Shortcrust or Sweet Shortcrust Pastry on pages 199 and 198, made with 175 g/6 oz flour, etc.
2 tablespoons icing sugar

for the filling
3 tablespoons raspberry jam
75 g/3 oz butter or margarine
75 g/3 oz caster sugar
few drops almond essence
2 eggs
25 g/1 oz plain flour
75 g/3 oz ground almonds
40 g/1½ oz soft fine sponge cake crumbs

Make, roll out the pastry and line a 20–23 cm/8–9 inch flan dish or tin or ring. Spread bottom of pastry with the jam.

Cream together the butter, sugar and almond essence until soft and light. Beat in the eggs then sift in the flour. Mix well then add the ground almonds and cake crumbs. Spoon over the jam.

Bake in the centre of a moderately hot oven, 200°C, 400°F, Gas Mark 6 for 15–20 minutes to set the pastry. Reduce the heat to very moderate, 160°C, 325°F, Gas Mark 3 and bake for a further 20 minutes until both pastry and filling are firm.

Cool slightly, remove from the tin or ring then sift the icing sugar over the top.

HIGHLAND TART

Serves 6

ingredients as Shortcrust Pastry on page 199, made with 100 g/4 oz flour, etc.

for the filling
50 g/2 oz butter or margarine
50 g/2 oz soft light brown sugar
1 egg
50 g/2 oz rolled oats
25 g/1 oz candied peel
25 g/1 oz glacé cherries
25 g/1 oz sultanas
25 g/1 oz currants

for the topping
25 g/1 oz blanched flaked almonds

Make, roll out the pastry and line an 18 cm/7 inch flan dish or tin or flan ring on an upturned baking tray. Chill well before proceeding further as the filling is light in weight and the pastry could lose its good shape.

Cream together the butter or margarine and sugar until soft, beat in the egg and the rolled oats. Finely chop the peel and cherries, add to the mixture together with the sultanas and currants. Spoon into the pastry case and top with the almonds.

Bake in the centre of a moderately hot oven, 190–200°C, 375–400°F, Gas Mark 5–6 for 15–20 minutes to set the pastry, then reduce the heat to very moderate 160°C, 325°F, Gas Mark 3 for a further 15 minutes. Serve hot as a dessert.

LEMON MERINGUE PIE

Serves 4–6

ingredients as Shortcrust Pastry on page 199, made with 175 g/6 oz flour, etc.

for the filling
1 large or 2 small lemons
water, see method
25 g/1 oz cornflour
25 g/1 oz butter
75–100 g/3–4 oz caster sugar
2 egg yolks

for the meringue
2 egg whites
50–100 g/2–4 oz caster sugar, see method

Make, roll out the pastry and line a deep 20 cm/8 inch flan dish, ring or sandwich tin. Bake 'blind' as described on page 206–207 in the centre of a moderately hot oven, 200°C, 400°F, Gas Mark 6 for 15 minutes.

Grate the top rind (the 'zest') from the lemon(s). Squeeze out the juice and add enough water to make a total of 300 ml/½ pint liquid. Blend the cornflour with this liquid, put into a saucepan; add the butter, lemon rind and sugar (amount depends upon personal taste). Stir over a low heat until thickened and smooth. Remove the pan from the heat, whisk in the egg yolks. Return the pan to a very low heat and stir until the mixture thickens again then spoon into the part baked pastry case.

Whisk the egg whites until stiff, add the sugar; see information on Meringues, pages 164 to 168, use the higher amount if serving the meringue cold. Pile on top of the filling, make sure there is no gap between the meringue and the pastry.

To serve hot: bake in the centre of a very moderate oven, 160°C, 325°F, Gas Mark 3 for 20 minutes.

To serve cold: set for 1 hour in a very cool oven, 130°C, 250°F, Gas Mark ½.

Note: See the comments about other types of meringue that could be put on to the filling on page 167.

MACAROON TARTLETS

Makes 12–18

ingredients as Shortcrust or Sweet Shortcrust or Flan Pastry on pages 198 and 199, made with 175 g/6 oz flour, etc.

for the filling
2–3 tablespoons apricot jam
2 egg whites
few drops almond essence
100 g/4 oz ground almonds
100 g/4 oz caster sugar

Make the selected pastry as page 199 or 198. Roll out very thinly for these tartlets, since the filling is a delicate one and it would be over-cooked if the pastry was too thick; cut into rounds and line 12 deep or 18 more shallow patty tins. Put a little jam into each pastry case. There may be a little pastry left over in which case re-roll this and cut into thin strips, make sufficient for two strips to form a cross for each tartlet case.

Whisk the egg whites until frothy, add the essence, ground almonds and sugar. Divide the filling between the pastry cases.

Damp the ends of the pastry strips with a little cold water. Place very lightly across the filling, but press the ends of the strips against the sides of the tartlet cases. Bake in the centre of a moderately hot oven, 200°C, 400°F, Gas Mark 6 for 10 minutes, then reduce the heat slightly and continue cooking for a further 5 minutes or until both the pastry and filling are firm.

RECIPES BASED ON MACAROON TARTLETS

Economical Macaroon Tartlets: Use half ground almonds and half fine sponge cake crumbs for a soft texture or 75 g/3 oz ground almonds and 25 g/1 oz semolina or ground rice for a firmer texture.

Almond Slices: Make the pastry as in Macaroon Tartlets, roll out and line a Swiss roll tin measuring approximately 25 × 18 cm/10 × 7 inches. Spread the base of the pastry with the apricot jam; top with the macaroon filling as in the Macaroon Tartlets then sprinkle with 25–50 g/1–2 oz flaked blanched almonds.

Bake in the centre of a moderately hot oven, 200°C, 400°F, Gas Mark 6 for 15 minutes; reduce the heat to moderate, 180°C, 350°F, Gas Mark 4 for a further 10 minutes or until both pastry and filling are set. Mark into 12 fingers while warm; lift from the tin and place on a wire tray.

Chocolate Walnut Tartlets: Make the pastry as in Macaroon Tartlets, roll out and line 12–18 patty tins. Put 1 teaspoon apricot jam into each tartlet case. Coarsely chop 50 g/2 oz walnuts. Cream together 75 g/3 oz butter or margarine and 75 g/3 oz caster sugar. Beat in 1 egg. Sift 75 g/3 oz self-raising flour, or plain flour with ¾ teaspoon baking powder, and 40 g/1½ oz chocolate powder. Fold into the creamed ingredients. Add the chopped walnuts. Continue as Macaroon Tartlets.

Melt 100 g/4 oz plain chocolate, cool slightly and blend with 25 g/1 oz butter. Sift 25 g/1 oz icing sugar into the melted chocolate. Spread a little over each cooled tartlet and top with walnut halves and chocolate vermicelli.

Frangipani Tartlets: Make the pastry as in Macaroon Tartlets, roll out and line 12–18 patty tins. Put 1 teaspoon raspberry jam into each tartlet case. Cream together 75 g/3 oz butter and 75 g/3 oz caster sugar. Beat in 2 eggs, a few drops of almond essence, 75 g/3 oz ground almonds and 2 teaspoons plain flour. Continue as Macaroon Tartlets. When cold these tartlets can be topped with Glacé Icing made with 175 g/6 oz icing sugar, etc., see page 146.

MINCE PIES

Makes 12

Mince pies can be made with Shortcrust Pastry – use 225 g/8 oz flour, etc. as page 199 or Puff Pastry – use 175 g/6 oz flour, etc., see recipe on page 212. Roll out just over half the pastry until approximately 5 mm/¼ inch in thickness. Cut into approximately 12 rounds, sufficient to fill fairly deep patty tins. Put in a little mince-meat, do not overfill the pastry. Roll out the remaining pastry, cut into slightly smaller rounds than used for the base. Damp the edges and put on the 'lids'. Seal well and make two slits on top.

Bake in the centre of the oven. For shortcrust pastry use a moderately hot oven, 200°C, 400°F, Gas Mark 6; for puff pastry use a hot oven, 220°C, 425°F, Gas Mark 7. Bake for 20–25 minutes; reduce the heat slightly after 10–12 minutes if necessary. Dust with caster or icing sugar.

MINCEMEAT

Makes a generous 885 g/2 lb

The amount of 110 g is given under metric weights to ensure total weight above.

Mix together 225 g/8 oz seedless or de-seeded and chopped raisins, 110 g/4 oz currants, 110 g/4 oz sultanas, 110 g/4 oz shredded suet or melted butter, 110 g/4 oz light brown or Demerara or caster sugar, 110 g/4 oz grated cooking apple, 110 g/4 oz blanched chopped almonds, ½–1 teaspoon ground cinnamon, ½ teaspoon grated nutmeg, the finely grated rind of 1 lemon, 2 tablespoons lemon juice and 4 tablespoons brandy, rum or whisky.

You can add 50–110 g/2–4 oz chopped glacé cherries too, plus 110 g/4 oz chopped candied peel.

APFEL STRUDEL

Serves 4–6

for the pastry
225 g/8 oz plain flour
pinch salt
2 tablespoons oil
1 egg
approx. 4 tablespoons water

for the filling
100 g/4 oz butter
50 g/2 oz soft breadcrumbs
900 g/2 lb cooking apples
50 g/2 oz currants
50 g/2 oz seedless raisins
50–75 g/2–3 oz caster sugar
½–1 teaspoon ground cinnamon

to decorate
25–50 g/1–2 oz icing sugar

Grease a large baking tray. Sift the flour and salt into a bowl, add the oil and egg, mix thoroughly with the flour. Warm the water, blend with the flour mixture to give a soft, pliable dough. Cover the bowl with a cloth; leave for 15 minutes.

Heat 50 g/2 oz butter in a frying pan; fry the breadcrumbs until golden. Peel, core and coarsely grate the apples; mix with the dried fruit, sugar and spice.

Cover a table with a cloth; flour this and a rolling pin. Roll and stretch the pastry until a large paper-thin oblong shape.

Melt the remaining butter, brush half over the pastry. Sprinkle on the crumbs; add the apple filling. Keep this well away from the edges of the pastry. Roll up like a Swiss roll; seal the edges; make a horseshoe shape. Lift on to the baking tray. Brush with the remaining butter.

Bake in the centre of a moderately hot oven, 190–200°C, 375–400°F, Gas Mark 5–6 for 20 minutes, then reduce the heat slightly for a further 25–30 minutes. Serve hot or cold. Sift the icing sugar over the Strudel just before serving.

MAKING QUICHES

A quiche, or savoury egg custard flan, is one of the most delicious dishes.

SPINACH QUICHE

Serves 4–6

ingredients as Cheese Pastry on page 198, made with 175 g/6 oz flour, etc.

for the filling
1 small onion
25 g/1 oz butter
350 g/12 oz spinach
salt and pepper
pinch grated nutmeg
2 eggs
150 ml/¼ pint single cream
150 g/5 oz Cheddar cheese
25 g/1 oz Parmesan cheese

Make, roll out the pastry and line a 20–23 cm/8–9 inch flan dish or tin. Chill well while preparing the filling. Peel and finely chop the onion. Heat the butter in a good sized saucepan. Toss the onion in the butter, do not allow to brown. Wash the spinach, do not dry, but put into the saucepan with the water adhering to the leaves, add a little salt, pepper and nutmeg. Cook until just tender, this takes 6–8 minutes. Drain away any surplus liquid, chop the spinach, blend with the eggs and cream. Grate the cheese and mix with the spinach; taste the mixture and season.

Meanwhile bake the pastry case 'blind' as described on page 207 in the centre of a moderately hot oven, 200°C, 400°F, Gas Mark 6 for about 12 minutes until just set but still pale. Remove from the oven, fill with the spinach mixture.

Return to a very moderate oven, 160°C, 325°F, Gas Mark 3 and bake for 30–40 minutes or until the filling is firm. Serve hot or cold.

CRUMB QUICHE

Serves 4–6

ingredients as Shortcrust Pastry on page 199, made with 175 g/6 oz flour, etc.

for the filling
50 g/2 oz bread, weight without crust
300 ml/½ pint milk
75 g/3 oz Cheddar cheese
1 small sprig parsley
3 eggs
1 teaspoon Worcestershire sauce
salt and pepper

Make, roll out the pastry and line a 20 cm/8 inch flan dish. Bake 'blind' in the centre of a moderately hot oven, 200°C, 400°F, Gas Mark 6 for 15 minutes.

Meanwhile make the bread into breadcrumbs. Heat the milk in a saucepan, add the crumbs, remove from the heat and allow to stand for a few minutes. Grate the cheese, chop the parsley. Add the cheese, parsley, well-beaten eggs, Worcestershire sauce, salt and pepper to the milk mix.

Spoon into the partially baked pastry case, reduce the heat to very moderate, 160°C, 325°F, Gas Mark 3 and bake for 35–40 minutes or until the filling is set.

CRUMB QUICHE LORRAINE

Serves 4–6

ingredients as Crumb Quiche
75 g/3 oz streaky or back bacon

Bake the pastry case 'blind' as above. Meanwhile chop the bacon into small pieces, fry for a few minutes until crisp; drain and add to the other ingredients for the filling. Put into the partially baked pastry case and continue cooking as above.

CHEESE AND ONION QUICHE

Illustrated in colour on page 197

Serves 4–6

Make a 20 cm/8 inch flan with shortcrust pastry using 175 g/6 oz flour etc. Bake 'blind' as under Crumb Quiche on page 204. Peel and thinly slice 1 large onion, fry in 25 g/1 oz butter, add to the flan. Blend 3 eggs, 150 ml/¼ pint milk, 150 ml/¼ pint single cream, 100 g/4 oz grated Samsø or Danbo cheese and seasoning. Pour into the pastry, top with a little cayenne pepper. Bake as the Crumb Quiche.

RICH CHEESE PASTRY

As this pastry is generally used for biscuits, i.e., Cheese Straws, you will find the recipe on page 171 in the Meringues, Biscuits and Cookies chapter. This pastry is too rich and brittle to use for general purposes. The Cream Cheese Pastry which follows can be used instead of the Cheese Pastry on page 198.

CREAM CHEESE PASTRY

225 g/8 oz plain flour
pinch salt
150 g/5 oz cream cheese
water or egg yolk and water to bind

Sift the flour and salt into a mixing bowl. Add the cream cheese, mix with the flour. Knead lightly and then add water or egg yolk and water to make a rolling consistency.

SUET CRUST PASTRY

This pastry uses the same proportions of fat (suet) to flour as Shortcrust Pastry, see page 199, but is different in texture and flavour because the pastry is made with self-raising flour, or plain flour with baking powder, and it is mixed with more liquid. It is used more often in steamed puddings than in baking.

The basic recipe is made just by mixing ingredients rather than 'rubbing-in'.

225 g/8 oz self-raising flour or plain flour
    with 2 teaspoons baking powder
pinch salt
110 g/4 oz shredded suet
approx. 150 ml/¼ pint water to bind

Sift the flour, or flour and baking powder, with the salt. Add the suet, then gradually add sufficient water to make a soft rolling consistency. Bind with a palette knife then knead quickly until smooth.

BACON AND APPLE ROLL

Illustrated in colour on page 197
Serves 6

Make Suet Crust as above. De-rind and chop 350 g/12 oz choice middle cut bacon rashers; peel and slice 1 large onion and 1 large cooking apple. Fry the bacon rinds, bacon and onion until soft. Remove the rinds, add the apple, 1 teaspoon brown sugar and a shake of pepper. Cool. Roll out the pastry to a rectangle, 25 × 20 cm/10 × 8 inches; spread with the filling; leave a 2.5 cm/1 inch border. Moisten edges, roll and place on a lightly greased baking tray, with the join underneath. Slash the top. Brush with milk. Bake in the centre of a moderately hot oven, 190–200°C, 375–400°F, Gas Mark 5–6 for 30 minutes or until firm and golden. Garnish with sliced dessert apple, dipped in lemon juice to keep white.

PASTRY MADE BY CREAMING METHOD

Although Flan Pastry can be made by rubbing fat into flour, see pages 198 and 199, creaming the fat and sugar produces a deliciously crisp pastry, ideal for sweet flans. This is known as Fleur or Flan pastry.

The information about creaming on pages 66 and 67 is important, although the pastry is firm and crisp, as opposed to the soft lightness of a cake.

You can use either a mixer or food processor for creaming and blending the ingredients. Although this pastry can be handled more firmly than other types, care must be taken that the appliance is not used for too long a period. For information see pages 68 and 69.

FLEUR PASTRY

150 g/5 oz butter or margarine
25–50 g/1–2 oz caster sugar
225 g/8 oz plain flour
pinch salt
1–2 egg yolks
cold water to mix

Important Points: Creaming the butter or margarine and sugar until soft; kneading the dough lightly and rolling out firmly.

Cream together the butter or margarine and sugar. Sift the flour and salt into the creamed mixture, mix well, then add the 1 or 2 egg yolks with a very little water if necessary. Form into a neat shape. If the dough is rather soft, wrap in foil or clingfilm and chill for a while before rolling out. This richer pastry is generally baked in a moderate to moderately hot oven, 190–200°C, 375–400°F, Gas Mark 5–6.
Note: You can omit 25 g/1 oz flour and use 25 g/1 oz cornflour instead.

APPLE HAZZELBACH

Serves 4

ingredients as Flan Pastry, made with 100 g/4 oz flour, etc.

for the topping
5 tablespoons apricot jam
50 g/2 oz ground almonds
50 g/2 oz Demerara sugar
pinch ground cinnamon
1 egg yolk
2 medium dessert apples

Make, roll out the pastry and line an 18 cm/7 inch flan dish or tin. Spread 2 tablespoons jam over the pastry. Blend the ground almonds, sugar, cinnamon and egg yolk and cover the jam with this mixture. Halve the apples, peel and core them, do not slice. Place the apples, with the cut side downwards, on the almond mixture, gently cut the top of the apples to make 3–4 slits, brush with half the remaining jam.

Bake in the centre of a moderate oven, 180°C, 350°F, Gas Mark 4 for 30 minutes. Spread the remaining jam over the apples and bake for a further 15 minutes.

TO MAKE AND BAKE A FLAN

Use any of the shortcrust pastries or Flan or Fleur Pastry made with:

100 g/4 oz flour, etc. will make a 15–19 cm/6–7½ inch flan
175 g/6 oz flour, etc. will make a 19–23 cm/7½–9 inch flan
225 g/8 oz flour, etc. will make a 23–25 cm/9–10 inch flan

The variation depends upon the richness of the pastry used and the depth of the flan ring or other container.
Grease the flan ring lightly and place on an

upturned baking tray, this makes it easier to slide the flan off the baking tray when cooked; if preferred use an ovenproof flan dish or a tin.

Make the pastry, support it over a rolling pin, lower into the flan ring, dish or container. Press down firmly. Either cut away the surplus pastry or roll the rolling pin firmly over the top of the flan ring or other container and the excess pastry drops away.

To bake the pastry flan without a filling, i.e. 'blind', it is important to prevent the bottom of the pastry rising. Put either a layer of foil into the pastry or a round of greased greaseproof paper (greasy side touching the pastry). Top with dried beans, crusts of bread or the modern plastic peas. Bake in the centre of a moderate to moderately hot oven, about 190–200°C, 375–400°F, Gas Mark 5–6, depending upon the pastry used, for 15 minutes. Remove the foil or paper and beans, bread or peas, you can also slip off the flan ring. Return the flan to the oven for a further 5 minutes.

FRUIT FLAN

Bake the flan as instructions on page 206 and above. Allow to cool. Fill with fresh soft fruit, such as strawberries or with very well-drained canned, frozen or cooked fruit. A 20 cm/8 inch flan takes from 450–550 g/1–1¼ lb fruit.

To glaze the fruit in a 20 cm/8 inch flan, put 5 tablespoons redcurrant jelly or sieved apricot jam into a pan. Add 3 tablespoons water and a squeeze of lemon juice. Stir over a low heat until the jelly or jam has melted; cool slightly then spread or brush over the fruit.

If using canned or cooked fruit you can strain off 150–200 ml/5–7½ fl oz of the juice or syrup, blend this with 1–1½ teaspoons arrowroot or cornflour. Tip into a saucepan, add any extra sugar required and stir over a low heat until thickened and clear. Cool slightly and brush over the fruit.

To make an authentic French fruit flan use the following method of making the pastry.

PÂTE SUCRÉE

110 g/4 oz butter
225 g/8 oz plain flour
pinch salt
50–110 g/2–4 oz caster sugar
2 egg yolks

Although like Flan Pastry, the method of making this French pastry produces a particularly light but crisp texture.

Allow the butter to become fairly soft but do not let it oil. Sift the flour and salt on to a large pastry board. Make a well in the centre, put the butter (in one piece), sugar and egg yolks into the centre space. Mix these ingredients with your finger-tips until well blended.

Gradually work the flour into this mixture with your finger-tips; start with the flour around the well. Do not try and make the butter mixture absorb too much flour at one time. When mixed use as Flan or Fleur Pastry, recipes on pages 198 and 206.

FRENCH APPLE TART

Make the pastry, line the flan dish or tin, spread with a layer of thick sweetened apple purée then top with sliced raw apples; sprinkle with sugar. Bake as the Fruit Flan, but allow an extra 15–20 minutes cooking time and a slightly lower setting to make quite sure the filling is cooked. Allow the flan to cool then top with a glaze made from apricot jam.

PECAN PIE

Serves 4–6

**ingredients as Fleur Pastry on page 206,
made with 175 g/6 oz flour, etc.**

for the filling
**100 g/4 oz pecan nuts
50 g/2 oz butter
225 g/8 oz light brown sugar
2 tablespoons golden syrup
¼–½ teaspoon vanilla essence
3 eggs**

Make, roll out the pastry and line a 20–
23 cm/8–9 inch flan ring. Bake 'blind' for
10 minutes only as described on page 207.
   Chop the nuts. Cream together the butter, sugar and golden syrup. Add the essence then gradually beat in the eggs and
finally add the nuts. Spoon into the pastry
case and return to the oven for 40 minutes,
reducing the heat to 160°C, 325°F, Gas
Mark 3. Serve hot or cold.

BRAZIL NUT PIE

Follow the recipe for Pecan Pie; omit the
pecan nuts. Use chopped Brazil nuts and
25 g/1 oz cake crumbs. Serves 4–6.

SHERRY FLAN

Serves 4–6

Make and bake 'blind', a 20–23 cm/8–9
inch flan, as pages 206–207. When cold,
spread the bottom with jam or thick
sweetened fruit purée. Blend 175 g/6 oz
sponge cake crumbs with 5 tablespoons
sweet sherry, 50 g/2 oz chopped glacé
cherries and 25 g/1 oz blanched chopped
almonds. Spoon into the flan. Top with a
thick layer of whipped cream, and with
glacé cherries and blanched almonds.

PASTRY MADE BY MELTING METHOD

Choux Pastry is surprisingly easy, the initial ingredients are melted and this stage is
an important one, see the comments about
melting on pages 108, 110–112.

A mixer or food processor is not a great
help for making Choux Pastry, it is better
to do this by hand.

CHOUX PASTRY

**150 ml/¼ pint water
50 g/2 oz butter or margarine
1 teaspoon sugar, or salt and pepper for
   savoury choux pastry
65 g/2½ oz plain flour
2 eggs**

Important Points: Heat the water only
until the fat has melted; dry the mixture
well when the flour is added. Beat the eggs
gradually into the flour mixture.

Put the water, butter or margarine and
sugar or seasoning into a good-sized saucepan. Heat until the fat has melted. Remove from the heat. Sift the flour, add to
the pan, stir well to blend, then return the
pan to a low heat and stir until the flour
mixture forms a ball and leaves the saucepan clean.
   Allow the mixture to cool; whisk the
eggs in a separate basin, then beat gradually into the flour mixture.
   Choux pastry should be baked in a hot
oven, so it rises well.

CHOUX PASTRY 2

A slightly more economical recipe is made
by using 85 g/3 oz flour and only 25 g/1 oz
butter or margarine.

RECIPES USING CHOUX PASTRY

The easiest way of shaping this pastry is to put it into a large piping bag, fitted with a 5 mm–1.5 cm/¼–½ inch plain pipe (the pipe depends upon the size of the shapes). The pastry can be spooned on to baking trays.

Always preheat the oven thoroughly before baking choux pastry; allow cooked pastry to cool away from a draught.

Cream Buns: Make the pastry as page 208. Pipe or spoon into 12 medium shaped rounds on one or two well greased baking trays. It is an advantage to use a single tray, but do not crowd the rounds.

Bake just above the centre of a moderately hot oven, 200°C, 400°F, Gas Mark 6 for 30–35 minutes until well risen and firm to the touch. Check carefully (do not open the door too wide) and if the buns are changing colour too much, lower the heat slightly.

If your oven tends to be a little cooler than average, cook the buns for 10–15 minutes at 220°C, 425°F, Gas Mark 7 then reduce the heat to 190°C, 375°F, Gas Mark 5 for the rest of the cooking time.

The more economical recipe given as Choux Pastry 2 on page 208 cooks in a slightly shorter time.

Lift the cooked buns from the baking tray(s) on to a wire cooling tray. When cold make a slit in each bun; should there be a small amount of uncooked mixture inside carefully remove this with a teaspoon; the buns could be returned to the oven for a few minutes to 'dry out' but this is rarely necessary.

Whip 150–300 ml/¼–½ pint double cream, sweeten this if desired. Spoon or pipe into the buns. Sift a little icing sugar over the top of the buns or ice, as given under Eclairs.

Fruit Choux: Fill the buns with fruit and whipped cream or ice cream, do this just before serving.

Eclairs: Make the pastry as page 208. It is better to use a pipe to obtain even-sized fingers. Lightly flour the greased baking tray(s); mark lines in the flour with the end of a wooden spoon; these will show the length of the fingers. If you have no piping bag then use a spoon, or put the mixture into well greased sponge finger tins.

Pipe or spoon the mixture into about 16 medium sized fingers. Bake as Cream Buns but allow only 20–25 minutes cooking time. When cool, slit and fill with whipped cream. Top with Chocolate, Coffee or tinted Glacé Icing, made as page 146, using 225 g/8 oz icing sugar, etc.

Gâteaux Paris Brest: Make the pastry as page 208. Pipe 12–16 narrow rings on well greased and floured baking trays; (mark the rings in the flour first). Brush the rings with a beaten egg, then top with 50 g/2 oz blanched flaked almonds and 25 g/1 oz sifted icing sugar. Bake as the Cream Buns, but allow only 20–25 minutes cooking time. When cold, split and fill with whipped cream or Crème Pâtissière, made as page 150. Top with more icing sugar.

Prawn-filled Choux: Use the Choux Pastry recipe on page 208 but add 50 g/2 oz grated Samsø or Danbo cheese after blending in the eggs. Cook as the Choux Buns on this page; if small (as in the picture on page 197) allow 15–20 minutes baking only. Cool; fill as below and garnish with paprika, lettuce, lemon slices and unpeeled prawns (optional).

The filling: Blend 75 g/3 oz cream cheese, 2 tablespoons grated Samsø or Danbo cheese, 1 teaspoon grated lemon rind, 1 teaspoon chopped chives and 100 g/4 oz peeled and chopped prawns. Makes 12–16. *Illustrated in colour on page 197.*

Miniature Choux or Eclairs: Form minute rounds or fingers (use only about 1 teaspoon of pastry). Bake as for Cream Buns but allow 10–12 minutes cooking time. Split and fill with cream cheese, mashed sardines or Savoury Butter as page 171. Makes about 50.

Gâteau St. Honoré: Make the Fleur Pastry, as page 206, using 100 g/4 oz flour, etc. Roll out to a round of 20–23 cm/8–9 inches in diameter. Make the Choux pastry as page 208. Put half into a piping bag and pipe a ring on top of the Fleur Pastry. Put the remaining Choux Pastry into the piping bag, make 9–10 small bun shapes on a greased baking tray.

Bake the round of the two pastries in the centre of a moderate oven, 190°C, 375°F, Gas Mark 5 for 30–35 minutes. Bake small buns above oven centre 25 minutes. Cool.

Slit the round and small buns. Whip 300 ml/½ pint double cream, sweeten to taste, pipe or spoon into all the Choux Pastry. Arrange the small buns on top of the round and decorate with fresh or glacé fruits. Serves 6–8.

Petites Religieuses: Make the Choux Pastry as page 208. Bake two-thirds as eight larger buns, see Cream Buns, and the rest as eight Profiteroles, below. Split and fill with whipped cream. Put the larger buns on a serving dish, top with a little cream and then the smaller buns. Dredge with sifted icing sugar. Makes 8.

Profiteroles: Make the Choux Pastry as page 208. Pipe into 24–30 small bun shapes on greased baking trays. Bake as Cream Buns on page 209 but allow only 20–25 minutes. Allow to cool. Whip 300 ml/½ pint double cream, sweeten if desired. Slit each small bun and fill with the cream. Put into a serving dish and top with Chocolate Sauce, made as below.

Chocolate Sauce: break 175 g/6 oz plain chocolate into pieces. Put into the top of a double saucepan or basin, add 25 g/1 oz butter, 3 tablespoons water, 25 g/1 oz caster sugar and 1 tablespoon golden syrup. Heat over hot, but not boiling water, or in a microwave cooker. Serves 4–6.

HOT WATER CRUST PASTRY

This pastry is made by melting; it is only for cold savoury pies. The pastry must be kept warm during all rolling and handling.

Veal and Ham Pie: Prepare the filling before making the pastry. Hard-boil and shell 2 eggs. Dice 550 g/1¼ lb veal fillet and a 175 g/6 oz slice of cooked ham. Mix the meats with ½ teaspoon grated lemon rind, salt and pepper and 2 tablespoons veal stock.

Hot Water Crust Pastry: Sift 350 g/12 oz plain flour and ¼ teaspoon salt into a mixing bowl. Melt 100 g/4 oz lard with 150 ml/¼ pint milk or water in a saucepan, pour on to the flour. You can add an egg yolk for extra flavour without affecting the amount of liquid. Knead the warm pastry, roll out on a lightly floured board; keep warm.

Take a 16.5 cm/6½ inch cake tin or special Raised Pie tin, grease it lightly. Cut two rounds the diameter of the tin and a band of pastry the depth and circumference of the tin.

Put in one round of pastry; fit the band of pastry around the inside of the tin, seal the edges firmly. Put in half the filling, the eggs, then the remainder of the filling. Moisten the rim of pastry with water. Place the round of pastry for the 'lid' on top of the filling, do not press this down too tightly; seal the edges.

Cut a definite hole in the centre of the pastry 'lid'; this is important – it enables the steam to escape. Roll out any trimmings; cut into leaves and a rose shape. Arrange *around* the hole.

Bake in the centre of a moderate oven, 190°C, 375°F, Gas Mark 5 for 1 hour; then at 180°C, 350°F, Gas Mark 4 for 1½ hours; cool. Dissolve 1 teaspoon gelatine in 5 tablespoons hot veal stock, allow to cool, pour through the centre hole. Leave for several hours until set before cutting and serving. Serves 6.

PASTRY MADE BY FOLDING

This is the method by which the very light pastries, i.e. flaky, puff and rough puff are produced. Although the amount of fat and number of rollings and foldings for each pastry varies, the way in which the dough is handled is very similar.

It has been found that white strong flour, the kind used in making bread, can be used for these pastries. If strong flour is not available use plain – not self-raising – white flour. Wholemeal or wheatmeal flours are unsuitable.

FLAKY PASTRY

225 g/8 oz strong or plain flour
pinch salt
175 g/6 oz fat – can be all butter or half butter or hard (not luxury) margarine and half lard. Shredded suet and half butter can be used
squeeze lemon juice
cold water to mix

Important Points: Using the proportions of fat above and never using over-soft fat. Rolling lightly but firmly; turning the dough at right angles and never stretching this. Keeping the pastry cool.

Sift the flour and salt into a mixing bowl. If using a mixture of fats, blend together, this action softens the fats to the right consistency. Divide the fat into three portions. Rub one third into the flour exactly as shown on page 39. Add the lemon juice and cold water to make an elastic and pliable dough; blend with a palette knife. Flours vary in the amount of liquid they absorb, but you will need appreciably more liquid than when making shortcrust.

Turn the dough on to a lightly floured surface and roll out into a neat oblong shape, use a short sharp movement, do not press down on the dough.

Divide the second third of the fat into small pieces and dot over the top two-thirds of the dough.

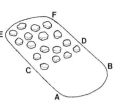
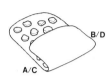

Bring up the fatless section, A to C; B to D; so covering the middle third of the dough – it now looks like an open envelope.

Bring down the top third of the dough E to A/C and F to B/D, so making a neat shape which looks like a closed envelope.

Turn the dough at right angles so you have an open end towards you, seal this and the other open end firmly with the rolling pin. Depress the pastry at intervals, this is known as 'ribbing' the pastry. Roll out the dough once more to an oblong shape and add the rest of the fat in exactly the same way as before, fold the dough, turn, seal the ends and 'rib'.

Allow the dough to rest (often known as 'relax') in the refrigerator. This makes sure it does not become over-sticky. Always cover with clingfilm to make sure the outer surface does not develop a hard skin.

Roll out the pastry to an oblong once more, this time you do not add fat, fold the dough, turn, seal the ends and 'rib'. Cover and relax until ready to use.

Flaky pastry has three rollings and three foldings although some people like to divide the fat(s) into four portions, rub in a quarter and add the rest in three not two batches.

Flaky pastry must be baked in a hot to very hot oven, 220–230°C, 425–450°F, Gas Mark 7–8 to encourage the light dough to rise well. If baking for a long time reduce the heat after 15–20 minutes when the pastry has risen well.

ROUGH PUFF PASTRY

Although this has the same proportions of fat as Flaky Pastry the method of mixing is quite different. Many people find it easier to make. Weigh out the ingredients as for Flaky Pastry, page 211.

Sift the flour and salt into a mixing bowl. Add all the fat. Take two knives and cut the fat into the flour until it has formed small pieces; do not rub it in. Blend the dough with lemon juice and cold water to a pliable and elastic dough. Roll out to a neat oblong on a floured surface.

Fold as Flaky Pastry and then proceed in same way but give a total of five rollings and foldings. Bake as Flaky Pastry.

PUFF PASTRY

This is richer than Flaky Pastry because equal amounts of butter and flour are used. The pastry is rolled and folded seven times, using exactly the same method as Flaky Pastry, page 211.

225 g/8 oz strong or plain flour
pinch salt
squeeze lemon juice
225 g/8 oz butter

Sift the flour and salt into a mixing bowl, mix to an elastic and pliable dough with the lemon juice and cold water. Roll out to a neat oblong, as Flaky Pastry.

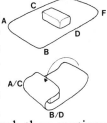

Place the block of butter in the centre of the oblong. Bring up the bottom third of the dough to cover the butter, i.e. A to C, B to D; then bring down the top third E to A/C and F to B/D. Turn the dough then continue as Flaky Pastry with the extra rollings and foldings. Puff Pastry is baked in a very hot oven, see under Flaky Pastry.

212

MILLE FEUILLES

Serves 6

This should, as the name suggests, look like a thousand layers, when baked. Make the Puff Pastry. Roll out into a square, about 30.5 × 30.5 cm/12 × 12 inches. Trim the edges (this encourages the pastry to rise). Cut the square into three equal sized oblongs. Place on one or two dampened baking trays, cover lightly with clingfilm; allow to relax for 20–30 minutes.

Preheat the oven at hot to very hot, 220–230°C, 425–450°F, Gas Mark 7–8. Bake the pastry just above the centre of the oven for about 20 minutes; reduce the heat slightly after 10 minutes if necessary. Remove from the baking trays on to a wire cooling tray.

Whip 300 ml/½ pint double cream; spread the first layer of pastry with jam or thick sweetened fruit purée and half the cream. Top with the second layer of pastry, more jam or fruit purée and the rest of the cream. Make a stiff Glacé Icing, as page 146, using 175 g/6 oz sifted icing sugar. Spread on the third layer of pastry. When set lift over the other two layers of pastry.

SAVOURY MILLE FEUILLES

Serves 6

Bake the pastry as above. Blend 350 g/12 oz cream cheese with 3–4 tablespoons double cream. Season to taste.

Top one layer of pastry with one third of the cheese mixture; garnish with sliced gherkins, radishes and herbs.

Blend 1 tablespoon chopped chives, 1 tablespoon chopped parsley together with 50 g/2 oz chopped lean ham and the rest of the cheese mixture. Use instead of whipped cream and jam in the sweet one.

BANBURY CAKES

Makes 10

ingredients as Eccles Cakes
50 g/2 oz fine cake or macaroon biscuit
**   crumbs**

Roll out the pastry as for Eccles Cakes but cut into large oval shapes instead of rounds. Cream the butter and sugar, add the other filling ingredients, including the crumbs. Proceed as for Eccles Cakes.

ECCLES CAKES

Illustrated in colour on the jacket

Makes 10

ingredients as Puff Pastry on page 212;
**   made with 175 g/6 oz flour, etc.**

for the filling
50 g/2 oz butter or margarine
50 g/2 oz caster or light brown sugar
50 g/2 oz sultanas
50 g/2 oz currants
2 tablespoons finely chopped candied
**   orange and lemon peel**
1 teaspoon grated lemon rind
1 tablespoon lemon juice
¼ teaspoon mixed spice

to glaze
little milk
caster sugar

Make, roll out the pastry until it is very thin; cut into 10 rounds (you need to cut around a large saucer, unless making very small cakes). Cream together the butter or margarine and sugar, then add the rest of the filling ingredients; blend thoroughly. Divide the filling between the rounds of pastry; damp the edges of the pastry and gather together, seal firmly, then turn the cakes upside down; roll and shape with your fingers very gently and carefully to make perfect rounds of about 6.5–8 cm/ 2½–3 inches in diameter.

Make two or three slits on top of each cake with kitchen scissors, brush the cakes with a very little milk and sprinkle lightly with the sugar. Lift on to an un-greased baking tray and bake in the centre of a hot to very hot oven, 220–230°C, 425–450°F, Gas Mark 7–8 for 15 minutes then reduce the heat to moderate, 180°C, 350°F, Gas Mark 4 for a further 5–6 minutes.

NUT BATONS

Makes 12–15

ingredients as Flaky, Puff or Rough Puff
**   Pastry on pages 211 and 212, made**
**   with approx. 100 g/4 oz flour, etc.**
3 tablespoons caster sugar
2 tablespoons finely chopped walnuts or
**   other nuts**
1 egg white

This is an excellent way of using up left over pastry. Form the pastry into a neat oblong shape. Sprinkle half the sugar on the pastry board and roll out the pastry until very thin, fold as Flaky Pastry, page 211, to make an oblong again. Roll out again and cut into neat fingers. Mix the remaining sugar and nuts. Whisk the egg white until frothy, brush over the pastry then roll each finger in the sugar and nuts. Grease a baking tray, place the pastry fingers on this.

Bake just above the centre of a hot to very hot oven, 220–230°C, 425–450°F, Gas Mark 7–8 for 10 minutes, check carefully after 5–6 minutes to make quite sure the sugar-coating is not becoming too brown. If necessary lower the heat.

213

RECIPES BASED ON THE RICHER PASTRIES

All the following recipes can be made with flaky, rough puff or puff pastry. The quantities are based on pastry using 225 g/ 8 oz flour, etc.

Cream Horns: Roll out the pastry and cut into 12 strips about 2.5 cm/1 inch in width and 28–30.5 cm/11–12 inches in length. Take great care that you do not stretch the pastry when rolling and cutting this or when winding it around the horn tins.

Grease 12 cream horn tins very lightly. Damp the edges of the pastry strips with a little cold water, then wind these around the tins. Start from the bottom pointed end; allow each strip to overlap by about 5 mm/¼ inch.

Place the horns on a baking tray, with the top joined end underneath. Check to see that the pastry has not come over the top of the tins, for this would make it very difficult to remove the tins after baking. Allow to relax for 30 minutes.

Bake just above the centre of a hot oven, 220°C, 425°F, Gas Mark 7 for 10–15 minutes or until the pastry begins to colour. Remove from the oven. Brush the shapes very lightly with either milk or an unwhisked egg white then dredge with caster sugar. Return to the oven for a further 5–10 minutes. By glazing during, rather than before, cooking you keep the pastry a better colour. Allow the pastry to cool for a good 5 minutes, then carefully slip the horn tins away. When the pastry is quite cold, fill firstly with jam, then top with whipped cream. You will need about 225 g/8 oz jam (or use a thick sweetened fruit purée) and at least 150 ml/¼ pint double cream.

Miniature Cream Horns: You can make very tiny horns by winding the pastry from the base only one third or half way up the tins. These can be partially cooked, glazed and then completed as above for only a total of 15–20 minutes cooking or glazed just with egg white and no sugar.

When cold, fill with cream cheese and garnish with tiny pieces of gherkins or tomato or finely chopped parsley.

Jam Puffs: Roll out the pastry until wafer thin. Cut into squares, the size is purely a matter of personal taste. Put a teaspoon of jam in the centre of each square. Damp the edges and fold the pastry to make triangles. Seal the edges; allow the pastry to relax for 30 minutes.

Bake for approximately 10 minutes as Cream Horns, glaze with milk or egg white and sugar and return to the oven for a further 10 minutes.

Thick sweetened fruit purée could be used instead of jam.

Pâté Puffs: Use liver pâté instead of jam. Omit the sugar glaze.

Palmiers Glacés: Make the pastry as usual but on the final rolling and folding, sprinkle the pastry board with 50 g/2 oz caster sugar; make sure all of this is absorbed by the pastry.

Roll out very thinly to make a large oblong shape. Take one long side and roll this towards the centre, as though making a Swiss Roll. Take the other long side and roll towards the centre, but on the reverse side of the pastry. Cut into an even number of slices of about 5–8 mm/¼–⅓ inch in thickness.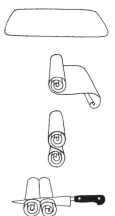

Bake towards the top of a hot to very hot oven, 220–230°C, 425–450°F, Gas Mark 7–8 for 6–7 minutes until brown on one side. Turn over and cook for the same time on the second side. Allow to cool. Serve plain or sandwiched together in pairs with firm jam and whipped cream.

VOL-AU-VENTS

Makes 12

ingredients as Puff Pastry on page 212, made with 225 g/8 oz flour, etc.

to glaze
1 egg yolk for savoury cases or 1 egg white plus a little sugar for sweet cases

Make the pastry as page 212 then follow one of the two methods given below for shaping the pastry.

Method 1: Roll out two-thirds of the pastry until about 5 mm/¼ inch in thickness, cut into rounds of approximately 6.5 cm/2½ inches in diameter. Put on to a slightly dampened baking tray. Roll out the remaining pastry to approximately the same thickness, or even slightly thinner. Cut into 6.5 cm/2½ inch rounds as before, but take a smaller cutter of approximately 3.5 cm/1½ inches in diameter and cut a circle from the centre of each round.

Damp the edges of the rounds on the baking tray and carefully place the rings of pastry on top, taking care you do not stretch these out of shape.

Re-roll any pastry left and use for more rounds and circles. Flake the edges (this helps the pastry to rise). If making savoury vol-au-vents brush the rims with the beaten egg yolk, if making sweet cases brush with lightly whisked egg whites, then sprinkle with a little caster sugar. Bake just above centre of a very hot oven, 230°C, 450°F, Gas Mark 8 for about 10 minutes or until the cases have risen well, then reduce the heat to moderate 190°C, 375°F, Gas Mark 5 for a further 5 minutes or until firm.

Method 2: Roll out all the pastry until 1.5–2 cm/½–¾ inch in thickness, cut into rounds of approximately 6.5 cm/2½ inches in diameter. Take a 3.5 cm/1½ inch cutter and press into the pastry, feel the cutter going approximately half way through the pastry, do not try and remove the dough.

Put on to the dampened baking tray, glaze as in Method 1 and bake in the same way. When cooked remove the centre part, which forms a 'lid', with the tip of a sharp knife.

If you find any slightly uncooked pastry in the centre, return the cases but not the 'lids' to the oven and cook for a further few minutes.

Cocktail Sized Vol-au-vents: Follow the directions but roll the pastry out rather more thinly and therefore bake for a slightly shorter time.

Large Vol-au-vents: Make one large round, oval or square of the pastry if following Method 2, roll either to the same thickness or a little thicker. Proceed as the recipe but allow slightly longer baking time at the lower temperature. This method is better for a large case, but you can use Method 1 if preferred.

FILLINGS FOR VOL-AU-VENTS

Savoury fillings are made by adding diced ingredients to a thick sauce. To fill the quantity of pastry above, heat 50 g/2 oz butter or margarine in a pan, stir in 50 g/ 2 oz flour, cook gently for 2–3 minutes; blend in 450 ml/¾ pint milk (or use a mixture of milk and cream). Bring to the boil, stir well until thickened and smooth. Add salt and pepper to taste and a little flavouring, such as chopped herbs then 225–350 g/8–12 oz diced cooked poultry or game or ham or flaked cooked salmon or shell-fish or fried mushrooms.

For a cold filling use a mixture of whipped cream and mayonnaise with the ingredients suggested above.

Sweet cases can be filled with whipped cream, jam or fruit or with ice cream.

SAUSAGE ROLLS

Makes 12–14

Sausage Rolls can be made with many kinds of pastry, but Flaky or Rough Puff are the most usual. To 225 g/8 oz sausagemeat use pastry made with 110 g/4 oz flour, etc. for a very thin crust or 175 g/6 oz flour, etc. for more substantial rolls, see pages 211 and 212 for the pastry recipes.

Make the pastry, roll out thinly and cut into two long strips, each measuring 13 cm/5 inches in width and 35.5 cm/14 inches in length; moisten the long edges with water. Form the sausagemeat into long rolls of the same length. Place in the centre of the strips, fold the pastry to completely enclose the sausagemeat. Seal the edges of the pastry, then flake these. Flaking means cutting horizontally into the pastry, this helps it to rise well. Cut each strip into 6–7 portions. Place on a baking tray; make 2–3 slits on top of each roll, brush with a beaten egg. Allow to relax for about 30 minutes.

Bake just above the centre of a hot oven, 220°C, 425°F, Gas Mark 7 for 20–25 minutes. Serve hot or cold.

Modern baking methods

In a Microwave Cooker

Although pastry needs the dry and even heat of an oven, it is possible to set it by using a microwave cooker. The most successful pastry is puff pastry, cut into narrow strips. This rises very well and does become pleasantly golden in colour.

Use the HIGH setting and allow from 3–4 minutes, but check carefully as cookers vary. Other pastries tend to look pale in colour and therefore less appetising than when cooked in the usual way but you can set the pastry for a Quiche, see page 204. Allow the timing as above.

In a Table Cooker

A small plate pie or flan can be cooked reasonably well. Preheat the cooker on the highest setting, put in the baking rack then the container of pastry. Bake for about 30 minutes, but check carefully during the cooking time. The pastry will look pale in colour.

Storing

Uncooked pastry can be wrapped and stored in the refrigerator for several days. Cooked pastry can be stored if the filling is sweet, or is not perishable. Put into an airtight container and reheat when required.

Do not try and store dishes made with Choux, Hot Water Crust or Suet Crust pastries, these must be frozen.

Store pastry away from cakes, bread and biscuits.

Freezing

Uncooked pastry can be wrapped and stored in the freezer for up to 4 months. Wrap the pastry in shallow packages (this hastens defrosting); label it carefully as to the type and weight.

Shortcrust pastry is better mixed with milk, rather than water, if it is to be frozen.

Cooked pastry dishes should be cooled, then frozen. Use within 6 months if containing sweet ingredients, 3 months with savoury ingredients.

PROBLEM SOLVING

Pastry often causes problems in making or baking; answers to the most usual queries are given below.

Q. *It is stressed that everything connected with pastry should be kept cold. Why is this?*
A. To prevent the dough becoming sticky and difficult to handle; also by keeping ingredients cold you trap more particles of air in the dough. It is these air particles that expand when heated to give light pastry.
Quick Remedy: In hot weather put the mixing bowl, water and flour into the refrigerator; keep fat well chilled but not too hard. Run cold water over your hands and wrists before you handle the ingredients.

Q. *Why is a raising agent not used in most types of pastry? Would this not make them lighter?*
A. No, it gives the pastry a sponge-like texture; pastry rises in a completely different way from a cake made with self-raising flour, it tends to lose its shape. The exception is Suet Crust Pastry which needs a raising agent, see page 205. You can use self-raising flour for economical Shortcrust Pastry, see page 199, if you reduce the fat slightly.

Q. *Why do Shortcrust and Flan Pastry break when rolled out?*
A. Too little liquid was used, or too much fat, or the pastry was over-handled in mixing. It is therefore brittle rather than pliable. Chill the pastry and support it over the rolling pin as it is used, see step 3 on page 199, in a pie, tart or flan.
Quick Remedy: Press out the pastry with your finger-tips into a flan shape, rather than rolling. It is not possible to do this for covering fruit or meat in a pie; in this case, work a little egg yolk into the crumbly pastry.

Q. *What makes Shortcrust Pastry tough?*
A. Too much liquid; always add this gradually; too little fat in proportion to the amount of flour; never be over-generous with flour when rolling out the dough, for, if you are, you lose the original ratio of fat to flour.
Over-handling the dough or too slow baking also causes toughness or hardness.
Quick Remedy: Leave over-moist pastry in the air for a short time before using; do not work in extra flour.

Q. *Why does pastry lose its shape?*
A. It was stretched in rolling; the dough was too moist.
Quick Remedy: Pastry should be chilled for 15–20 minutes before being rolled out and again before being baked; this allows the dough to relax.

Q. *Why do the richer pastries, Puff, Rough Puff and Flaky Pastry, sometimes fail to rise well?*
A. Incorrect rolling and folding; too cool an oven, see pages 211 and 212.
If the pastry does not rise as high as expected, it should still taste good.

Q. *Why does some fat run out of Puff and Rough Puff Pastry?*
A. Insufficient rolling and folding or because the oven was not sufficiently hot.

Q. *What makes Choux Pastry collapse after baking?*
A. The shapes were probably not 100% cooked, they should feel firm to the touch. Cool away from draughts.

Q. *Why does Choux Pastry sometimes fail to rise well?*
A. The flour was overcooked when added to the water and butter; the egg(s) were added too quickly to the flour mixture; allow this to cool before beating in the egg(s). The oven was too cool or inadequately preheated, pages 208–210.

217

Batch Baking

A great deal of time can be saved by preparing large quantities of a basic mixture and using this to make a variety of different dishes.

MAKE A BASIC SCONE MIXTURE

Sift together 1.35 kg/3 lb self-raising flour, or plain flour with raising agent, as described on page 182 and 1–2 teaspoons salt. Rub in 350 g/12 oz butter or margarine. Store in a covered container in the refrigerator or freezer or make up the various batches of scones and freeze these.

BASIC SCONES

Makes 16–20

Take 350 g/12 oz of the Basic Scone Mixture. Add sugar, seasoning, flavouring and liquid as the suggestions on pages 182 and 183. You need about 25% more of the extra ingredients suggested on these pages, since you have more scone mix than used in the recipes on pages 182 and 183. Bake as page 182.

CHEESE AND PARSLEY SCONE ROUNDS

Makes 12

Take 450 g/1 lb of the Basic Scone Mixture. Add ¼ teaspoon cayenne pepper, 2 tablespoons chopped parsley, 175 g/6 oz grated Cheddar cheese. Add sufficient milk to bind. Divide the mixture into two portions. Form each portion into a 15 cm/6 inch round. Place on to two lightly greased and floured baking trays. Mark each round into six portions, cutting nearly halfway through the dough.

Brush the scone round with milk and sprinkle with 25 g/1 oz grated cheese. Bake in the centre of a moderately hot oven, 200°C, 400°F, Gas Mark 6 for 25–30 minutes.

APRICOT AND RAISIN SCONES

Makes 14

Soak 50 g/2 oz dried apricots in water to cover for 12 hours, drain well, chop fruit.

Take 450 g/1 lb of the Basic Scone Mixture. Add 25 g/1 oz caster sugar, the finely grated rind of 1 orange, the apricots and 50 g/2 oz seedless raisins. Add sufficient milk to make a soft rolling consistency. Roll out the dough to 2.5 cm/1 inch in thickness and cut into 14 × 6.5 cm/2½ inch rounds.

Grease and flour two 18 cm/7 inch sandwich tins. Arrange seven scone rounds in each tin; six round the edge and one in the centre. Brush the tops of the scones with a little milk and sprinkle with Demerara sugar. Bake as the recipe above.

APPLE CINNAMON SCONE SQUARES

Makes 16

Take 450 g/1 lb of the Basic Scone Mixture. Add 1–2 teaspoons ground cinnamon, 50 g/2 oz caster sugar, 100 g/4 oz peeled and finely chopped cooking apples and enough milk to make a soft rolling consistency. Roll out to a 20 cm/8 inch square and cut into 16 × 5 cm/2 inch squares. Place on a greased and floured baking tray.

Bake above the centre of a moderate to moderately hot oven, 190–200°C, 375–400°F, Gas Mark 5–6 for approximately 20 minutes. Brush the scones with a little warm honey just before serving.

MAKE A BASIC VICTORIA SANDWICH MIXTURE

Follow the directions for mixing as given in the Master Recipe at the beginning of the Creaming Section on pages 66 and 67. If you prefer to use the soft type of margarine you can make a One-stage mixture as the advice given on page 70.

Cream together 350 g/12 oz butter or margarine and 350 g/12 oz caster sugar. Gradually beat in 6 large eggs. Sift 350 g/12 oz self-raising flour, or plain flour with 3 teaspoons baking powder, fold into the creamed mixture. This produces a mixture weighing:
4 × 350 g = 1.4 kg/4 × 12 oz = 48 oz.

MANDARIN GLORY GÂTEAU

Illustrated in colour on page 85

Serves 6–8

Grease and flour, or line, two 20 cm/8 inch round sandwich tins.

Take 600 g★/1¼ lb of the Basic Victoria Sandwich Mixture. Divide this between the prepared sandwich tins and bake above the centre of a moderate oven, 180°C, 350°F, Gas Mark 4 for 20–25 minutes or until firm to the touch. Allow to cool. Place sponge layers on to a flat dish.

Drain a 312 g/11 oz can mandarin oranges. Mix 4 tablespoons of syrup from the can with 2 tablespoons sherry, spoon over the sponges and allow this mixture to soak in for a few minutes.

Whip 300 ml/½ pint double cream. Carefully lift one moistened sponge on to the serving plate, spread with 3 tablespoons jelly-type marmalade, then with half the cream and half the mandarin oranges. Place the second sponge on top and cover this with another 3 tablespoons jelly marmalade, the remaining cream and then the mandarin oranges.

Melt 25 g/1 oz plain chocolate and drizzle over the mandarins; do this from the tip of a teaspoon. ★Metrication different.

CHERRY COCONUT FINGERS

Illustrated in colour on page 85

Makes 10–12

Grease and flour, or line, an 18 cm/7 inch square sandwich tin.

Take 450 g/1 lb of the Basic Victoria Sandwich Mixture. Add 75 g/3 oz desiccated coconut. Put into the prepared tin and bake in the centre of a moderate oven, 180°C, 350°F, Gas Mark 4 for 30–35 minutes until firm to the touch. Turn out and allow to cool.

Cover the top with 100 g/4 oz quartered glacé cherries. Blend 100 g/4 oz sifted icing sugar with 1 tablespoon lemon juice. Spoon carefully over the cherries; allow to set then cut into fingers.

WALNUT SULTANA LOAF CAKE

Illustrated in colour on page 85

Makes a 675 g/1½ lb loaf-shaped cake

Line a 675–900 g/1½–2 lb loaf tin with a double thickness of greased greaseproof paper.

Take 400 g/14 oz of the Basic Victoria Sandwich Mixture. Gently fold in 1 tablespoon extra flour (preferably self-raising) sifted with ½ teaspoon mixed spice, together with 50 g/2 oz sultanas, 50 g/2 oz chopped mixed peel and 25 g/1 oz chopped walnuts.

Spoon into the prepared tin and flatten the mixture. Top with another 25 g/1 oz chopped walnuts. Bake in the centre of a very moderate oven, 160°C, 325°F, Gas Mark 3 for 1 hour or until firm.

Index

Alcohol:
  as flavouring 17, 147
  moistening with 93, 107
allspice 18
almond 20:
  essence 17
  paste 148
  almond and apricot crumble 56
  almond and apricot rock cakes 42
  almond cake 50
  almond gingerbread 114
  almond glacé icing 146
  almond macaroons 177
  almond rock cakes 42
  almond scones 183
  almond shortbread 170
  almond slices 202
  almond sponge 75
  almond truffles 178
  apricot almond slices 122
  cherry almond cake 88
  cherry almond loaf 89
  golden almond cake 116
  ground almond butter icing 147
  iced golden almond cake 116
  orange almond gâteau 103
  rich almond cake 87
  rich almond sponge 75
American butter cookies 175
American frosting 152
angelica 19
Anzacs 172
apfel strudel 203
apple:
  apfel strudel 203
  apple bread 188
  apple brownie 60
  apple cinnamon scone squares 218
  apple and ginger squares 36, 51
  apple hazelbach 206
  apple juice 118
  apple sauce buns 42
  apple sauce cake 50
  apple shortcake 102
  bacon and apple roll 196, 205
  cider and apple pudding 118
  date and apple crumble 56
  Dutch apple cake 52
  French apple tart 207
  rosy apple flan 137
  streusel apple cake 52
apricot:
  almond and apricot crumble 56
  almond and apricot rock cakes 42
  apricot almond slices 122
  apricot and honey squares 53
  apricot layer sponge 74
  apricot and raisin scones 218
  apricot torta 52
  apricot upside down pudding 101
  apricot and walnut bread 180, 185
  orange apricot bread 185
Austrian chocolate cake 121
Austrian coffee gâteau 138
Australian icing 151

Babas au rhum 180, 193
bacon and apple roll 196, 205
bacon and onion crumble 59
baked Alaska 169
baked puddings 60
Bakewell tart 200
baking powder 13

baking 'blind' 207
baking soda: see bicarbonate of soda
banana:
  banana buns 43
  banana cream sponge 74
  walnut banana bread 185
Banbury cakes 213
Barbados sugar 15
basic fruit crumble 56
basic scones 218
basket cakes 84
batch baking 84, 188, 218
Bath buns 192
Battenburg cake 81
batter 140, 194
beating method of mixing 23
bicarbonate of soda 13
birthday cakes, novelty 158–9
biscuit crust pastry 198
biscuits 133, 164, 170–9:
  modern baking for 178
  storing and freezing 179
Black Forest gâteau 134
bloomer loaf 187
'boiled' fruit cake 51
boiling method of mixing 23
boudoir biscuits 133
Bourbon biscuits 175
bran:
  bran cakes 48
  chocolate bran brownies 108, 119
  honey bran muffins 184
brandy cornets 176
brandy snaps 176
Brazil nut pie 208
Brazil nuts:
  to blanch 20
  as filling 154
bread 180–95: see also loaf
  problem solving 195
  storing and freezing 195
  apple bread 188
  apricot and walnut bread 180, 185
  bread pudding, luxury 142
  bread roulade 131
  brown bread 188
  cheese bread 188
  French bread 195
  fruit bread 188
  granary bread 188
  milk bread 188
  oatmeal bread 188
  orange and apricot bread 185
  rye bread 188
  sweet bread 185, 188
  walnut banana bread 185
  white bread 186–9, 194
brioches 193
brown sugars 15:
  to soften 15
brown and white cobbler 55
brownies:
  apple 60
  chocolate bran 108, 119
Bûche de Noel 131
buns:
  apple sauce 42
  banana 43
  Bath 192
  carrot 43
  Chelsea 192
  chocolate 44
  coconut 45
  coffee walnut 43
  cream 209
  date and walnut 45
  fresh cherry 45

ginger 46
honey and spice 46
hot cross 191
iced coffee walnut 43
jam 46
lemon peel 47
marzipan 46
mocha 47
Swiss 191
butter 14, 20:
  adding to sponges 129
  savoury 171
butter icing 144, 147:
  flavourings for 147
butter sponges 73
butterfly cakes 84, front cover
butterscotch walnut crisps 172

Candied peel 19
caramel butter icing 147
caramel coffee gâteau 77
carrot buns 43
carrot cake 50
cashew nuts, as filling 154
caster sugar 15
cauliflower cakes 133
celebration cakes 144, 156–163
cereals, making cakes with 48
chamonix 169
cheese:
  cheese bread 188
  cheese crumble 58
  cheese meringue 168
  cheese and onion quiche 196, 205
  cheese and parsley scone rounds 218
  cheese pastry 198
  cheese scones 183
  cheese soufflé 141
  cream cheese pastry 205
  rich cheese biscuits 171
  rich cheese pastry 205
cheesecakes:
  citrus 99
  coffee raisin 98
  hot lemon and orange 100
  lemon 99
  vanilla 64, 98
Chelsea buns 192
cherry:
  making cherry cakes 88
  cherry almond cake 88
  cherry almond loaf 89
  cherry cakes 84
  cherry cobbler 55
  cherry coconut fingers 84, 219
  cherry cornflour cake 88
  cherry rock cakes 44
  cherry topped round cake 162
  economical cherry cake 50
  fresh cherry buns 45
  ginger cherry cake 50
  pinwheel cherry cobbler 55
  rich cherry cake 88
chestnuts, to prepare fresh 20:
  chestnut filling 131
  chestnut gâteau 135
chocolate:
  Austrian chocolate cake 121
  chocolate boxes 133
  chocolate bran brownies 108, 119
  chocolate buns 44
  chocolate butter icing 147
  chocolate corn oil sponge 120
  chocolate cream sponge 74
  chocolate cream roll 124, 130
  chocolate fruit gâteau 139

chocolate fudge icing 147
chocolate glacé icing 146
chocolate layer sponge 74
chocolate macaroons 177
chocolate meringues 167
chocolate orange sponge 77
chocolate orange rock cakes 44
chocolate petits fours 177
chocolate sauce 210
chocolate shortbread 170
chocolate sponge 76
chocolate sponge gâteau 76
chocolate sultana cake 50
chocolate walnut tartlets 202
crisp chocolate icing 146
Jamaican chocolate cake 119
moist chocolate cake 119
pear chocolate upside down
    pudding 60
rum and chocolate gâteau *124*,
    138
choux pastry 196, 208–10, 217
christening cake 161
Christmas cake:
    economical 94
    icing and piping 160
    last minute 94
    light coloured 94
    rich dark 93
    various sized 95
cider:
    cider and apple pudding 118
    cider cake 50
    cider dripping cake 118
cinnamon 18:
    apple cinnamon scone squares
        218
    cinnamon date loaf 116
citrus cheesecake 99
citrus loaf 91
cloves 18
cob loaf 187
cobbler 55:
    brown and white 55
    cherry 55
    pinwheel cherry 55
    savoury potato 59
cobnuts 20
cocktail-sized vol-au-vents 215
coconut:
    cherry & coconut fingers *84*,
        219
    coconut buns 45
    coconut butter icing 147
    coconut gingerbread 114
    coconut kisses 173
    coconut layer sponge 74
    coconut macaroons 177
    coconut meringues 167
    coconut pyramids 177
    coconut scones 183
    coconut shortbread 170
    economical coconut cake 50
    golden coconut cake 91
coffee:
    Austrian coffee gâteau 138
    caramel coffee gâteau 77
    coffee butter icing 147
    coffee corn oil sponge 120
    coffee gâteau 78
    coffee glacé icing 146
    coffee layer sponge 74
    coffee meringues 167
    coffee raisin cheesecake 98
    coffee sponge gâteau 78
    coffee walnut buns 43
    coffee walnut cake 50
    coffee walnut layer cake 78,
        front cover
    iced coffee walnut buns 43

consistency of mixture, types of 24
cooked fondant icing 152
cooked marzipan 152
cookies 175
coriander 18
corn oil sponges 120
cornflake macaroons 177
cottage loaf *180*, 187
cracks in cakes 107
cranberry nut loaf 184
cream:
    curdling 155
    banana cream sponge 74
    cream buns 209
    chocolate cream roll *124*, 130
    chocolate cream sponge 74
    home-made cream 76
    cream horns 214
    cream scones 183
cream cheese pastry 205
creaming method of mixing 23, 64:
    biscuits made by *164*, 171
    freezing mixture 105
    modern baking for 104
    pastry made by 206
    storing mixture 105
    using modern equipment 68
crème Chantilly 153
crème pâtissière 150
crisp chocolate icing 146
crisp jam filling 153
crock pot, using 62, 104, 122, 143
croissants 189
crumb quiche 204
crumb quiche Lorraine 204
crumble flavourings 57
crumble mixtures 56, 63:
    freezing 62
    sweet
    almond and apricot 56
    basic fruit 56
    crunch oat 121
    date and apple 56
    flapjack 121
    rhubarb and orange 56
    spiced crum 57
    spiced ginger 57
    spiced nut 57
    savoury
    bacon and onion 59
    cheese 58
    lemon 58
    paprika and onion 59
crumpets 194
crunchy oat crumble 121
crystallised fruit 19
cup cakes 82–3, 107
curdling 106, 155
custard tart 200
cutting in method of mixing 23

Dark brown sugar 15
dark Dundee cake 94
date:
    dried 19
    cinnamon date loaf 116
    date and apple crumble 56
    date and ginger loaf 116
    date loaf 185
    date scones 183
    date and walnut buns 45
    date and walnut cake 50
    date and walnut layer cake 79
    date and walnut squares 53
    marmalade and date cake 117
    sticky marmalade date cake 117
decorated sponge cakes 133
decorations, for cakes 133, 144–55,
    158–63
Demerara sugar 15

Devonshire splits 190
diabetic diets, baking for 16, 72, 74
dobos torte 136
dough 186, 191
doughnuts 190, *front cover*
dried fruits 19
dried fruit gingerbread 114
dripping 14:
    to clarify 118
    cider dripping cake 118
    dripping cake 118
drop scones 194
dropping consistency 24
Dundee cake 90, 92, *front cover*:
    dark Dundee cake 94
Dutch apple cake 52

Easter nests 82
Eccles cakes 213, *front cover*
éclairs 209
economical:
    cherry cake 50
    Christmas cake 94
    citrus loaf 91
    coconut cake 50
    gingerbread 113
    lemon cake 50
    luncheon cake 49
    macaroon tartlets 202
    Madeira cake 87
    rock cakes 41
    seed cake 50
    Victoria sandwich 71
economy cream 119
eggs, types and sizes 8, 16:
    vinegar in place of 51
eggless large fruit cake 51
eggless rock cake 41
eggless 'sponge' 72
elastic dough 24
electric frying pan: *see* table cooker
electric mixer, using 29, 40, 68–9,
    112, 128, 154, 168, 182
enriched yeast dough 191
equipment, types of 25–31
essences, types of 17

Fairy cakes 83
fat rascals 183
fats, types of *8*, 14–15
fillings, for cakes 153
firm rolling consistency 24
flaky pastry 211, 217
flan 206:
    French apple tart 207
    fruit flan 207
    rosy apple flan 137
    sherry flan 208
    sponge flan 137
flan pastry 198, 217
flapjack crumble 121
flapjacks 176
flavourings *8*, 17–18:
    for biscuits 171
    crumble mixtures 57
    gingerbread 114
    icings 146–7
    meringues 167
    shortbread 170
    soufflés 141
    Victoria sandwich 75
    whisked sponge 129
fleur pastry 206
flour:
    types of *8*, 12
    for sponges 129
flouring tins 32
folding method:
    of making pastry 210
    of mixing 23

food processor, using 29, 40, 69, 112, 128, 154, 168, 182
frangipani tartlets 202
freezing cooked and uncooked mixtures 62, 105, 123, 143, 154, 179, 195, 216
French apple tart 207
French bread 195
fresh cherry buns 45
frostings:
    American 152
    jam 154
    redcurrant 154
fruit:
    to clean 19
    essences 17
    sinking 106
    types of *8*, 19
    basic fruit crumble 56
    'boiled' fruit cake 51
    chocolate fruit gâteau 139
    dried fruit gingerbread 114
    eggless large fruit cake 51
    fruit bread 188
    fruit choux 209
    fruit doughnuts 190
    fruit flan 207
    fruit oaties 48
    fruit pie 199
    fruit scones 183
    fruity squares 54
    rich fruit cakes 92–7
    rich fruit loaf 191
    wheatmeal fruit cakes 95
fudge icing 152

Garland cake 163
gâteaux:
    Austrian coffee 138
    Black Forest 134
    caramel coffee 77
    chestnut 135
    chocolate fruit 139
    chocolate sponge 76
    coffee 100
    coffee sponge 78
    gâteau Paris Brest 209
    gâteau St. Honoré 209
    mandarin glory *84*, 219
    meringue 169
    nut 169
    orange almond 103
    orange rum 134
    rum and chocolate *124*, 138
    Viennese May 134
Genoa cake 90
Genoese pastry (sponge) 132, 143
gilacgi *108*, 122
ginger 18:
    apple and ginger squares *36*, 51
    date and ginger loaf 116
    ginger buns 46
    ginger cherry cake 50
    ginger jumbles 45
    ginger shortbread 170
    gingerbread *108*, 110–15
    spiced ginger crumble 57
gingerbread *108*, 110–11, 123:
    cookies 171
    as desserts 113
    men *108*, 115
gingerbreads *108*, 113–15:
    flavourings for 114
glacé fruits 19, 88
glacé icing *144*, 146
glazes 154
glycerine 149
golden almond cake 116
golden coconut cake 91
golden peanut biscuits *164*, 172

golden syrup loaf 184
granary bread 188
granulated sugar 15
greasing tins 32
griddle scones 183
ground almond butter icing 147
gum nut chews 178

Ham:
    shortcakes 61
    veal and ham pie 210
harlequin cakes 48
harvest upside down pudding 101
herbs, how to use 18
highland tart 201
holes in cakes 107
honey:
    apricot and honey squares 53
    honey bran muffins 184
    honey filling 153
    honey (or treacle) loaf 184
    honey and spice buns 46
hot cross buns 191
hot lemon and orange cheesecake 100
hot water crust pastry 210

Iced coffee walnut buns 43
iced fancies 133
iced golden almond cake 116
icing *144*, 144–7, 149–52, 154–5:
    feathering 146
    modern methods of icing 154
    storing and freezing 154
    American frosting 152
    Australian 151
    butter icing, flavourings for 147
    chocolate fudge icing 147
    cooked fondant 152
    crisp chocolate icing 146
    fudge icing 152
    glacé icing, flavourings for 146
    ground almond butter icing 147
    jam frosting 154
    redcurrant frosting 154
    royal 149
icing sugar 15
Irish soda bread 194
Italian meringue 168

Jam:
    crisp jam filling 153
    jam buns 46
    jam frosting 154
    jam glaze 154
    jam puffs 214
Jamaican chocolate cake 119
jelly glaze 154
jumbles:
    ginger 45
    lemon 46

Kneading 23

Lamingtons 81
langues de chat 172
lard 14
large light cakes 86–91
large Madeira cake 86
last-minute Christmas cake 94
layer sponges 74
lemon:
    economical lemon cake 50
    hot lemon and orange cheesecake 100
    lemon butter icing 147
    lemon cheesecake 99
    lemon crumble 58
    lemon filling 153
    lemon gingerbread 114

lemon glacé icing 146
lemon jumbles 46
lemon meringue pie 201
lemon and orange corn oil sponge 120
lemon peel buns 47
lemon rice cake 91
lemon shortbread fans *164*, 173
lemon sponge 79
Windsor lemon cake 87
light brown sugar 15
light coloured Christmas cake 94
light large cakes 86–7
light shortcake 102
light small cakes 82–5
lining tins 32
liquer glacé icing 146
liquids, types to use *8*, 16
loaf:
    bloomer 187
    cherry almond 89
    cinnamon date 116
    citrus 91
    cob 187
    cottage *180*, 187
    cranberry nut 184
    date 185
    date and ginger 116
    golden syrup 184
    luncheon 49
    marzipan nut 89
    mocha 54
    nut 89
    rich fruit 191
    tin 187
    treacle or honey 184
    treacle and raisin 50
    walnut sultana loaf cake *84*, 219
loaf sugar 15
loaf tin 25
low calorie recipes 16, 72
low fat spread 14
luncheon cakes 49
luncheon loaf 49
luxury bread pudding 142

Macaroons 177
macaroon tartlets 202
mace: *see* nutmeg
madeleines *64*, 83
Madeira cake:
    economical 87
    large 86
    rich 86
mandarin glory gâteau *84*, 219
margarine, types of 14
marmalade cakes 47, 117
marmalade and date cake 117
marshmallow gingerbread 114
marzipan 148, 155:
    cooked marzipan 152
    marzipan buns 46
    marzipan nut loaf 89
master recipes:
    gingerbread 110
    meringues 166
    rock cakes 38
    sponge cake 126
    Victoria sandwich 66
    white bread 186
measuring spoons 22
melting method of mixing 23, *108*, 108, 210:
    biscuits made by 176
    freezing mixture 123
    modern baking for 122
    pastry made by 208
    storing mixture 123
    using modern equipment 112
meringue cuite 168

meringues 166–9, 179, 201:
  modern baking for 178
  storing and freezing 179
microwave oven, using 62, 104, 122, 142, 154, 178, 194, 216
milk bread 188
mince pies 203
mincemeat 203
mille feuilles 212
miniature choux 209
miniature cream horns 214
miniature éclairs 209
miniature rock cakes 42
mixing:
  methods 23–4
  techniques of 10
mocha buns 47
mocha loaf 54
moist chocolate cake 119
molasses sugar 15
muesli cakes 48
muffins, honey bran 184
muscovado sugar 15
mushroom cakes 83

No-bake biscuits 178
non-stick (silicone) baking tins, care of 26
Norfolk pudding 140
novelty cakes 158–60
nuss roulade 131
nutmeg 18
nuts 8, 20: see also almond etc
  coating with 136
  in fillings 154
  Brazil nut pie 208
  cranberry nut loaf 184
  marzipan nut loaf 89
  nut batons 213
  nut gâteau 169
  nut loaf 89
  nut meringues 167
  nutty apple dumplings 205
  nutty pastry 198
  spiced nut crumble 57
nutty pastry 198

Oatcakes, sweet 174
oaties 174
oatmeal bread 188
oatmeal gingerbread 114
oil 14:
  baking with 120–21
old-fashioned strawberry shortcakes 61
one-stage sponges and cakes 70, 71, 90
onion:
  bacon and onion crumble 59
  cheese and onion quiche 196, 205
  paprika and onion crumble 59
orange:
  chocolate orange rock cakes 44
  chocolate orange sponge 77
  hot lemon and orange cheesecake 100
  lemon and orange corn oil sponge 120
  orange almond gâteau 103
  orange apricot bread 185
  orange butter icing 147
  orange gingerbread 114
  orange glacé icing 146
  orange rock cakes 47
  orange rum gâteau 134
  orange scones 183
  orange sultana squares 36, 54
  rhubarb and orange crumble 56
  rum and orange truffles 178

oven:
  position of food in 33–5
  temperatures 10, 33–5

Palmiers glacés 214
paprika and onion crumble 59
pastries 196–219
pastry 196:
  freezing and storing 216
  modern baking 216
  problem solving 217
pâté puffs 214
pâté sucrée 207
Pavlova 169
peach shortcake, spiced 61
peanut 20:
  golden peanut biscuits 164, 172
  peanut butter 20
  peanut butter cup cakes 83
  peanut butter fillings 153
pear:
  pear chocolate upside down pudding 60
  pear upside down pudding 101
pecan nuts 20
pecan pie 208
peppermint essence 17
petits fours, chocolate 177
petites religieuses 210
petticoat tails 170
pies:
  Brazil nut pie 208
  fruit pie 199
  lemon meringue pie 201
  mince pies 203
  pecan pie 208
  veal and ham pie 210
pinwheel cherry cobbler 55
piping 150, 155, 156
pistachio nuts 20
Pitcaithley bannock 170
pizza alla Napoletana 190
plain sweet scones 182, front cover
plum torta 53
portion sizes 11, 97
potato cobbler, savoury 59
pouring consistency 24
praline:
  to make 137
  praline sponge 137
prawn-filled choux 196, 209
preserving sugar 15
pressure cooker, using 62, 104, 122, 143
profiteroles 210
pruna torta 53
puddings:
  apricot upside down 101
  baked 60
  cider and apple 118
  Norfolk 140
  pear chocolate upside down 60
  pear upside down 101
puff pastry 212, 217

Queen cakes 84
quiches 196, 204–5

Raisin:
  apricot and raisin scones 218
  coffee raisin cheesecake 98
  raisin cake 90
  treacle and raisin loaf 50
raising agents 8, 13–14, 217
ratafia essence 17
ratafias 177
redcurrant frosting 154
rhubarb and orange crumble 56
rice cake, lemon 91
rich almond cake 87

rich almond sponge 75
rich cheese biscuits 171
rich cheese pastry 205
rich cherry cake 88
rich dark economical Christmas cake 93
rich fruit cakes 92–97
rich fruit loaf 191
rich gingerbread 108, 115
rich luncheon cake 49
rich Madeira cake 86
rich rock cake 41
rich scones 183
rich seed cake 89
rind, of fruits 19
ring cake 79
ring sponge 79
rock cakes 38–47, 63
rolled oats:
  crunchy oat crumble 121
  flapjacks 176
  fruit oaties 48
  oaties 174
  oatmeal bread 188
  shortbread crisps 174
rolls, bread 192
rose petal cakes 133
rosy apple flan 137
rough puff pastry 212, 217
roulade:
  bread 131
  nuss 131
rout biscuits 177
royal icing 149, 155
rubbing-in method of mixing 23, 36:
  baked puddings made by 60
  biscuits made by 170
  freezing mixture 62
  large cakes made by 36, 49–54
  modern baking 62
  pastry made by 199
  small cakes made by 42–8
  storing mixture 62
  using modern equipment 40
rum:
  essence 17
  orange rum gâteau 134
  rum babas: see babas au rhum
  rum butter icing 147
  rum and chocolate gâteau 124, 138
  rum and orange truffles 178
rye bread 188

Sachertorte 139
saffron cakes 47
Sally Lunns 192
sand cake 87
sandwich:
  sponge 72–9
  Victoria 64, 66, 72, 75
sandwich tins 26
sausage rolls 216
savarin 193
savoy finger:
  biscuits 133
  soufflé 142
savoys 133
savoury butter 171
savoury scones 183
savoury mille feuilles 212
savoury potato cobbler 59
scones 182:
  modern baking for 194
  storing and freezing 195
  apple cinnamon scone squares 218
  almond scones 183
  apricot and raisin scones 218

cheese scones 183
cheese and parsley scone rounds 218
coconut scones 183
cream scones 183
date scones 183
drop scones 194
fat rascals 183
fruit scones 183
griddle scones 183
orange scones 183
plain sweet scones 182–3, *front cover*
rich scones 183
savoury scones 183
treacle scones 183
wholemeal scones 183
Scotch pancakes 194
Scotch shortbread 170
Scots bun 163
seed cake:
    economical 50
    rich 89
seeds, types of 17
sherry flan 208
shortbread crisps 174
shortbread:
    flavourings for 170
    coconut kisses 173
    lemon shortbread fans *164*, 173
    petticoat tails 170
    Scotch 170
    shortbread crisps 174
    vanilla shortbreads 173
shortcake:
    apple 102
    ham 61
    light 102
    old-fashioned strawberry 61
    spiced peach 61
    strawberry 102, *front cover*
shortcrust pastry 198–9, 217
Shrewsbury biscuits 171
silicone (non-stick) baking tins 26, 38
simnel cake 92
slab, sponge 80
slice:
    almond 202
    apricot almond 122
small light cakes 82–5
small sponge cakes 133
soda bread, Irish 194
soft consistency 24
soft rolling consistency 24
soufflés *124*, 141–2
spices 18
spiced cakes 114
spiced crumb crumble 57
spiced ginger crumble 57
spiced nut crumble 57
spiced peach shortcake 61
spiced treacle cakes 117
spinach quiche 204
sponge 129, 143:
    decorations for 133
    almond sponge 75
    banana cream sponge 74
    butter sponge 73
    chocolate corn oil sponge 120
    chocolate cream sponge 74
    chocolate layer sponge 74
    chocolate orange sponge 77
    chocolate sponge 76
    chocolate sponge gâteau 76
    coconut layer sponge 74
    coffee corn oil sponge 120
    coffee layer sponge 74
    coffee sponge gâteau 78
    corn oil sponge 120

eggless 'sponge' 72
Genoese pastry 132
layer sponge 74
lemon sponge 79
praline sponge 137
rich almond sponge 75
ring sponge 79
savoy fingers 133
savoys 133
small sponge cakes 133
sponge cake 126
sponge flan 137
sponge fingers 133
sponge sandwiches 136–7
sponge slab 80
squares:
    apple cinnamon scone 218
    apple and ginger 36, 51
    apricot and honey 53
    date and walnut 53
    fruity 54
    orange sultana 36, 54
sticky consistency 24
sticky marmalade date cake 117
storing cooked and uncooked
        mixtures 62, 92–4, 97, 105,
        123, 143, 154, 179, 195, 216
stirring method of mixing 23
strawberry:
    old-fashioned strawberry
        shortcakes 61
    strawberry shortcake 102, *front cover*
streusel apple cake 52
suet crust pastry 205
sugar, types of 8, 15–16, 18
sultana:
    chocolate sultana cake 50
    orange sultana squares 36, 54
    walnut sultana loaf cake *84*, 219
sweet oatcakes 174
sweet shortcrust pastry 198
sweeteners 15–16
Swiss buns 191
Swiss roll 130, 143:
    individual 131
    small 130
Swiss roll tin 25
syrup:
    golden syrup loaf 184
    tart 200

Table cooker, using 62, 105, 123,
        143, 194, 216
tarts:
    Bakewell 200
    custard 200
    French apple 207
    highland 201
    macaroon tartlets 202
    syrup 200
teacakes 180:
    Bath buns 192
    Chelsea buns 192
    fat rascals 183
    honey bran muffins 184
    Sally Lunns 192
testing, of cooked food 10, 106–7
temperature chart, oven 35
tiger cakes 175
tin loaf 187
tins, baking 30–2
tipsy cake 103
toad in the hole 140
torta:
    apricot 52
    plum 53
    pruna 53
torte:
    dobos 136

tutti-fruitti 135
traditional buns 192
tray bakes 80
treacle:
    spiced treacle cakes 117
    treacle or honey loaf 184
    treacle and raisin loaf 50
    treacle scones 183
truffles 178
tutti-fruitti torte 135

Unrefined granulated sugar 15
upside down puddings:
    apricot 101
    harvest 101
    pear 101
    pear chocolate 60

Vacherin 169
valentine cake 160
vanilla 17, 18:
    vanilla butter icing 147
    vanilla cheesecake *64*, 98
    vanilla meringues 167
    vanilla shortbreads 173
veal and ham pie 210
vegetable soufflé 141
Victoria sandwich *64*, 66, 107:
    economical 71
    one-stage 70
    one-stage economical 71
    wheatmeal 72
Viennese May gâteau 134
vinegar, in place of eggs 51
vinegar cake 51
vol-au-vents 215

Walnut 20:
    apricot and walnut bread *180*,
        185
    butterscotch walnut crisps 172
    chocolate walnut tartlets 202
    coffee walnut buns 43
    coffee walnut cake 50
    coffee walnut layer cake 78,
        front cover
    date and walnut buns 45
    date and walnut cake 50
    date and walnut layer cake 79
    date and walnut squares 53
    iced coffee walnut buns 43
    walnut banana bread 185
    walnut sultana loaf cake *84*, 219
water icing: *see* glacé icing
wedding cakes 96–7, *156*, 161, 162
weights and measures, 21–22
wheatmeal fruit cakes 95
wheatmeal gingerbread 113
wheatmeal rock cakes 41
wheatmeal Victoria sandwich 72
whisking method of mixing 24,
        124, *124*
    biscuits made by 177
    modern baking 142
    oven hot water 129
    storing and freezing mixture
        143
    using modern equipment 128
whisks, types of 29
white sugars 15
wholemeal bread 189
wholemeal flour in pastry 198
wholemeal scones 183
Windsor lemon cake 87

Yeast 13, 180, 186, 191, 194–5
yogurt cakes 138
Yorkshire pudding 140

Zest 19